ADVERTISEMENTS.

SOUTH EASTERN R[AILWAY]

THE DIRECT MAIL SHORT SEA-ROUTE TO ALL PART[S]

FOUR COMMUNICATIONS DAILY.

THE OVERLAND ROUTE TO INDIA, AND FOR OFFICERS RETURNING FROM THE CRIMEA AND TURKEY.

London to Paris in 12 Hours.   London to Brussels in 12¾ Hours.
London to Cologne in 19½ Hours. London to Marseilles in 35 Hours.

Sea Passage only two Hours.

THE DAILY TIDAL SERVICE,
VIA FOLKESTONE AND BOULOGNE,

PERFORMED always at tide time and by daylight, the hours of which are published in the front page of *The Times*, affords the most advantageous means of communication between London and Paris, and possess specially attractive features. Passengers are conveyed by express train to Folkestone, where they walk on board a powerful steamer, from which they are landed in less than two hours and proceed at once to Paris by express train, making the journey in about *Twelve Hours*. The same correspondence of trains and steamer is arranged from Paris to London.

Through Conductor.—A Special Guard accompanies each train throughout the entire journey between London and Paris, and *vice versa* whose duty is to attend to the luggage, act as interpreter, and give all information and assistance to Passengers.

Through Registering of Luggage.—Passengers by the above Trains can Register their Luggage for Paris direct, thereby avoiding Customs examination at Boulogne, or any care of their Luggage until arrival at Paris. Luggage for Paris can also be registered at Redhill and Folkestone. Charge for registering, 1s. per package; and the Luggage must be at Folkestone 1 hour, and the other stations 20 minutes before the hour for starting.

Through Tickets, as above, at the same rates as from London, are issued at Redhill (where the Train stops for Passengers and from whence also Luggage can be registered) for the convenience of those proceeding *via* Reading Branch, and to facilitate communication between the Midland Districts and the Continent.

FIXED CONTINENTAL SERVICE, VIA DOVER AND CALAIS.

FROM LONDON.

London	depart.	8 10 a.m.	*1 30 p.m.	8 30 p.m.
Dover	,,	11 0 ,,	4 30 ,,	11 15 ,,
Calais	,,	2 0 p.m.	8 0 ,,	2 0 a.m.
Paris	arrive.	10 20 ,,	5 30 a.m.	9 10 ,,
Brussels	,,	8 50 ,,	†5 30 ,,	10 15 ,,
Cologne	,,	5 0 a.m.		4 0 p.m.

* Sundays excepted.   † *Via* Valenciennes.

TO LONDON.

Cologne	depart.	11 30 p.m.	......	6 30 & 9 15 a.m.
Brussels, North Stat.	,,	*7 0 a.m.	*12 20 a.m.	*6 0 p.m.
Brussels, South Stat.	,,	†8 0 ,,	‡2 0 p.m.	‡7 0 ,,
Paris	,,	8 0 ,,	1 45 ,,	7 30 ,,
Calais	,,	3 30 p.m.	§10 30 ,,	2 30 a.m.
Dover	,,	7 30 ,,	2 0 a.m.	5 20 ,,
London	arrival.	10 5 ,,	4 30 ,,	7 45 ,,

* *Via* Ghent.   † *Via* Jurbise and Tournay.   ‡ *Via* Valenciennes.
§ This Steamer does not sail from Calais on Saturdays.

Luggage.—By the 8 30 p.m. train from London and the 7 30 p.m. train from Paris, Passengers Luggage can be registered for London direct, and *vice versa*, avoiding the Customs examination at Dover and Calais.

Offices for Through Tickets and Information.—London: Chief Offices, London Bridge Station; 40, Regent Circus, Piccadilly; 147, Cheapside. Paris: 4, Boulevard des Italiens. Brussels; 74, Montagne de la Cour.

For Fares and all further particulars, see Time Books, to be had as above.

C. W. EBORALL, Manager.

Manager's Office, London, 1856.

ADVERTISEMENTS.

LONDON, BRIGHTON, AND SOUTH COAST RAILWAY.

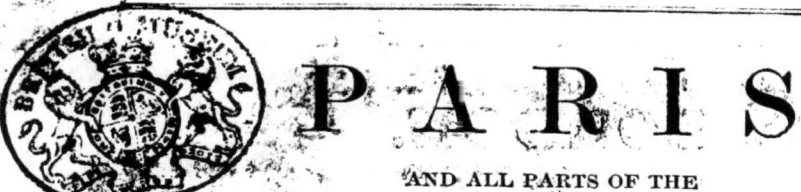

PARIS
AND ALL PARTS OF THE
CONTINENT,
VIA NEWHAVEN AND DIEPPE.

THE SHORTEST AND CHEAPEST ROUTE.

FARES THROUGHOUT:

First Class............28s. | Second Class..........20s.

FOR Times of Sailing, and full particulars, see Advertisements in BRADSHAW'S GUIDE FOR GREAT BRITAIN AND IRELAND; also BRADSHAW'S CONTINENTAL GUIDE; the TIMES Newspaper; the TIME TABLES of the BRIGHTON AND SOUTH COAST, AND THE LONDON & NORTH WESTERN RAILWAY COMPANIES.

Every information may be obtained respecting this *Pleasant and Beautiful Route* on application in LONDON to H. P. MAPLES, 5, Arthur Street East (opposite the Monument), London Bridge; at the LONDON AND BRIGHTON RAILWAY OFFICES, London Bridge, and at all their various Stations; also at the COMPANY'S OFFICES, 43, Regent's Circus, Piccadilly.—In PARIS; to A. D. BOSSON, 7, Rue de la Paix; and at 35, Quai Henry IV., DIEPPE.

ADVERTISEMENTS.

CHINA & GLASS ROOMS,

Nos. 49 & 50, OXFORD STREET,

LONDON.

JOHN W. SHARPUS

Begs respectfully to call the attention of the Public to his IMMENSE STOCK, which is now replete with all the most Modern and Classic Designs in China, Glass, Earthenware, Parian Statuary and Bohemian Glass.

DINNER SERVICES.

	£	s.	d.
Dinner Services, in a variety of colours, richly gilt............from	3	3	6
Handsomely Painted and Gilt ditto .... ,,	5	15	6
Handsome Coloured Bands, richly gilt............	7	7	0

A variety of rich patterns, equal to China, without its expense, at the same moderate prices.

DESSERT SERVICES.

Dessert Services for 12 persons, in neat coloured borders............from	1	1	0
Ditto ditto antique Pugin's wreaths	1	8	0
Ditto ditto or a variety of coloured bands, with gold and flowers, from	3	15	0

300 PATTERNS OF TEA SERVICES.

White and Gold	0	17	6
Neat bands and flowers	1	8	0
Neat pattern, handsomely gilt and painted ....from	2	2	0
Rich pattern, splendidly gilt and painted, of most elaborate workmanship ....to	14	14	0

GLASS DEPARTMENT.

Particularly neat cut Wine Glasses............	£0	5	6	per dozen.
And an immense variety............to	6	6	0	,,
Good Strong Tumblers	0	4	6	,,
A great choice ....to	2	2	0	,,
Decanters ....from	0	8	6	per pair.
Handsome cut and engraved ditto	1	1	0	,,
Custard and Jelly Glasses ....from	0	4	6	per dozen.

PARIAN FABRICS.

The largest choice in London of Artistic Statuary, Vases, &c.

BOHEMIAN GLASS.

A choice selection from the two most renowned makers.

ADVERTISEMENTS.

THE NEW REGISTERED PORTMANTEAU,

REGISTERED AND MANUFACTURED BY

JOHN SOUTHGATE,

76, WATLING STREET,

LONDON.

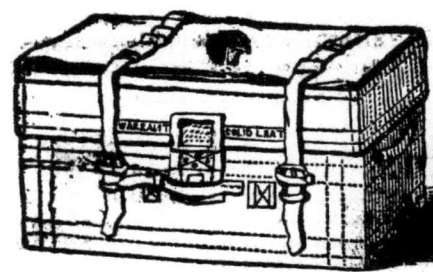

THIS PORTMANTEAU is admitted by all who have used it to be the most PERFECT and USEFUL of any yet invented, and to combine all the advantages so long desired by all who travel.

The peculiar conveniences of this Portmanteau are, that it contains separate compartments for each description of Clothes, Boots, &c.; each division is kept entirely distinct, and is immediately accessible on opening the Portmanteau, without lifting or disturbing anything else. Every article is packed perfectly flat, and remains so during the whole of the journey.

It may be obtained of MR. WILKINSON, 30, Cockspur Street; of MESSRS. MOORE and Co., 14, St. James's Street, London; of MR. HUNT, Above-Bar, Southampton; of MR. BAYS, Hatter, Cambridge; of MR. ELLENGER, Granger Street, Newcastle-on-Tyne; MR. POOL, Trunk Maker, Hull and Leeds; MR. LOVE, Trunk Maker, Hull; MR. NORTHAM, Trunk Maker, opposite St. Sidwell's Church, Exeter; of most Outfitters and Saddlers throughout the Kingdom; and of

JOHN SOUTHGATE,

MANUFACTURER OF

Every Description of Portmanteaus and Travelling Equipage,

76, WATLING STREET, CITY.

ADVERTISEMENTS.

J. W. AND T. ALLEN,
Manufacturers, 18 and 22, West Strand, London.

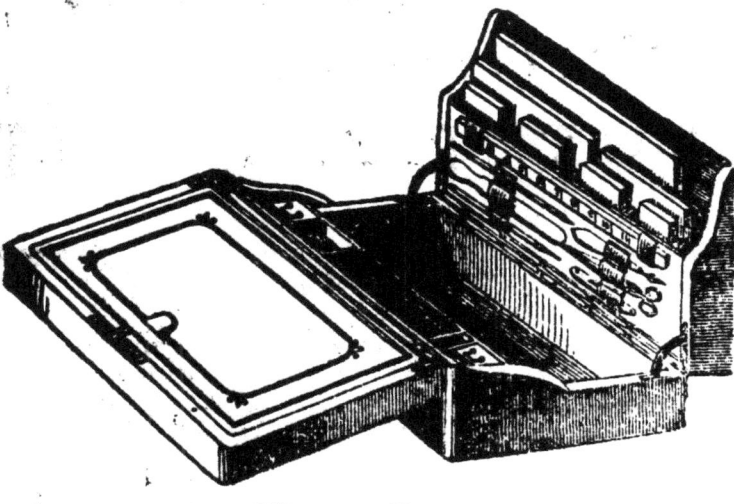

ALLEN'S
PATENT DISPATCH BOX
AND
TRAVELLING WRITING DESK

Is the most complete and convenient article of the kind yet produced. It contains Stationery and all Writing requisites, with ample space for papers, and is so arranged that any article is instantly accessible without disarranging the remainder.

OPEN   SHUT

ALLEN'S
PATENT
TRAVELLING BAG,

The opening of which is as large as the bag itself, thus allowing coats, linen, &c. to be packed without injury, and more conveniently than in the ordinary carpet bag.

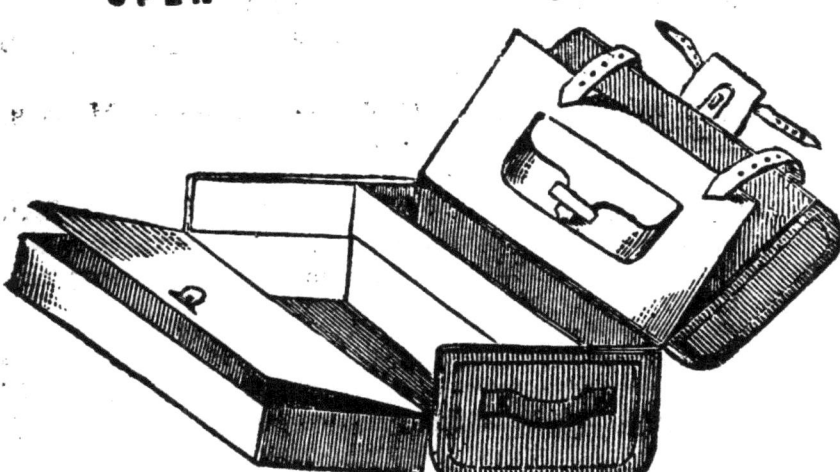

ALLEN'S
NEW
PATENT SOLID LEATHER
PORTMANTEAU

Contains four distinct compartments, all accessible at the same time, and secured by a Bramah lock; it affords greater facilities for arranging a wardrobe than any other Portmanteau, and is as light and portable as the ordinary kinds.

Illustrated Catalogues, with size and price of more than 150 other articles, forwarded on receipt of two Stamps; also Allen's Catalogue of Portable Barrack-room Furniture (see separate Catalogue.)

ADVERTISEMENTS.

LIGHT, CHEAP, AND DURABLE ROOFING.

CROGGON'S
PATENT ASPHALTE ROOFING FELT,

AS ADOPTED BY

Her Majesty's Woods and Forests,	The Corporation of the City of Edinburgh,
Her Majesty's Board of Ordnance,	The Duke of Buccleugh,
The Royal Agricultural Society of England,	The Marquis of Anglesea,
The Leeds and Manchester,	The Marquis of Westminster,
The London and North Western,	The Birkenhead Dock Company,
The Liverpool and Manchester,	The Dock Trustees of Liverpool,
The Chester and Holyhead,	Most of the Nobility, Gentry, and Agricul-
The Norfolk, and other Railways,	turists,

And many Members of the Royal Agricultural Societies of England, Scotland, and Ireland; Effects a saving of half the Timber usually required; has been extensively used and pronounced efficient, and particularly applicable for

WARM CLIMATES.

It is a non-conductor.—It is portable, being packed in rolls, and not liable to damage in carriage.—It can be easily applied by any unpractised person.—From its lightness, weighing only 42lbs. to the square of 100 feet, the cost of carriage is small.

UNDER SLATES, &c.,

in Church and other Roofs, the Felt has been extensively used to REGULATE THE TEMPERATURE.

INODOROUS FELT,

For damp walls, and for damp floors under carpets and floor-cloths; also for LINING IRON HOUSES, to equalise the temperature.

PRICE ONE PENNY PER SQUARE FOOT.

PATENT FELTED SHEATHING FOR COVERING SHIPS' BOTTOMS, &c., ON WHICH THE COPPER LIES SMOOTH.

DRY HAIR FELT,

For Deadening Sound, and Covering Steam Boilers, Pipes &c., preventing the Radiation of Heat thereby saving

TWENTY-FIVE PER CENT. OF FUEL.

SAMPLES, TESTIMONIALS, AND FULL INSTRUCTIONS, ON APPLICATION TO

CROGGON & CO., 2, Dowgate Hill, London.

CORDING'S WATERPROOFS

AND

CORDING'S FISHING BOOTS

ARE THE BEST THAT CAN BE HAD.

USED BY OFFICERS OF BOTH SERVICES, AND FIRST SPORTSMEN IN THE WORLD.

J. C. CORDING,
231, STRAND, TEMPLE BAR, LONDON.

WATCHES, CHAINS,
AND JEWELLERY

OF FIRST QUALITY, AT

LOWEST POSSIBLE PRICES.

SPOONS AND FORKS ELECTRO-PLATED WITH PUREST SILVER.

GEORGE CORDING,
232, STRAND, TEMPLE BAR, LONDON.

PALACE OF INDUSTRY, PARIS.

BRADSHAW'S
ILLUSTRATED
GUIDE THROUGH PARIS
AND ITS ENVIRONS;

EXHIBITING IN A NOVEL AND COMPREHENSIVE FORM

ALL THAT CAN BE SEEN
AND
HOW TO SEE IT

WITH THE LEAST FATIGUE, TIME, AND EXPENSE; FORMING A COMPLETE AND INDISPENSABLE
COMPANION TO THE VISITOR TO PARIS, AND CONTAINING

A SPLENDID (STEEL ENGRAVED)

MAP OF THE FRENCH EMPIRE;

ALSO A BEAUTIFUL AND DISTINCT

PLAN OF PARIS AND ITS ENVIRONS,

AND OTHER WELL EXECUTED STEEL

ENGRAVINGS, ILLUSTRATIVE OF THE FRENCH METROPOLIS.

LONDON:
W. J. ADAMS (BRADSHAW'S GUIDE OFFICE), 59, FLEET STREET;
MANCHESTER:—BRADSHAW AND BLACKLOCK, 47, BROWN STREET;
LIVERPOOL:—T. FAIRBROTHER, 46, DALE STREET;
BIRMINGHAM:—JAMES GUEST, 52, BULL STREET; SHEFFIELD:—R. CHADDERTON, MARKET PLACE;
EDINBURGH:—MOODIE & LOTHIAN, 76, PRINCES STREET; GLASGOW:—JAMES REID, 138, ARGYLE STREET;
DUBLIN:—A. CARSON, 51, GRAFTON STREET (CORNER OF STEPHEN'S GREEN);
PARIS:—LOUIS NICOUD BELLENGER, 212, RUE RIVOLI, & J. DAWES, 3, PLACE VENDOME (3 Doors from the Rue St. Honore),
FRANKFORT:—MESSRS. JUGEL;
BRUSSELS:—94, MONTAGNE DE LA COUR;
UNITED STATES:—EDWARDS, SANDFORD, & CO., NEW YORK, BALTIMORE, AND PHILADELPHIA.
And Sold by all Booksellers, and at all Railway Stations throughout Great Britain, Ireland, and the Continent.

Communications having reference to this work to be addressed to the Editor, 59, Fleet Street, London.

1856.

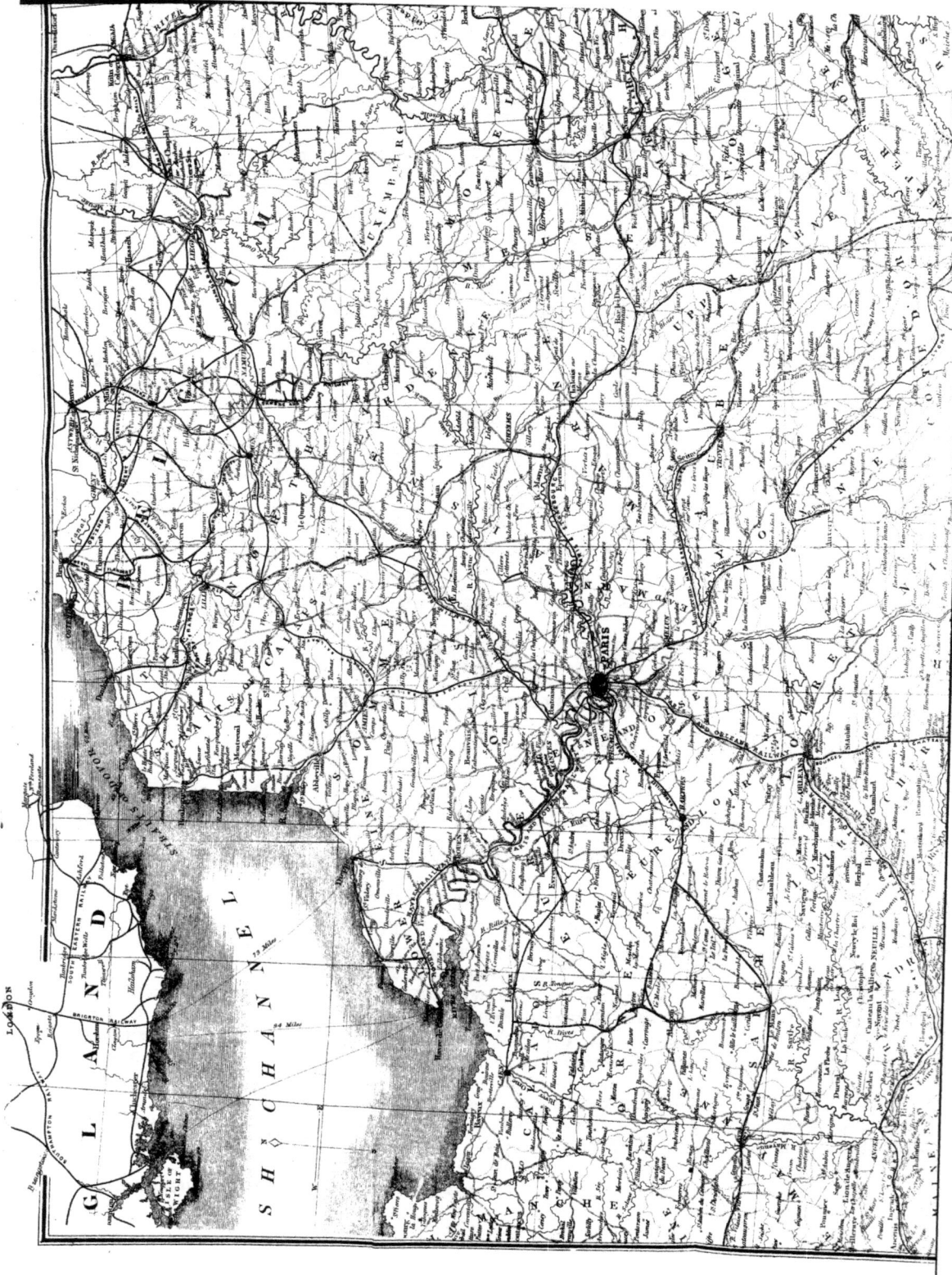

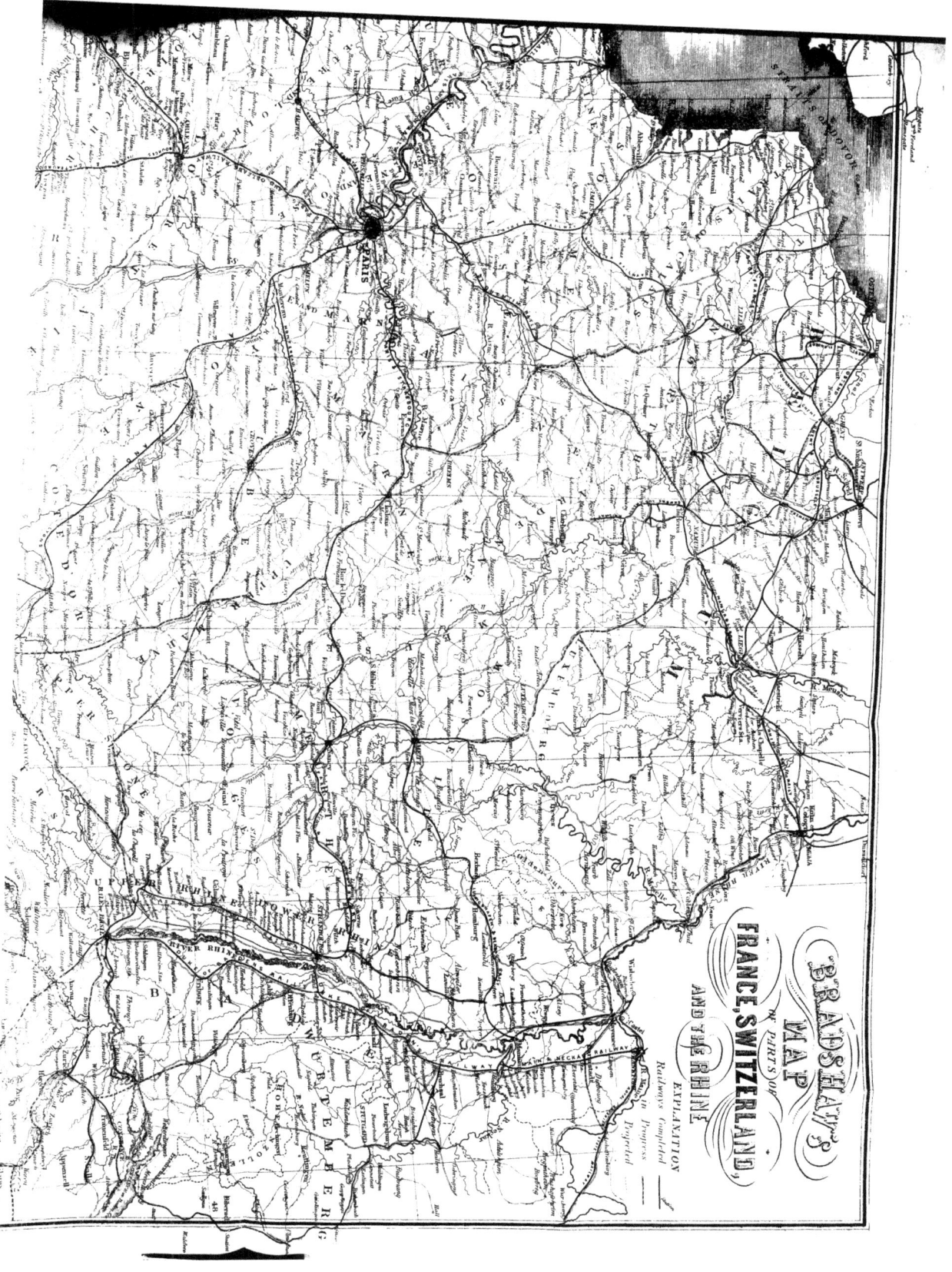

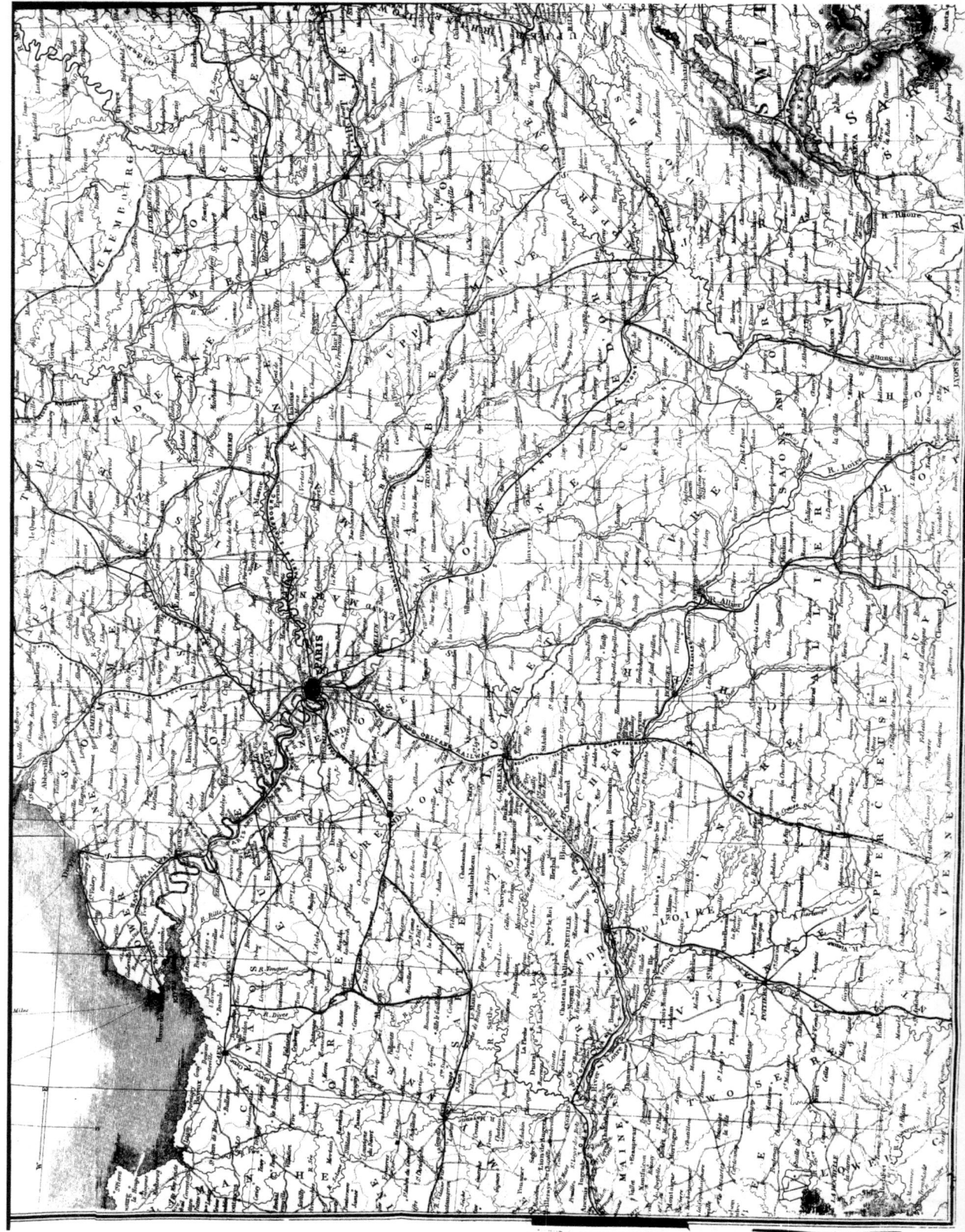

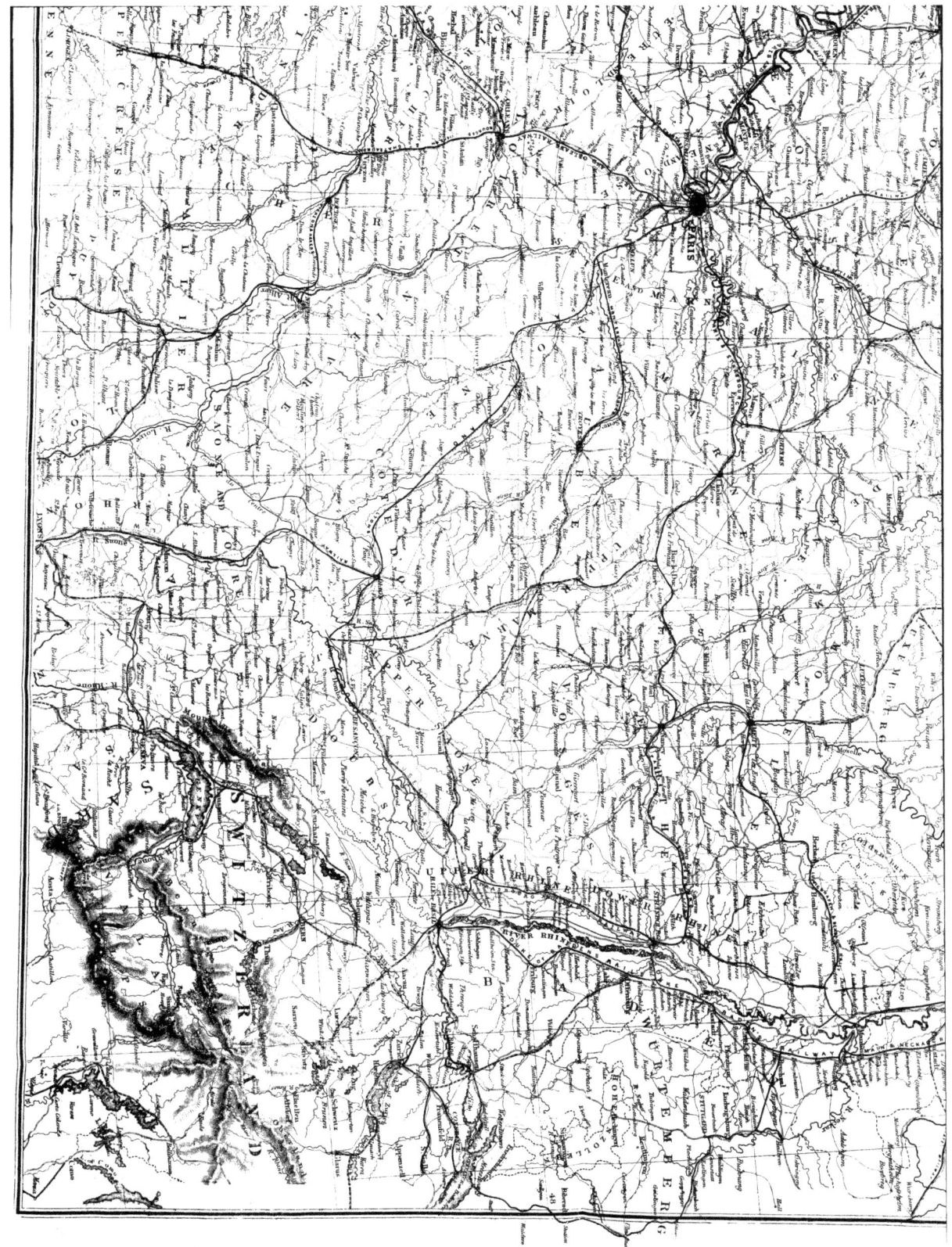

HINTS TO VISITORS GOING FROM LONDON TO PARIS.

We give at page XX. the necessary information respecting the different routes to Paris, to enable the traveller to select that which suits him best. If a person, however, be limited to a certain number of days, the direct routes *via* Calais or Boulogne will, of course, be preferred; but if time be of no object, the scenery between those two places and Paris is somewhat too flat and monotonous to offer sufficient attraction to the generality of travellers, who will, no doubt, consider it desirable to go and return during the summer months by the two routes that afford the greatest novelty and interest to persons who have not yet visited the Continent, and who should avail themselves of this opportunity to visit the picturesque banks of the Seine, and the charming scenery and beauties of the Rhine.

With this view, the traveller can proceed to Paris *via* Brighton, Dieppe, and Rouen, and return from thence by rail to Strasburg, Baden Baden, Frankfort, &c.: visit the principal towns on his route down the Rhine to Cologne, take the rail at this place for Belgium, and embark at Antwerp or Ostend for London, or proceed through Belgium first, thence up the Rhine to Strasburg, and on to Paris; returning thence to London *via* Rouen, Dieppe, and Brighton. The advantages by either of these routes are, that the traveller is amused and interested by a variety of scenery and remarkable objects on his journey. For instance, Dieppe is the favourite and fashionable watering place of the Parisians, and is much frequented for its excellent sea bathing. The environs are exceedingly pretty, comprising the Chateau of Louis Philippe at Eu, the ruins of the castle of Arque, in the valley of Bethune, and the Château d'Ange, &c. The railway from Dieppe to Rouen passes through a highly-cultivated portion of Normandy, the scenery being diversified with villas and Chateaux up to the very walls of Rouen, one of the finest provincial cities in France; and to which the traveller should devote at least a whole day, to visit the several remarkable objects and scenes for which it is celebrated. The Cathedral and Churches, the Hotel de Ville and Museum, &c., and the memorable places of surpassing interest connected with the tragic martyrdom of the unfortunate Joan of Arc, who was burnt at the stake, in the Place de la Pucelle, and whose statue now ornaments the square.

The scenery between Rouen and Paris, along the banks and valleys of the Seine, is exceedingly pretty; and the traveller who enters Paris by this route will have his mind already stored with a variety of the most pleasing souvenirs, predisposing it to a better appreciation of the wonders of Paris than if he went direct from London. The route via Southampton and Havre offers nearly the same variety of attractive views, especially if the visitor can ascend the Seine by steamer from Havre to Rouen, as the scenery of the lower Seine is peculiarly picturesque, and in some parts wild and rugged, resembling in many features the characteristics of the Rhine, with its wooded heights and ruined castles.

After passing a week or two in Paris, the traveller will find it a delightful change proceed thence by rail, direct to Strasburg and Frankfort, whence he can make excursions to the celebrated watering places and towns in the vicinity of the Rhine, such as Heidelberg, Homburg, Wiesbaden, Baden Baden, Mayence, Coblentz, Stolzenfels, &c., and explore from these and other places the inland beauties of the countries bordering the Rhine between Mayence and Cologne. From Cologne the tourist should proceed to Belgium, to visit the fine old cities of Liege, Antwerp, Brussels, Ghent, and Bruges, with their splendid cathedrals, town-halls, and churches, museums, and magnificent collections of paintings—for all of which Belgium is so celebrated—and then embark at Ostend or Antwerp for London. Or, as already mentioned, by inverting the order of the routes or places, the traveller can proceed by whichever route he deems most agreeable, whether by Brighton, Dieppe, and Rouen, or Havre or *via* Antwerp, or Ostend, Cologne, Frankfort, and Strasburg. The expense by either of these routes will be little more than by Boulogne or Calais, and whatever the difference may be, will be more than compensated for, by the additional pleasure afforded in visiting so many places of engrossing interest, in seeing so much beautiful and picturesque scenery, in inspecting the splendid and noblest specimens of Gothic architecture, and works of art; in observing the manners and customs of the French, the Germans, and the Belgians, and all this in addition to the attractions of Paris, and during one tour on the Continent. Many persons will probably extend their journey up the Rhine into Switzerland, and return *via* Paris, or *vice versa*, which will be adding so many more pleasing souvenirs and reminiscences. The hotel accommodation at Dieppe and Rouen, as well as in Belgium, and all up the Rhine, is particularly good, and this will not only enhance the pleasure of the journey, but prove beneficial to the health of the traveller before he reaches the French capital in the hot months of summer.

INDEX.

	PAGE
Abbey St. Denis	xvii., 54
Abelard	29
Advertisements	77
Anne of Austria	40, 43
Anteuil	xvii., 34, 49
Arc de Triomph	xvi., 2, 16, 34
Archives Imperiàles	58
Archives Judiciares	24
Armand	12
Arsenal	68
Asnières	34, 71
Avenue de Neuilly	15
Banque de France	31
Barrière Blanche	xxv.
Barrière de l'Etoile	xvi., xxiv.
Barrière de la Gare	xxiv.
Barrière de Monceaux	xxv.
Barrière du Roule	xxv.
Barrière de Long Champs	xxiv.
Barrière du Trone	xxv., 61
Barrière d'Enfer	xxiv.
Barrière des Martyrs	xxiv.
Barrière du Maine	xxv.
Barrière Montparnasse	xxv.
Barrière Poissonnière	xxv.
Barrière St. Jacques	xxiv.
Bastille	xxiv., xxv.
Batignollaises	xxiv.
Batignolles Monceaux	xxiv.
Bayard	35
Bearnaises	xxiv.
Belleville	xxiv., 34, 71
Belle Fermiere	60
Bercy	xxv.
Bertrand	19
Bibliothèque de l'Arsenal	68
Bibliothèque du Commerce	53
Bibliothèque St. Geneviève	45
Bibliothèque Imperiàle	52
Bougival	71
Bois de Bologne	xvi., xvii., 34, 48
Boulevards	xv., xxiv., xxv., 32
Boulevards des Italiens	xv.
Boulevard des Filles du Calvarie	xxv.
Boulevard de la Madeleine	xxv.
Boulevard du Temple	xxv., 57
Boulogne	xx.
Bourdon	28
Bourse	53

	PAGE
Cabs	xxi.
Calais	xx.
Camille Demoulins	10
Cardinal Mazarin	52
Carrefour de l'Odeon	47
Caserne Napoleon	30
Casimir Perier	61
Catherine de Medicis	5, 31
Champs Elysées	xvi., xxii., 15
Champs de Mars	xvii., xxiv., 19
Chapelle du Calvaire	23
Chapelle St. Denis	xxiv.
Chapelle Expiatoire	12
Chapel St. Ferdinand	xvi.
Charenton	xxv.
Charles V	1
Charles IX	8
Chateau d'Eau	32
Chateau des Fleurs	xvi., 15
Chateau de Fontainebleau	63
Chateau of Meudon	xvii., 51
Chateau Rouge	xxv.
Chateau de Vincennes	61
Chemin de Fer de Lyon	xxv.
Chemin de Fer du Nord	xxiv.
Chevalier Bernini	7
Cirque de l'Imperatrice	15
Cirque Olimpique	33
Citadines	xxiv.
Closerie de Lilacs	xvi.
Clovis	1
Colbert	35
College de France	2
College of Henri IV	46
College Louis le Grande	46
Colonnade	1
Column of July	60
Column Vendome	22
Compiègne	xiv.
Conciergerie	26
Condé	35
Conservatoire des Arts, &c.	54
Constantines	xxiv.
Corps Legislatif	20
Count de Paris	21
Daguesclin	35
Damas	12
Damien	26
Dames-Reunies	xxiv.
Delapierre, Mr.	xxv.

	PAGE
Delorme	
Devienne	
Dieppe	
Diorama of M. Langlais	
Docks Napoleon	
Dover	xx.,
Duchess de Bourbon	
Duchess of Orleans	
Duguesne	
Duguay-Trouin	
Duke of Cambridge	15,
Duke of Orleans	10,
Duke of Wellington	
Dunkirk	
Duroc	
Eaubonne	
Ecole de Medicine	
Ecole Militaire	2,
Ecole Polytechnique	
Elysée National	
Emperor of Russia	15
English Directory of First-rate Houses and best Shops in Paris	xxxvi.
Enghien	56, 71
Ermont	
Esplanade des Invalides	17
Excellentes	xxiv.
Exhibition	16, 74
Faubourg St. Martin	xxiv.
Favourites	xxiv.
Fix, Mdm.	
Fleury	12,
Folkestone	
Fontainebleau	xiv., xvii.,
Fontaine St. Antoine	
Fontaine des Capucins	
Fontaine des Innocents	
Fontaine St. Martin	
Fontaine Molière	
Foret de Fontainebleau	
Francis I	1,
French Phrases	xxvii.
Gazelles	xxiv.
General Hoche	
Girondists	
Gobelin's Manufactory	xvi., 1,
Gobelins	xxiv.

INDEX.

	PAGE
Grand Trianon	38
Gravesend	xxi.
Grenelle	xxiv.
Grenier de Reserve	68
Gros-Caillou	xxiv.
Halle aux Blés	31
Halles Centrales	30
Halle aux Vins	69
Havre	xx.
Heloise	29
Henry IV.	1, 68
Henry IV., Bath	24
Hippodrome	16
Hirondelles	xxiv.
Hopital Militaire	43
Hospital St. Louis	1
Hotels	xxii.
Hotel de Cluny	xvi., 46
Hotel Dieu	27
Hotel des Invalides	xv., xvii., 1, 17
Hotel des Monnaies	47
Hotel de Praslin	22
Hotel de Sully	68
Hotel de Ville	xiv., xvii., 2, 29
Hugh Capet	1
Imprimérie Imperiàle	59
Isle de la Cité	1, 2
Jacques Molay	24
Jardin d'Hiver	16
Jardin de Luxembourg	42
Jardin Mobile	xvi., 15
Jardin des Plantes	xvi., 67, 69
Joinville	72
Jourdan	35
Lannes	35
Larochelle	12
Law	23
La Villette	xxiv.
Letters	xvii.
London	xvii., xxi.
Lord Raglan	15, 19
Louis Philippe	xiv., 23, 35
Louis XIII.	4, 10, 35
Louis XIV.	1, 2, 6, 10, 23, 35
Louis XV.	61
Louis XVI.	12, 14, 58
Louvre	xv., xvii., xxv., 7
Lucian Buonaparte	11
Lycée Charlemagne	67
Madame Elizabeth	27
Madame de Maintenon	38
Madame de Pompadour	15
Madeleine	xv., xxv., 1, 2, 13
Madeleine Broham, Mdm	12
Maillotins	30
Maison de Cluny	46
Maison Dorée	32
Mars	12
Marie Antoinette	12, 14, 23, 26, 38, 50, 56

	PAGE
Marie de Medicis	14
Marseilles	xx.
Marshal Turenne	18
Marshal Ney	61
Massena	35
Maurice de Saliac	27
Meudon	xvii., 51
Mc.Henry	xxv.
Mirabau	44
Molé	12
Molière	11
Money	xvii., xxv.
Monrose	12
Monteaux and Co.	xxv.
Montmartre	34, 72
Montmorency	34, 56
Montrouge	xxv.
Montrougiennes	xxv.
Morgue, La	27
Mortier	35
Murat	15
Musée d'Artillerie	xvii., 39
Musée des Beaux Arts	xvii.
Napoleon	13, 14
Newhaven	xx.
Neuilly	xxv., 72
Nôtre Dame	xv., 1, 2, 27
Obelisk de Luxor	2, 14
Observatory	1, 43
Odeon	xxv.
Omnibuses	xxv.
Opera Comique	33
Opera Francais	33
Palace of Industry	74
Palace of Versailles	85
Palais des Beaux Arts	2, 40
Palais de Justice	xv., 25
Palais de la Legion d'Honneur	21
Palais du Luxembourg	xv., xvii., 41
Palais du Quai d'Orsay	2, 21
Palais du Prior	57
Palais Royal	xv., xxiv., 10
Palais des Thermes	46
Pantheon	xvi., xxv., 1, 43
Paris	xiii., xxi., xxiii., 1
Passports	xvii.
Passy	xxv., 34, 48
Père la Chaise	xvi., xxv., 60
Petits Pères	32
Petit Trianon	38
Philip Augustus	1
Place de la Bastille	60
Place Cadet	xxiv.
Place du Carousel	xv., xxv., 2, 6
Place du Châtelet	24
Place de la Concorde	xv., xiv., 2, 14
Place Dauphine	xxiv., 25
Place de l'Ecole	24
Place du Havre	xxiv.
Place du Palais Royal	xxiv.
Place de Richelieu	53
Place St. Sulpice	xxiv., 40

	PAGE
Place Vendome	22
Place des Victoires	31
Place des Vosges	59
Pont d'Austerlitz	68
Pont du Carousel	3
Pont de la Concorde	20
Pont d'Iena	17
Pont des Invalides	17
Pont Neuf	1, 24
Pont Royal	1, 22
Pont de la Reforme	29
Pope Alexander III.	27
Porte St. Denis	1, 32
Porte St. Martin	xxv., 1, 32
Post Office	xxv.
Prince de Condé	20
Prince Jerome Bonaparte	xv., 51
Prince Napoleon	11
Prince Polignac	49
Prince de Salm	21
Provost, Mr.	12
Quai Conti	47
Quai de Voltaire	22
Rachel, Mlle.	12
Ravaillac	30
Reynier, Mr.	12
Richelieu	35
Robespièrre	27, 30
Rouen	xx.
Rueil	73
Rue St. Antoine	30, 60, 67
Rue Castiglione	xxv.
Rue du Faubourg St. Honoré	xxv.
Rue Franc Bourgois	59
Rue Grenelle St. Honoré	xxv.
Rue St. Honoré	xxv.
Rue Jean Jacques Rousseau	xxv.
Rue Mouffetard	xxiv.
Rue de la Paix	xxii., xxv.
Rue du Rempart	12
Rue Richelieu	xxv.
Rue de Rivoli	xv.
Rue Vivienne	xxv., 54
Sainte Chapelle	xv.
Samaritan Bath	24
Samsons, Mr.	12
Sceaux	73
Seine (river)	45
Sèvres	xvii., 2, 51
Sorbonne	1, 46
Southampton	xx.
St. Cloud	xvi., 34, 49
St. Denis	55
St. Etiénne du Mont	45
St. Eustache	30
St. Germain	xvii., 71
St. Germain l'Auxerrois	10
St. Gervais	30
St. Jacques	23
St. Lazare	xxv.
St. Louis	26
St. Ouen	73

INDEX.

	PAGE		PAGE		PAGE
St. Paul and St. Louis	67	Theatre des Folies Dramatiques	33	Tomb of Napoleon	18
St. Roch	23	Theatre Francais	12	Tomb of Princess Demidorf	61
St. Sulpice	2, 40	Theatre des Funambules	33	Tomb of St. Geneviève	45
St. Vincent de Paul	57	Theatre de la Gaîte	33	Tourville	35
Ste Genevieve	1	Theatre Gymnase	33	Tuilleries	xv., xvii., xxii., 3
Suffren	35	Theatre Lyrique	53	Turenne	35
Suger	35	Theatre de St. Martin	33		
Sully	35	Theatre Odeon	47	Val de Grace Church	43
		Theatre des Varieties	33	Vaugirard	xxv.
Talma	12	Theatre du Vaudeville	53	Versailles	xvi., 33
Tapisseries des Gobelins	67, 70	The Temple	57	Ville d'Avray	34
Terrace of Bellevue	xvii., 51	Tobacco Manufactory	17	Vincennes	2
Theatre de l'Ambigu	33	Tomb of Colbert	31	Visconti	7, 11
Theatre du Boul, Beaumarchais	33	Tomb of Cath. de Medicis	56	Voitures à Remise	xxiii.
Theatre des Delassements	33	Tomb of Dagobert	56	Voitures de Place	xxiv.

CONTENTS.

INTRODUCTION.

	PAGE.
Address to the Traveller	xiii.
Addresses of Embassies and Consulates in Paris	74
Cabs	xxi.
Cardinal Numbers	xxxv.
Choice of Locality	xxii.
Days and Hours for visiting Public Buildings, Palaces, Museums, &c.	xxxix., xl.
English Directory of First-rate Houses and Best Shops in Paris	
Form of Address	xxvi.
Fortifications	74
French Phrases	xxvii. to xxxv.
Hotels	xxii.
Hints to Visitors going from London to Paris	iii.
Letters	xviii.
List of Custom Duties	75
Luggage	xxi.
Money	xvii., xxv.
Money Changers	xxv.
Ordinal Numbers	xxxv.
Passports	xvii.
Post Office	xviii., xxv., 75
Postal convention with France	xviii.
Preface	xi.
Public Conveyances	xxiii. to xxv.
Routes.—Boulogne, Calais, Dieppe, Dunkirk, and Havre	xx. and xxi.
Visitors passing only One Day in Paris	xv.
Ditto Two Days ,,	xvi.
Ditto Three Days ,,	xvi.
Ditto Four Days ,,	xvii.
Ditto Five Days ,,	xvii.
Ditto Six Days ,,	xvii.
Ditto Seven Days ,,	xvii.

PARIS—Historical and Descriptive .... 1 to 4

FIRST DAY.

PAGES

The Tuilleries—Place du Carousel—Louvre—St. Germain l'Auxerrois—Palais Royal—Fontaine Molière—Theatre du Palais Royal—Rue du Remparts—The Tuilleries .... 4 to 12

SECOND DAY.

Chapelle Expiatoire—Madeleine—Place de la Concorde—Champs Elysées—Cirque de l'Imperatrice—Exhibition—Place des Champs Elysées—Arc de l'Etoile—Pont des Invalides—Pont d'Iena—Manufactory of Tobacco—Invalides—Champs de Mars—Ministere des Affaires Etrangeres—Corps Legislatif—Pont de la Concorde—Palais de la Legion d'Honneur—Palais du Quai d'Orsay—Barracks—Pont Royal—Quai de Voltaire .... 12 to 22

x.

CONTENTS.

PAGES

THIRD DAY.

Place Vendome—Fontaine des Capucins—St. Roch—St. Jacques de la Boucherie—Pont Neuf—Place Dauphine—Palais de Justice—Sainte Chapelle—Conciergerie—La Morgue—Hotel Dieu—Notre Dame—Pont de la Reforme—Hotel de Ville—Caserne Napoleon—St. Gervais—Henry IV. Assassinated—Halles Centrales—Fontaine des Innocents—St. Eustache—Halle Aux Bles—Bank of France—Place des Victoires.. 22 to 33

FOURTH DAY.

Versailles .... 33 to 39

FIFTH DAY.

Musee d'Artillerie—Palais des Beaux Arts—Place, Fountain, and Church of St. Sulpice—Palais du Luxembourg—Statue of Marshal Ney—Observatoire—Val de Grace—Pantheon—Bibliothèque—Ste. Geneviève—St. Etienne du Mont—Ecole Polytecnique—College Louis le Grand—Sorbonne—Hotel de Cluny—Theatre Odeon—Hotel des Monnaies .... 39 to 48

SIXTH DAY.

Bois de Bologne, St. Cloud, Sevres, Meudon .... 48 to 52

SEVENTH DAY.

Bibliothèque Imperiale—Place Richelieu—Bourse—Conservatoire des Arts et Metiers—St. Denis—Enghien—Montmorency and St. Vincent de Paul ...... 52 to 57

EIGHTH DAY.

Le Temple—Archives Imperiales—Imprimerie Imperiale—Place des Voges—Bastille—Pere la Chaise—Place du Trone—Vincennes............................... 57 to 62

NINTH DAY.

Fontainebleau... 63 to 67

TENTH DAY.

Rue St. Antoine—St. Pierre et St. Paul—Fontaine St. Antoine—Hotel de Sully—Temple Protestante—Arsenal—Grenier de Reserve—Pont d'Austerlitz—Jardin des Plantes—Halle aux Vins—Manufacture des Gobelins .... 67 to 70

Environs of Paris .... 71 to 73

PREFACE.

The rapid and extensive sale of the first edition of this work, has induced the proprietors to publish the present improved edition.

The work is in the form of an Itinerary, and is divided into such portions, or routes through Paris, as the Visitor will be able to accomplish in a given time. Everything worthy of attention is distinctly noticed, and each day's walk is so carefully arranged, that the trouble and confusion generally arising from the indiscriminate view of numerous objects, are by this means avoided. Many useful hints respecting hotels, lodgings, &c., have been added to the present edition—and the whole carefully revised, so as to render it a complete Guide to the objects of attraction in the French capital.

MAPS AND ILLUSTRATIONS.

	PAGE.
CHAPEL OF THE PALACE OF VERSAILLES	27
CHAPELLE DES INVALIDES	61
CHATEAU DE FONTAINEBLEAU	63
CLERMONT, VIEW OF	1
DANJAN DU CHATEAU VINCENNES	61
ENTREE DU PALAIS DU LUXEMBOURG	27
EXHIBITION, VIEW OF (BAXTER'S PROCESS)	Face Title.
FONTAINE DES INNOCENTS	61
FRANCE, MAP OF	After Contents.
JARDIN DES PLANTES	69
LOUVRE, COURT OF THE	5
MUSEES DU LOUVRE	7
NOTRE DAME	27
PARIS, PLAN OF	Face Title.
PARIS, VIEW OF	1
PASS OF VIRON	63
PERE LA CHAISE, VIEW OF	63
PERE LA CHAISE, PLAN OF	60
PLACE DU CAROUSEL	5
PORTE D'ENTREE CHATEAU DE VINCENNES	61
RIVOLI, RUE DE	27
ST. CLOUD, VIEW IN	1
ST. GENEVIEVE, EGLISE DE	61
TUILLERIES, THE	5
VAL DE GRACE	27

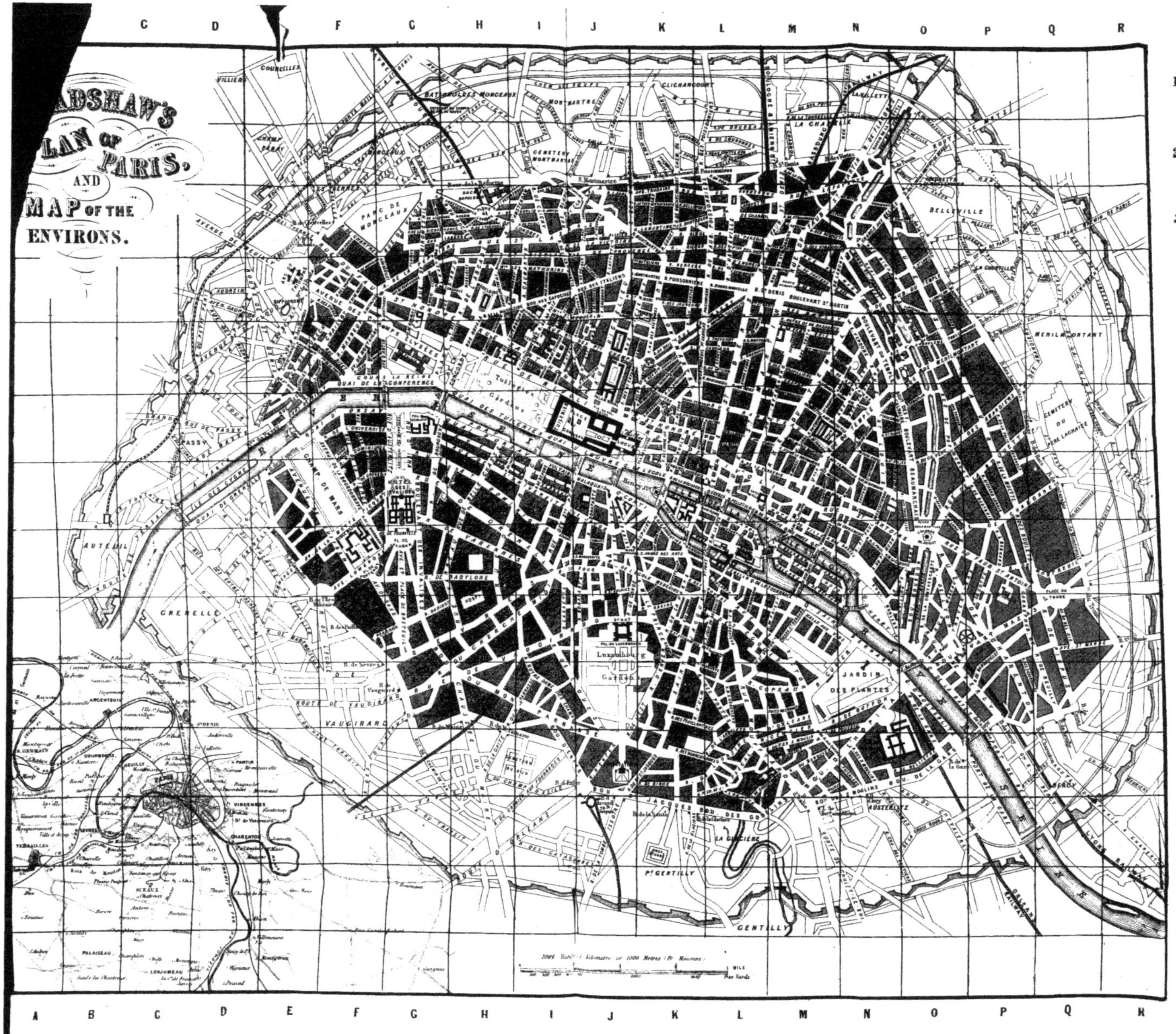

BRADSHAW'S PLAN OF PARIS AND MAP OF THE ENVIRONS.

REFERENCE TO THE PLAN.

In order to make the stranger to find on inspection the situation of any Street, &c., the Map is divided into Squares, by means of vertical and horizontal lines. The vertical lines are marked at the top of the plan by letters A, B, C, &c., and the horizontal ones by figures 1, 2, 3, &c., on the side. To use it, the operation is as follows:—Opposite the name of the Street, &c., of which the situation is enquired, will be found letters and figures: the letter corresponds to one on the top or bottom, and the figures to one on the sides; and the intersection of the vertical line with the horizontal line indicates the square in which the object sought will be found.

STREET REFERENCE

(Street index, illegible)

ENVIRONS OF PARIS

(Index of environs, illegible)

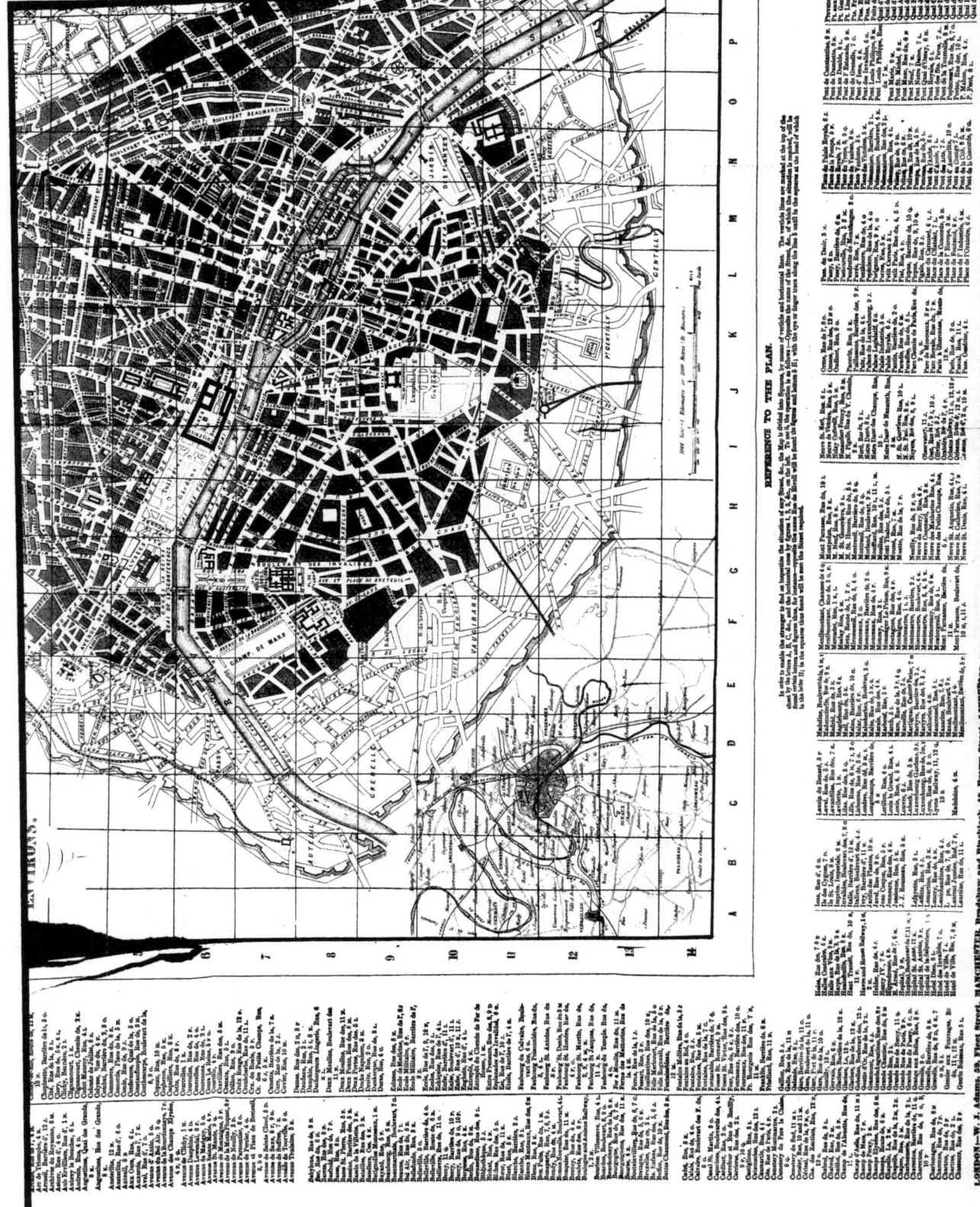

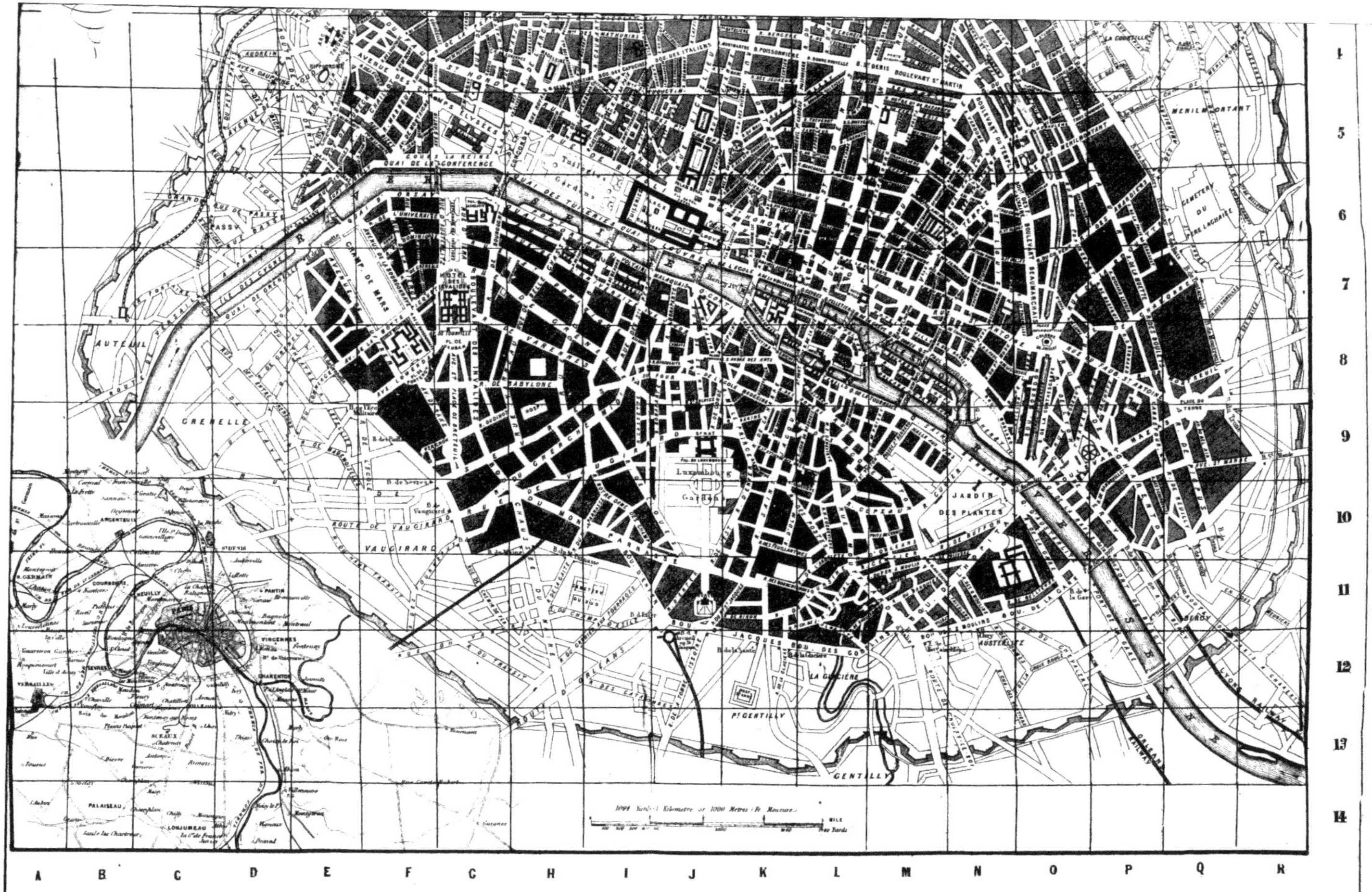

REFERENCE TO THE PLAN.

In order to enable the stranger to find on inspection the situation of any Street, &c., the Map is divided into Squares, by means of verticle and horizontal lines. The verticle lines are marked at the top of the sheet by the letters A, B, C, &c., and the horizontal ones by figures 1, 2, 3, &c., on the left. To use it, the operation is as follows:—Opposite the name of the Street, &c., of which the situation is required, will be found certain letters and figures thus, for instance—opposite the name Rue de Rivoli will be found the figures and letters 5 H; with the eye or finger trace along the line 5 until in the squares at the head of which is the letter H; in the squares thus found will be seen the Street required.

Iena, Rue d', 6 G.
Ile des Cygnes, 7 D.
Ile St. Louis, 8 M.
Imprim. Imperiale, 6 M.
Invalides, Boulevart des, 7, 8 G.
Italie, Barrière d', 12 M.
Italiens, Boulevart des, 4 J.
Ivry, Barrière d', 11 N.
Jardin des Plantes, 10 N.
Javel, Rue de, 9 D.
Jean Coujon, Rue, 5 F.
Jenneurs, Rue des, 4 K.
Jussienne, Rue, 5 K.
J. J. Rousseau, Rue, 5 K.

Lafayette, Rue, 3 L.
Laffitte, Rue, 4 J.
Lamartine, Rue, 3 K.
Lancry, Rue de, 4 N.
Lanichandiere, Rue, 4 J.
L pe, Rue de, 7, 8 O.
Laurent Jussieu, Rue, 7 F.
Laursine, Rue de, 11 L.
Lauzin du Renard, 3 F.
Laval, Rue de, 3 J.
Lavandilas, Rue des, 7 K.
Lavilette, 1 N.
Lilas, Rue des, 3 Q.
Lille, Rue de, 6 H, 7 I, 2 O.
Lisbonne, Rue de, 3 G.
Londres, Rue de, 3 H, I.
Longchamps, Barrière de, 5 E.
Lorillon, Rue, 4 O.
Louis le Grand, Rue, 4 I.
Louis, Rue, 4, 5 K.
Louvre, 6 J.
Lubeck, Rue de, 5 E.
Luxembourg Gardens, 9 J.
Luxembourg, Rue de, 5 H, I.
Lyon, Rue de, 8, 9 O.
Lyons Railway, 11, 12 Q, 13 R.

Madeleine, 4 H.
Madeline, Boulevart de la, 4 H, I.
Mademoiselle, Rue de, 9 E.
Madrid, Rue de, 3 H.
Magdebourg, Rue, 6 E.
Mail, Rue du, 5 K.
Maine, Barrière du, 10 H.
Malar, Rue, 6 F.
Malesherbes, Boulevart, 3 G.
Malte, Rue de, 5 N, O.
Marais, Rue des, 4 N.
Marbeuf, Rue, 5 F.
March, 5 I.
Mare, Rue de la, 3 P, 4 Q.
Marseille, Rue de, 2 O.
Martignac, Casimir Perier, 7 H.
Martyrs, Barrière des, 2 J.
Martyrs, Rue des, 2, 3 J.
Mathurins, 4 H.
Mauconseil, Rue, 5 L.
Mazarine, Rue, 7, 8 J.
Mazas, Boulevart, 9 P.
Menilmontant, 5 Q.
Menilmontant, Barrière de, 5 P.
Menilmontant, Chaussee de 4 Q.
Menilmontant, Rue de, 5 O, P.
Mercadet, Rue, 1 K, L.
Meslay Rue, 4 M.
Metz, Route de, 1, 2 P.
Miromesnil, Rue de, 3, 4 G.
Monceaux, 2 G.
Monceaux, Barrière de, 2 G.
Monceaux, Rue de, 4 F.
Moncey, Rue, 3 I.
Monseignr Le Prince, Rue, 9 K.
Montagnes, Rue des, 4 P.
Montaigne, Rue, 4 G.
Montmartre, 1 I, J.
Montmartre, Barrière, 2 J.
Montmartre, Boulevart, 4 K.
Montmartre, Rue, 3, 4, 5 K.
Montmorency, Rue de, 6 M.
Montorgeuil, Rue, 5 L.
Mont Parnasse, Barrière du, 11 H.
Mont Parnasse, Boulevart du, 10 H, I, 11 J.
Mont Parnasse, Rue du, 10 L.
Montpolon, Rue, 8 K.
M. Neuf, Rue, 8 K.
M. St. Genevieve, 9 L.
M. St. Honore, Rue du, 5 I.
Montreuil, Barrière de, 8 Q.
Montreuil, Rue de, 8 Q.
Morland, Boulevart, 9 N.
Moufftard, Rue, 10 L, 11 L, M.
Moulins, Rue des, 5 J.
Mont Thabor, Rue du, 5 I.
Moussi, Rue, 7 M.
Muette, Rue de la, 7 P.

Neuilly, Rue de, 2 F, G.
Neuve de Berry, Rue, 4 F.
Neuve Coqenard, Rue, 3 K.
Neuve des Mathurins Rue, 4 I.
Neuve des Petits Champs, Rue, 5 J.
Neuve St. Augustin, Rue, 4 I, J.
Neuve St. Catherine, Rue, 7 N.
Neuve St. Denis, Rue, 4 L.
Neuve St. Meri, Rue, 6 L.
Neuve de Victoire, Rue, 5 K.
Nolay Caffarelli, Rue, 5 N.
Nonandiers Foucy, Rue, 8 M.
N. Pigalle, Rue du V. Chemin, 2 K.
Nord, Rue du, 2 L.
Notre Dame, 8 L.
Notre Dame des Champs, Rue, 10 I.
Notre Dame de Nazareth, Rue, 5 M.
N. St. Genevieve, Rue, 10 L.
N. St. Paul, Rue, 8 N.
Noyers, Rue des, 8, 9 L.

Observatory, 11 J.
Oest, Rue de l', 9 I, 10 J.
Olivier, Rue, 3 J.
Oratoire, Rue de l', 4 F.
Orleans Railway, 11 O, 12, 13 P.
Orleans, Route d', 12 H, I.
Orleans, Rue d', 2 G, 10 M.
Orme, Rue de l', 8 O.
Ormes, Rue des, 12 N O.
Oudinot, Rue, 9 G.

Pacevin, Rue, 5 K.
Paillassons, Barrière des, 9 F.
Paix, Rue de la, 4 I.
Palace du Luxenbourg, 9 J.
Palace Legislatif, 6 G.
Palais Industrie, 5 G.
Palais Royale, 6 J.
Pantin, Barrière de, 2 O.
Paradis, Rue de, 6 M.
Paradise, Rue de, 3 L.
Parc Chemin de Paris, Rue du, 2 Q, R.
Parc de Monceaux, 3 F G.
Parc Royale, Rue du, 7 N.
Paris à Charenton, Route de, 12 R.
Paris, Rue de, 2 G.
Pascal, Rue, 11 L.
Pass. Ocudrier, 4 I.
Pass. du Desir, 3 M.
Passy, 6 D.
Passy, Barrière de, 6 E.
Pastourelle, Rue, 5 6 M.
Pandrette de Montfaugon 2 O.
Pavée, Rue, 7 N.
Penthieore, Rue de, 4 G.
Pepiniere, Rue de la, 4 G.
Perignon, Rue, 9 F, G.
Perres, Rue, 5 N.
Petit Carreau 5 L.
Petit Paris, Rue du, 4, 5 D.
Piat, Rue, 4 P.
Picpus, Barrière de, 10 Q.
Picpus, Rue de, 9, 10 Q.
Pigale, Rue, 3 J.
Place du Carousel, 6 I, J.
Place du Chatelet, 7 L.
Place de la Concorde, 5 H.
Place de l' Europe, 3 H.
Place de Fontenoi, 8 F.
Place de l' Industrie, 4 M.
Place de l'Oratoire, 6 J.
Place du Palais Royale, 6 J.
Place de la Pompe, 5 F.
Place Royale, 7 N.
Place du Trone, 8, 9 Q.
Place de Vauban, 8 G.
Place Vendome, 5 I.
Place des Victoires, 5 K.
Poissonniere, Barrière, 2 L.
Poissonniere, Boulevart, 4 K.
Poissonnieres, Rue des, 2 L.
Poissonniere, Rue, 4 L.
Poissy, Rue de, 9 M.
Poitou, Rue de, 6 N.
Poliveau, Rue de, 10 N.
Pompe, Rue de la, 5 D.
Ponceau, Rue du, 5 L.
Pont de l'Arche, 8 L.
Pont d'Arcole, 7 L.
Pont des Arts, 7 J.
Pont d' Austerlitz, 10 O.
Pont au Change 7 L.
Pont de la Cité, 8 L, M.
Pont de la Concorde, 6 G.
Pont de Constantine, 9 N.
Pont de Damiette, 8 N.
Pont au Double, 8 L.
Pont de l' Estacade, 9 N.
Pont de Grenelle, 7 C.
Pont d' Iena, 6 E.
Pont des Invalides, 6 G.
Pont Louis Philippe, 8 M.
Pont Louis Philippe, Rue du 7 M.
Pont Marie, 8 M.
Pont St. Michel, 8 K.
Pont Musc, Rue du, 8 N.
Pont Neuf, 7 K.
Pont Notre Dame, 7 L.
Pont Quai d'Orsay, 6 H.
Pont Royale, 6 I.
Pont des Sts. Peres, 7 J.
Pont de la Tournelle, 8 M.
Popincourt, Rue de, 6, 7 O.
Postus, Rue des, 10 L.
P. Mahon, Rue, 4 J.
P. Pont, 8 L.
Provence, Rue de, 3 K, 4 J.
Pt. aux Choux, 6 N.
Pt. Gentilly, 13 K.
Pt. Lion, Rue du, 5 L.
Pte. Friperie, Rue, 6 K.
Ptes. Ecuries, 3, 4 L.
Ptes. Ecuries, Rue des, 3, 4 L.
Puits de l' Ermite, 10 M.
Quai d' Anjou, 8 M.
Quai des Augustins, 8 K.
Quai d' Austerlitz, 10 O.
Quai Aux Fleurs, 7 L.
Quai de Bethune, 8 9, M.
Quai Bourbon, 8 M.
Quai des Celestins, 8 N.
Quai de la Conference, 5 F, G.
Quai Conti, 7 J.
Quai Debilly, 6 E.
Quai de l' Ecole, 7 K.
Quai des Gevres, 7 L.
Quai de Grenelle, 7 D.
Quai Henry IV., 9 N.
Quai de l' Horloge, 7 K.
Quai de la Loire, 2 O.
Quai du Louvre, 6 I, J.
Quai de la Megisserie, 7 K.
Quai Montebello, 8 L.
Quai Napoleon, 8 L.
Quai des Orfevres, 7 K.
Quai d' Orleans, 8 M.
Quai des Ormes, 8 M.
Quai d' Orsay, 6 F.
Quai Pelletir, 7 L.
Quai de la Rapée, 10 O.
Quai St. Benard, 9 M, N.
Quai St. Martin, 4 N.
Quai St. Michel, 8 K.
Quai St. Paul, 8 M.
Quai de la Seine, 2 N, O.
Quai de la Tournelle, 8 L, M.
Quai de Tuileries, 6 H, I.
Quai Voltaire Malaquaise, 7 I, J.
Quatre Fils, Rue des, 5 M, N.

Racine, Rue 9 K.
Rambouillet Rue de, 9, 10 P.
Rosiers, Rue des, 7 M N.
Roule, Barrière du, 3 E.
Roule, Rue du, 6, 7 K.
Royale, Rue, 2 K, 5 H.

Sante, Barrière de la, 12 K.
Saus-Saies, Rue des, 1, 2 J.
Seine, Rue de, 7, 8 J.
Senat, 9 J.
Sentier, Rue du, 4 K.
Sevres, Barrière de, 10 F.
Sevres, Rue de, 9. 10 D, E, F, G, H.
Sorbonne, Rue de, 9 K.
Soulances, Rue, 11 P, Q.
St. Aune, Rue, 5 J.
St. Andre, Rue, 6, 7 Q.
St. Andre des Arts, Rue, 8 K.
St. Antoine, Rue, 7, 8 N.
St. Bernard, Rue, 8 P.
St. Ch. de la Bretonnerie, Rue, 7 M.
St. Claude, Rue, 6 N, O.
St. Dominique, Rue, 6 F, 7 H, I.
St. Denis, Barrière, 2 M.
St. Denis, Boulevart, 3 Q, 4 M.
St. Denis, Route de, 4, 5 E.
St. Denis, Rue, 4, 5, 6 L, 2 P.
St. Etienne des Cres, Rue, 9 K.
St. Ferdinand, Rue, 4 O.
St. Florentine Ritchepansie, Rue, 5 H.
St. Genevieve, 9, 10 L.
St. George's, Rue, 3 J.
St. Germain l' Auxerrois, Rue, 7 K.
St. Germain, Rue, 6, 7 H.
St. Honoré, Rue, 5 H, I, J, K.
St. Hyacinthe, Rue, 9 K.
St. Jacques, Bould., 11, 12, J, K.
St. Jacques, Rue, 9, 10 K, J, K.
St. Jean de Beauvaise, Rue, 9 L.
St. Laurent, Rue, 3 M, O, P.
St. Lazare, Rue, 3 H, I, J.
St. Louis, Rue, 7, 8 D, 4 O.
St. Marguerite, Rue, 8 J.
St. Marie, Barrière, 6 E.
St. Marie, Rue, 5 E.
St. Martin, Boulevart 4 M, N.
St. Martin, Rue, 5, 6. 7 L.
St. Maude, Barrière, 9 R.
St. Maur, Rue, 4, 5 O, 6 P.
St. Nicolas, Rue, 4 H, I.
St. Paul, Rue, 8 N.
St. Peres, Rue des, 7, 8 I.
St. Petersbourg, Rue, 3 H.
St. Roch, Rue, 5 I.
St. Sauveur, Rue, 5 L.
St. Sebastian, Rue, 6 O.
St. Sulpice, Rue, 8 J.
St. Thomas, Rue, 4 J.
St. Victor, Rue, 9, 10 L, M.
Stockholm, Rue de, 3 H.
Strasbourg, Boulevart de, 3, 4 M.
Strasbourg Railway, 1, 2, 3 M, N, O.
Strasbourg, Rue de, 3 N.
Surennes, Rue de, 4 H.

Tacherie S. Bon, Rue, 7 L.
Taitbout, Rue, 4 J.
Taranne, Rue, 8 I.
Temple, Boulevart du, 5 N.
Temple, Rue du, 5, 6 M, N.
Theatre, Rue du, 8 D E.
Thermes Demours, Rue des, 3 E.
Thermes, Les, 3 F.
Thermes, Route des, 3 E.
Thevenot, Rue, 5 L.
Thorigni, Rue, 6 N.
Tiron, Rue, 7 M.
Tivoli, Rue de, 3 I.
Tomb Issoire, Rue de la, 12 J.
Tour d' Auvergne, Rue la, 3 K.
Tour, Rue de la, 6 D.
Tournelle, Rue de la, 2 M.
Tournelles, Rue des, 7 O.
Tourtille, Rue de, 4 P.
Transit, Rue du, 12 G.
Traversiere, Rue, 9 O.
Trois Bornes, Rue des, 5 O.
Trois Chandelles, Rue des, 10 F.
Trois Couronnes, Barrière des, 4 P.
Trois Couronnes, Rue, 5 O.
Trois Frères, Rue des, 3 J.
Trone, Barrière du, 9 Q.
Tuilleries, 6 I.
Tuilleries Gardens, 5, 6 H, I.
29 Juillet, Rue du, 5 I.

Ulm, Rue, 10 K.
Universite, Rue de l', 6 F, 7 H, I.

Valois, Rue de, 9 G.
Vanneau, Rue, 8, 9 H.
Varennes, Rue, 8 H.
Vaugirard, 10 F.
Vaugirard, Barrière de, 10 G.
Vaugirard, Route de, 10 E, F.
Vaugirard, Rue de, 9, 10 G, H, I.
Vauvres, Rue du, 11, 12 F, G, H.
Vendome, Rue, 5 N.
Verneuil, Rue de, 7 I.
Verrerie, Rue de la, 7 L, M.
Versailles à Paris, Route de, 7, 8 C D.
Vert Bois, Rue du, 5 M.
Vertus, Barrière de, 2 N.
Veux Augustins, Rue des, 5 K.
V. Haudriettes, Rue des, 6 M.
Viarmes, Rue de, 6 K.
Victoire, Rue de la, 3 J.
Vierge, Rue de la, 7 F.
Vignes, Rue des, 6 C.
Vignes, Rue des, 4 F.
Villeju, Rue, 11 M.
Villiers, 1 D.
Vienne, Rue de, 3 H.
Vierge, Rue de la, 4 P.
Ville l' Evèque, Rue de la, 4 G.
Vinaigriers, Rue, 2 K, 3 M.
Vincennes, Route de, 4 R.
Violet, Rue, 8, 9 D.
Vivienne, Rue, 4, 5 J, K.
Volta, Rue, 5 M.
V. St. Catherine, Rue, 7 N.

Bue, 13 A.

Cella, La, 12 A.
Champlan, 13, 14 B.
Chapelle, La, 11 C.
Charenton, 12 D.
Charonne, 11 D.
Chatenai, 13 C.
Chatillon, 12 C.
Chaton, 11 A.
Chaville, 12 B.
Chemin de Fer de Corbeil, 12, 13, 14 B.
Chemin de Fer d' Havre, 10 A, 11 B.
Chemin de Fer du Nord, 10 C.
Chemin de Fer de St. Germain 11 A, B.
Chemin de Fer de Versailles, 11 B, C., 12 B, C.
Chilly, 14 C.
Choisy le Roi, 13 D.
Clamart, 12 B.
Clichy, 11 C.
Colombes, 10 B.
Cormeil, 10 B.
Courbevoie, 11 B.
Cr de France, La, 14 D.

Deuil, 10 C.
Draved, 14 D.

Epinay, 10 C.
Ermont, 9 B.

Fleury, 12 B.
Fontenay, 12 B.
Fontenay aux Roses, 13 C.
Foret de St. Germain, 10 A.
Franconville, 10 B.
Frette, La, 10 B.

Garches, 12 B.
Gennevilliers, 10 C.
Gentilly, 12 C.
Gingues, 14 G.
Grenelle, 12 C.
Gros Bois, 13 B.

Houilles, 10 B.

Isle St. Denis, 10 C.
Issy, De, 12 B.
Ivry, 12 D.

Joinville, 12 E.
Juvisy, 14 C.

Lhay, 13 C.
Lonjumeau, 14 C.
Louveciennes, 11 A.

Maisons, 10 A.
Mandé, 12 D.
Marly, 13 B.
Marnes, 12 A.
Masons, 12 D.
Massy, 14 C.
Menilmontant, 11 D.
Meud, Bs, 12 B.
Meudon, 12 B.
Meudon, Bois de, 13 B.
Montesson, 11 A.
Montgeron, 14 D.
Montigny, 9 B.
Montmartre, 11 C.
Montreuil, 11 D.
Montrouge, 12 C.
Morangis, 14 C.
Moulineau, Les, 12 B.

Nanterre, 11 B.
Neuilly, 11 B.
Noissy le Pt. 14 D.

Orgement, 10 B.
Orsay, 14 B.

P. Marly, 11 A.
P. à l' Anglais, 12 D.
Palaiseau, 14 B.
Pantin, 11 D.
Paris, 11, 12 C.
Passy, 12 C.
Pluris Picquet, 13 B.
Puteoux, 11 B.

Rocquencourt, 12 A.
Romainville, 11 D.
Rueil, 11 B.
Rungis, 13 C.

S. Aubin, 14 A.
S. Claud, 11 C.
St. Cloud, 12 B.
St. Denis, 10 D.
St. Germain, 11 A.
St. Gervais, Pre, 11 D.
St. Gratie, 10 C.
St. Maur, 12 E.
St. Ouch, 11 C.
Sannors, 10 B.
Sartrouville, 10 A.
Satong, 13 A.
Saule les Chartreux, 14 B.
Sceaux, 13 C.
Sevres, 12 B.
Soclay, 14 A.
Solsy, 10 C.
Suresnes, 11 B.

Thiais, 13 D.
Tournam, 13 G.
Tousus, 13 A.

Vanves, 12 C.
Vancresson, 12 A.
Vaugirard, 12 C.
Verrigres, 13 B.
Versailles, 12 A.
Vigneux, 14 D.
Villetaneuse, 10 C.
Villette, La, 11 D.
Ville d'Avray, 12 B.
Villejuif, 13 C.
Villeneuve, 14 D.
Vincennes, 12 D.
Vincennes, Bs. de, 12 D.
Viroflay, 12 A.
Vitry, 13 D.

Wissous, 14 C.

…ER, Bradshaw and Blacklock, 47, Brown Street; LIVERPOOL, T. Fairbrother, 46, Dale Street; BIRMINGHAM, James Guest, 52, Bull Street; SHEFFIELD, Robert Chadderton, Market Place; EDINBURGH, Moodie and Lothian, 76, Princes Street; GLASGOW, James Reid, 138, …rson, 51, Grafton Street; PARIS, Louis Nicoud Bellenger, 212, Rue Rivoli, and J. Dawes, 3, Place Vendome; BRUSSELS, W. Middleton, 94, Montagne de la Cour; UNITED STATES, Edwards, Sandford, and Co., New York, Baltimore, and Philadelphia.

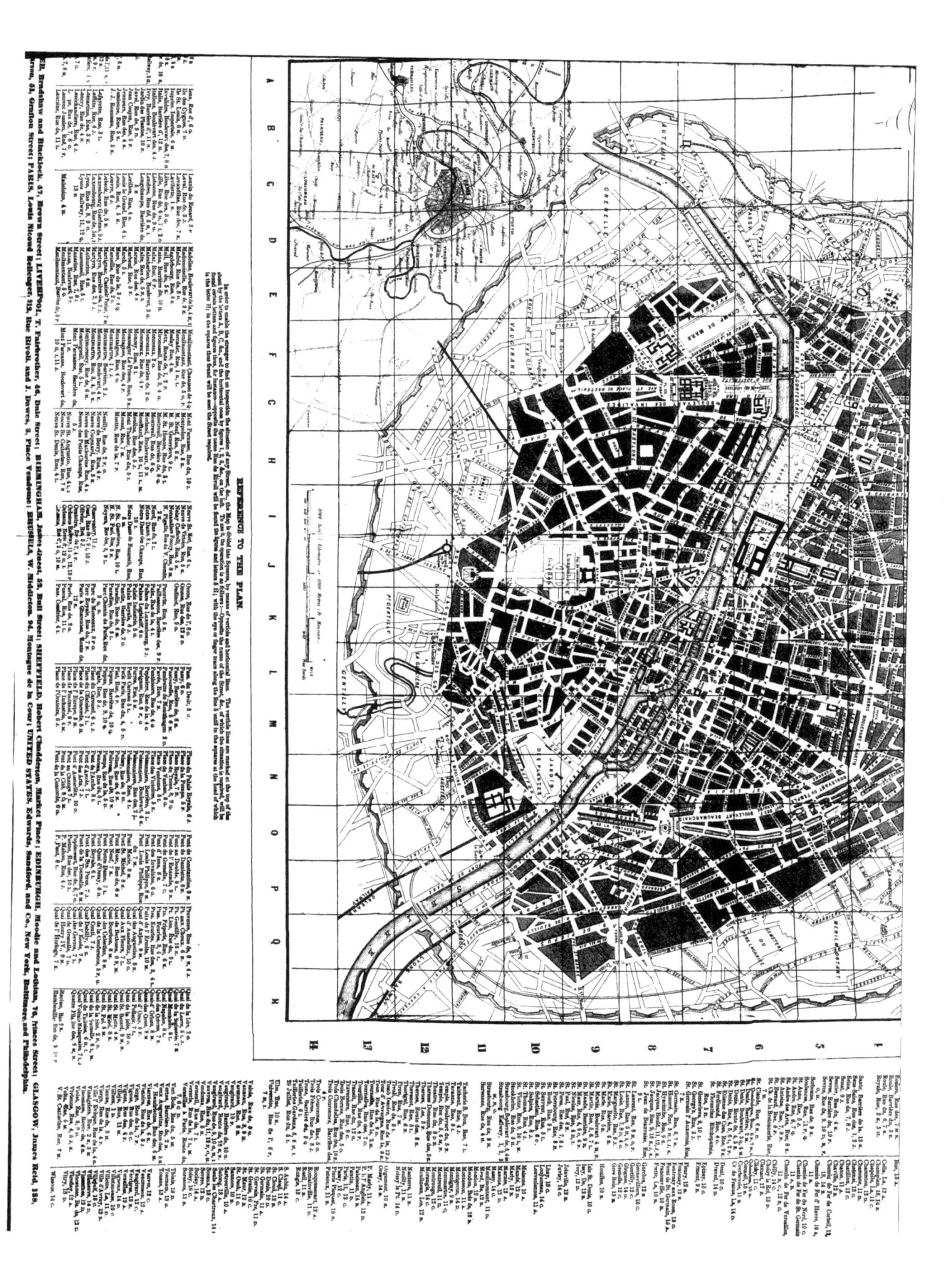

TO THE TRAVELLER.

In publishing the following Guide for Paris, the proprietors have had the same object in view which has always stimulated them in their former publications, viz.: giving to the public the most full and at the same time the most concise information they had it in their power to collect. Every one on arriving at a new city naturally asks, *What is to be seen here, and How is it to be seen?* and this question, not easily solved from the elaborate and learned guides now published, becomes more and more pressing, in proportion to the shortness of his stay which the visitor is about to make. In Paris, more especially is this difficulty felt. There are so many objects to be seen, so many more which the visitor desires to see, that he is perplexed and distressed what to do. If he apply to friends, one directs him to one place, another to another, each according as his taste inclines him to prefer one public monument or one public institution to another; and so the unfortunate sight-seeker finds that, in following the advice of friends, he loses a large portion of that which is most valuable to be seen, from the mere want of duly economising his time.

But, this presupposes that his friend is thoroughly acquainted with Paris and its environs, and is gifted with the capacity of acting as a guide. Whereas every day's experience teaches that people residing in a place are actually often the least qualified to act as guides; and there are many Parisians residing in Paris, as well as many Londoners residing in London, who know comparatively nothing of the interior of the public places of their respective cities of residence.

If, on the other hand, the visitor throw these kind friends or relations overboard, and apply himself to a Guide-Book, he discovers that the generality of them contain either too much or too little, and that none of them inform him how so to divide his time as to combine objects the most interesting, in, as it were, a coup d'œil.

The object of the present guide, is not only to answer the question, *What is to be seen?* but the not less essential one, *How is it to be seen?* and this too in a convenient and methodical form. By arranging the places to be visited each day, according to their proximity to each other, a great advantage is gained. The tourist will have no wild chase after a "lion" in one quarter of the town, and another immediately after in an opposite and distant locality. More may therefore be seen in the same time and with less fatigue.

A short historical and descriptive notice is appended to each object of interest, giving the most important particulars, and yet brief enough to be gathered in at a glance on the spot. This necessarily adds to the pleasure of the visit, by recalling the principal events, and arousing those associations which would otherwise, in the excitement and hurry of seeing so many material things before us, remain unawakened.

The plan of the work divides the time of the visitor into *ten* days, allotting to him so much for each day. By pursuing the arrangement thus laid down, he cannot fail to be made acquainted with the greater part of all that is most important, and most capable of affording him pleasure in Paris and its distant environs, for even Compiègne and Fontainebleau are included in its environs. But there may be others who will be unable to stay out the time allotted, and who therefore adopting this plan, would lose the sight of several of the finest monuments of the metropolis of France.

It has therefore been thought advisable for the benefit of such, to give a preparatory arrangement of the objects to be seen, so that the stranger entering Paris *for a single day*, may know at once what he should see, as well as the readiest means of seeing it in that limited time. The same is done for a visitor *having two days at his disposal*; the same again for a person *having three days, and so on*.

And here a few words of remark may be offered on the *order of selection*. Of course there can be no greater difficulty than that of catering for the tastes of so many as will naturally be led to visit Paris, since so great a variety of opinion and criticism exists in the world. Taking the Hotel de Ville for example. One person visiting it, is struck with the beauty of its construction, and regards it as one of the finest monuments of the reign of Louis Philippe, judging it little inferior to the Hotels de Ville of Calais and Brussels. If he penetrate into the interior, and visit the private apartments of the Prefect or the public salons, he admires the paintings on the walls, the gildings of the ceilings, the graceful fall of the draperies, the richness of the silk decorations, the magnificence of the furniture, the brilliance of the mirrors, the style of the architecture, and the superb disposal of the whole. Another person visiting it the same day, and under the same auspices, judges it but a waste of time to have come out of his way to see it. This is no unusual occurrence and that too amongst persons professing a refinement of taste. The difficulty has been then to strike the average, and make such an arrangement as may satisfy all parties. In directing the steps of the stranger from one object to another, the most judicious choice has been made, and those monuments which excite the most general interest, first selected. We may therefore confidently anticipate that such an order will produce the greatest amount of entertainment, and give universal satisfaction.

TO VISITORS PASSING ONLY ONE DAY AT PARIS.

Take up your abode at one of the Hotels which you will find mentioned at page XXII, but let it be, if possible, near the Boulevards, or the Rue St. Honoré. Breakfast at 8 o'clock, walk along the Boulevards, from the Boulevards des Italiens to the Madeleine, one of the most beautiful and modern churches of Paris. Here you may take a Remise (a superior kind of cab, something like an English Brougham), for which you will have to pay two francs an hour. This is only five sous more than the fare of a common cab, but you gain your money in having a better horse, and going over your ground in less time. The coachman expects about five sous the hour. If you give the driver to understand that your object is to see all you can of Paris, he will take you by the most public streets, and point out the principal public buildings, that lie in your route. It should be observed that you will find Remises in nearly every street. They stand always under some shed or building, and not, as the cabs, in the open air. They are always ready, and you will find the coachman generally civil and obliging.

Drive then to *Nôtre Dame*, visit the *Palace de Justice* and the *Sainte Chapelle*,* which is very near it. Then proceed to the *Gardens and the Palace of the Luxembourg*. You will only have time to view the exterior, and take a momentary glance at the *Picture Gallery*, filled with the works of living artists, which it contains. Direct your course next to the *Hotel des Invalides* where your passport will gain you admission to see the church and tomb of Napoleon, one of the richest sights in Paris, if on a Monday, Wednesday, Thursday, Saturday, or Sunday, after twelve o'clock. From the Invalides drive to the *Place de la Concorde*, and (here discharging your Remise) walk through the *Gardens of the Tuilleries*, to view their beauties, and the Palace, whose principal front faces them. Go out by one of the gates on the left, into the Rue de Rivoli, and cross over to the *Palace Royal*, which, with its beautiful shops, cafés, and restaurants, is always interesting. At the southern extremity, the end facing the Louvre, is the Palace now inhabited by Prince Jerome Bonaparte, uncle to the present Emperor. In the Palace Royal you will find a luncheon at any price you desire, from 1 franc 25 centimes (14½d.), or upwards. After lunch a few minutes' walk will take you to the *Louvre* and the *Place du Carousel*. In this Place you will do well to pause a moment, to reconnoitre the extensive pile of buildings that surround you on every side, and the two palaces, the palaces of the Louvre and the Tuilleries, that

---

* Look in the Index for the names of the different places, and then to the page, where an account of them, as well as their situation, is given.

are on the right and left of you, as well as the triumphal arch which rises before the entrance into the chateau. After this, you will be able to spare a little time to inspect some of the galleries of paintings and curiosities, which the Louvre contains. The Louvre may be entered any day of the week, except Monday, by a passport. On Sundays it is open to the public without restriction, and always closes at four in the afternoon.

When you leave the Louvre, you would do well to take another Remise by the hour, drive through the Place de la Concorde, and the Champs Elysées to the Barrière de l'Etoile. Out side this Barrière is the magnificent arch, the Arc de Triomph, which it will well repay you to mount. Should you like it you can prolong your drive to the Bois de Bologne, remembering to visit the *Chapel of St. Ferdinand* which is situated a hundred yards or so in the avenue opposite the Port Maillot. The Bois de Bologne, in which two lakes have lately been constructed, is a most fashionable resort between the hours of 4 and 6; and here about the same time when they are in town or at St. Cloud, the Emperor and Empress may almost invariable be seen. The charge for the Remise for coming outside the Barrière, it must be recollected, is three francs per hour, instead of two.

On your return to the city, you will find good dinners at any of the Restaurants named in the introduction, after which amusement of every description will be open, to drive away the ennui of the next three or four hours. The Theatres, or the Circus, or one of the Operas, or some other diverting spectacles of the kind are always open; but should none of these gay sights attract you, you will be much amused by walking along the Boulevards, taking your coffee or an ice on the outside of one of the Cafés, and watching the curious stream of human beings that rolls by you.

Should your stay be prolonged for *two* days, you would do well to take a run down and see the chateau and gardens of Versailles. This is an occupation that will fill up the whole day. In the evening you will again be at liberty to select which of the many places of amusement you may like best. There are many gardens open after sunset, brilliantly lighted up with variegated lamps, where dancing and other gay scenes of delight take place; such as the *Jardin Mobille*, the *Chateau des Fleurs*, the *Closerie de Lilacs*, &c. There are also in the Champs Elysées, cafés, where you may hear pretty good singing and sip your coffee, or have an ice, or indulge in brandy and water, or beer, at your leisure. The *Jardins* alluded to above are not visited by the elite of the Parisian society, but they give to a foreigner a good insight into the habits and amusements of the French people.

Should your stay extend over *three* days, a visit to *Père la Chaise*, the *Jardin des Plantes*, the *Gobelin's Manufactory* (should it be on a Wednesday or Saturday), the *Pantheon*, and the *Hotel de Cluny* is recommended. An examinatian of these places will fully occupy your day until five or six o'clock, when the evening attractions of Paris are again open to your choice.

INTRODUCTION.

Should your visit extend over *four* days, you will find the Chateau and Park of St. Cloud, a short distance out of town, and the Museums of the porcelain manufactory at Sèvres, very interesting. You may go to St Cloud by the railway to Anteuil, where an omnibus will be waiting to take you for two sous, by a pleasant drive through the Bois de Bologne, the town of Bologne, and across the Seine to the park gates. From Sèvres to St. Cloud is only a short walk through the park. If you are a good walker, you should visit the *Terrace of Meudon*, about a mile and a half beyond Sèvres on the hill. This spot commands a magnificent view of Paris and the river. Cabs may be obtained at St. Cloud to take you to Sèvres and Meudon, should you prefer to ride.

Should it be your intention to remain *five* days, on your return from Meudon, or Sèvres, you should, immediately on your arrival in Paris, apply for permission to visit the Tuilleries and the interior of the Hotel de Ville. If your stay be over a Sunday, you might witness mass at any of the principal churches. The service commences exactly at ten o'clock.

Should your visit extend over *six* days, the *Hotel de Cluny*, the *Musée des Beaux Arts*, and the *Musée d'Artillerie* should be visited; also *St. Germain* and the *Abbey of St. Denis*, which, though on different lines of railway, may easily be accomplished in a day. St. Denis should be seen first.

Should you remain *seven* days, a trip to Fontainebleau, will be highly interesting; and should you have more days than these, you would do wisely to go over some of those public places which the visitor for one day is invited to go to, and which he had scarcely time to inspect, as for example the *Louvre*, the *Luxembourg*, the *Hotel des Invalides*, the *Champs de Mars, &c.*

GENERAL REMARKS FOR TRAVELLERS.

In drawing up the following instructions, it has been presumed that the traveller will have provided himself with *Bradshaw's Continental Railway Guide*, as indispensable to railway travelling on the Continent.

WHAT SHOULD BE DONE IN LONDON —PASSPORTS—MONEY—LETTERS. The first thing the traveller must see about is his passport, for which ample instructions are found at pp. 19-22 of *Bradshaw's Continental Guide*. Mr. W. J. Adams, our London Agent, will answer any inquiries on this head, or take the necessary steps to procure a passport, and have it mounted in a case, for those who desire it. It is recommended that the passport be always carried about with the traveller, as it procures admission to many public places, where a native only is admitted on certain days, and thus, what is generally considered a source of annoyance, proves an advantage to the traveller.

B

MONEY.—See pp. 23-5 of *Bradshaw's Continental Guide*, also page xxv. Bank-notes are negociable in Paris, and sovereigns are received, but the best plan is to change your English money into French napoleons at a respectable money-changer's at London or in France (*changeur*). English gold however will pass anywhere (silver is useless), so will the louis d'or or napoleon, and the five-franc piece. As to expenses, 10s. to 20s. per head per day may be allowed. The latter sum will cover all charges of living in the best hotels, and travelling by first class railway and the best places in the coach.

LETTERS.—The traveller will find it convenient to have his letters addressed to him to the "Poste Restante." They will be delivered on the passport or name-card being shewn. There are now two posts daily (one in the morning and the other in the evening) leaving London for France. All letters for France go through the London post-office, and for the morning mail must be in the London office before 7-45 a.m., and the evening mail before 6 p.m.

POSTAL CONVENTION WITH FRANCE.—In accordance with the provisions of a new Postal Convention with France, the entire postage, British and French, chargeable upon Newspapers and other Printed Papers posted in the United Kingdom addressed to France or Algeria, or, when they are conveyed by the French Mediterranean Packets, to any of the places in Turkey, Syria, and Egypt at which France maintains Post Offices, must, on the 1st of January, 1856, and thenceforward, be paid in advance, and no further charge of any kind will be levied upon their delivery.

Under the new arrangement many kinds of books and other printed matter, which have hitherto been liable to the letter rate of postage, will be forwarded at a greatly reduced charge; and as the charges on newspapers and other periodical literature levied on delivery in France have, in most instances, been much greater than that now to be paid in advance, a considerable reduction of postage will be made in their case also.

The following Table shows the charge which must be paid hereafter on the Printed Papers above referred to:—

	Not exceeding 4 oz.	Above 4 oz. and not exceeding ½ lb.	Above ½ lb. and not exceeding 1 lb.	Above 1 lb. and not exceeding 1½ lb.	Above 1½ lb. and not exceeding 2 lb.
	s. d.	s. d.	s. d.	s. d.	s. d.
For a Packet of British Newspapers duly registered at the General Post Office for Transmission abroad	0 1	0 2	0 4	0 6	0 8
For a Packet of Printed Papers other than British Newspapers duly registered at the General Post Office for Transmission Abroad	0 3	0 6	1 0	1 6	2 0

and so on, adding twopence or sixpence, as the case may be, for each additional half-pound.

The same rates of postage must be paid in advance upon newspapers and other printed papers addressed to any of the following countries and places, the correspondence for which is forwarded, as a rule, through France; viz.,—Baden, Bavaria, Greece, Lucca, Majorca, Minorca, Modena, the Papal States, Parma, Placentia, Sardinia, Two Sicilies, Spain, Switzerland, Syria, Tripoli, Tunis, Tuscany, Venetian Lombardy, and Wurtemberg, or addressed to any other foreign country, and specially directed to be forwarded " viâ France."

On this class of printed papers the rate paid in this country will cover the whole charge, either to the extreme frontier of France or to the port of disembarkation if they are conveyed from France by one of the French Mediterranean Packets.

Upon Newspapers addressed to the Ionian Islands, *specially directed to be sent viâ France*, and upon Newspapers for Malta, *specially directed to be sent " by French Packet viâ Marseilles*," the same rates of postage must also be paid in advance; but printed papers other than newspapers, addressed to the Ionian Islands and Malta, will not be sent at a reduced rate of postage by way of France. They may, however, be forwarded *viâ* Southampton under the Colonial Book Post Regulations.

The following is a list of the places in Turkey, Syria, and Egypt at which France maintains Post Offices; viz., Alexandria, Jaffa, Beyrout, Tripoli in Syria, Latakia, Alexandretta, Mersina, Rhodes, Smyrna, Mytelene, Dardanelles, Gallipoli, and Constantinople.

All newspapers, to be forwarded at the lower of the two rates mentioned above, must be posted within fifteen days from the date of publication; but newspapers of an older date may be forwarded at the rate set down for ordinary printed papers. If any printed paper, not a newspaper, be enclosed in the same packet with one or more newspapers, the whole will be chargeable at the higher of the two rates of postage.

Under the term "Printed Papers" are included periodical works, other than registered newspapers, stitched or bound books, pamphlets, sheets of music, catalogues, prospectuses, announcements, and notices of every kind, whether printed, engraved, or lithographed.

The following regulations must be strictly observed:

1. Every packet must be sent without a cover, or in a cover open at the ends or sides.

2. There must be no enclosure, except newspapers or other printed papers.

3. There must be no other writing or marks upon the newspapers or printed papers than the name and address of the person to whom they are sent, nor anything upon the cover but such name and address, the printed title of the papers, and the printed name and address of the publisher or vender who sends them.

If any of the above regulations be disregarded, or if the whole postage be not paid in advance, the packets will either be detained or forwarded charged as unpaid letters.

Newspapers addressed to the Mediterranean or the East Indies, and intended to be sent in the closed mails by way of Marseilles, will continue liable to the existing regulations, including the present rates of postage.

The time required for conveying Letters, &c., to any part of France, can be ascertained by reference to *Bradshaw's Continental Railway Guide*, and in very little more than this time the traveller may expect them at their appointed place.

WAY TO GET TO FRANCE AND LANDING THERE.—See pp. 140-1 of *Bradshaw's Continental Guide*, from which the following is extracted:—

ROUTES.

CALAIS ROUTE.—London to Paris direct, *via* Dover and Calais, 346 miles in 12½ hours, viz :—Departure from London for Dover (1st class only) at 8 30 *p.m.*; arrival at Dover at 11 15 *p.m.*; departure from Dover 11 30 *p.m.*; arrival at Calais 2 20 *a.m.*; arrival at Paris 9 50 *a.m.* (See page 30, *Bradshaw's Illustrated Hand Book to France.*) Through tickets, 61s. There are 26 miles only of sea by this route, which in the old coach days took 58 to 60 hours between London and Paris. By the direct train the luggage is examined only on arrival at Paris. Another direct train (1st and 2nd class) starts at 8 10 *a.m*, reaching Dover at 11 *a.m.*, Calais at 2 30 *p.m.*, and Paris at 11 15 *p.m.*; through tickets, 61s. and 43s. 9d. Travellers for Marseilles, on landing at Boulogne or Calais, should have their passports *viséd* for that place direct, to save delay at Paris; they will receive a provisional passport for 2 francs. The station, refreshment room, and douane at Calais are close to the quay. Three departures from Calais for Dover daily. Calais may be also reached by the General Steam Navigation Company's steamers, direct from London Bridge Wharf, twice a-week, in 8 to 9 hours. Fares 14s. and 10s. [As the Railway Trains are subject to change every month, the information given here respecting them had better be compared with *Bradshaw's Continental Guide.*]

BOULOGNE ROUTE.—London to Paris direct in about 12 hours, by South Eastern Railway and Packets from Folkestone, according to tide. *See pp.* 35-6, *Bradshaw's Hand-Book to France.* Through tickets, 51s. 6d. and 37s. Or by General Steam Navigation Company's boats twice a-week, direct from London Bridge Wharf, in 10 hours. Fares 14s. and 10s.; or through 31s. and 22s.

DIEPPE ROUTE.—Direct, in 12 to 15 hours, by Brighton Railway, steamer from Newhaven to Dieppe, according to tide, and railway to Rouen and Paris. *See pp.* 12-13, *Bradshaw's Illustrated Hand-Book to France.* About 72 miles of sea passage. Through fares, 28s. and 20s.

HAVRE ROUTE.—By South Western Railway to Southampton, steam to Havre, and railway to Rouen and Paris. (See pp. 10-12, *Bradshaw's Illustrated Hand-Book to France*). Through fares 28s. and 20s. N.B.—Steamer three times a-week; sea passage 102 miles.

DUNKIRK ROUTE.—By screw steamer direct from Irongate Wharf, two or three times a-week, in about 12 hours. Fares 10s. and 7s. (See pp. 38-9, *Bradshaw's Illustrated Hand-Book to France.*)

No baggage, except it may be a small parcel, or a carpet bag (if at night) is allowed to be taken ashore by the passengers, but is detained at the Douane (custom-house), where you may clear it yourself or pay a porter (*commissionnaires*, as they are called) to clear it.

Your passport is taken from you at the Douane, and a provisional passport given you instead, which will take you on to Paris. Or if you make a stay of a day or two at the port, you apply for provisional pass on leaving it. This you may do through the commissionnaire, who will also clear your baggage. It is much better in either case to make use of such an agent, who will for a franc or two take all the trouble off your hands, and save much bother and loss of time. The regular charge when you clear it, is, per package, 7 sous (3½d.) if under 10lb., 14 sous from 10 to 56lb., 1 franc above that weight; every package being charged, so that the fewer you have the better. For carriage to the hotel you pay a porter 50 cents (5d.) for the first package, and 25 cents for each of the others. When leaving a French port for England, a *permis d'embarquement* may be had at the Douane one hour before the steamer starts, or between one and three p.m. when she leaves at night. Once on board you cannot go ashore again without special permission. You may bring back, free of duty, a pint of spirits, and half a pint of eau-de-Cologne. By a new arrangement, luggage direct to London, by some of the trains on the South Eastern Railway, is not examined at Dover or Folkestone, but at the London Bridge station. Luggage, also, in Steamers from abroad, is now examined by the officers of customs on board, between Gravesend and London.

On alighting from the train in Paris, the passenger need give himself no anxiety about his luggage. What he has to do is quietly to follow the others, and he will enter a spacious room where he will find his trunk and boxes, as well as those of his fellow voyagers arranged on a long platform. Selecting his own, he will give up the keys to the nearest officers, who are the *customs officers* for Paris. They will at their leisure proceed to unlock, open and examine his various packages, and when they have satisfied themselves, re-deliver him his keys with permission to pass. The passenger will then ask a porter, who can easily be distinguished by his special dress, to take his trunks, &c. for him to a conveyance.

CALL A CAB.—We give the traveller the following advice. By all means call for a cab, you will find a variety of omnibuses waiting at the station, ready to seize upon you and carry you to what they call a good Hotel, professedly for less than a cab. But their object is to drive you to one of *their* Hotels, we say *their* Hotels, because either the driver or conductor is invariably paid for each passenger he brings to the Hotel. This of course is made up for by the exorbitant charges which the hotel-keepers to which you are conducted, manage to make.

CHOICE OF A LOCALITY.—There are many parts of Paris in which a person intending to reside for some time, would find very commodious and cheap lodgings, which, however, would be perfectly unsuited for a traveller who wishes to spend only a few days, and to see as much in that limited time as he can. We therefore recommend him, although perhaps he may have to pay a little dearer, to take up his quarters *somewhere near* the Madeleine. This is not only the most delightful quarter of Paris, but it is the centre from which nearly all the principal monuments may be visited, and has besides a great number of English residents in it. In fact it might almost be called an English quarter. In the neighbourhood are the Tuileries, the Champs Elysées, the Rue de la Paix, the Boulevard, and a few moments' walk will take you to either of the Operas or the principal French theatres.

HOTELS.—Having then made a choice of your locality, the next thing is the choice of your hotel. This we might observe should be made before arriving at the station, that you may at once order the cabman where to drive you, and being decided upon this point you will not suffer interruption from the importunities of the conductors of the omnibus. As it may be difficult for the traveller to determine where to put up on his arrival in Paris, without some idea of the hotels in this metropolis, we subjoin a list of the best.

The principal hotels such as Meurices, the Bristol, the Rhine, and des Princes, are first class—with first-rate charges—and therefore somewhat to expensive for the generality of English travellers, who will experience more attention and find greater comfort at those recommended in the following list.

HOTEL DU LOUVRE.—A first-rate establishment, situated between the Rue de Rivoli, Rue St. Honoré, and the place du Palais Royal.

HOTEL WAGRAM.—One of the best in Paris.

HOTEL DES ETRANGERS.—3, Rue Vivienne, worthy of the very highest recommendation.

HOTEL BEDFORD.—11, Place de l'Arcade, near the Madeleine, excellent in every respect.

HOTEL DES DEUX MONDES ET D'ANGLETERRE.—First-rate, cannot be too highly recommended for its comforts, cleanliness, and charges.

HOTEL D'YORK, Rue St. Anne, is a new house, well furnished; everything very clean and comfortable.

HOTEL FOLKESTONE.—9, Rue Castellane, very comfortable, and charges moderate.

GRAND HOTEL D'ANGLETERRE.—10, Rue des Filles, St. Thomas, between the Rue Richelieu and the Place de la Bourse, a first-rate house, and highly recommended.

GRAND HOTEL D'OXFORD ET CAMBRIDGE.—Exceedingly good in every respect.

GRAND HOTEL DE LYON.—12, Rue des Filles St. Thomas, with a large frontage in the Rue Richelieu, very comfortable, and charges moderate.

HOTEL DE LILLE ET ALBION.—223, Rue St. Honoré, a well-conducted, good house.

GRAND HOTEL LOUVOIS.—Place Louvois, in the Rue Richelieu, most centrally situated, and a well-conducted, clean house.

HOTEL DE NORMANDIE.—240, Rue St. Honoré, good and moderate.

The principal Restaurants are sumptuous establishments, but a good dinner at one of the following houses will be found an expensive affair. Visitors should endeavour to make a party of three or four, and then, by ordering one dish for two persons, or two dishes for four; they can then have a considerable variety of particular dishes at a moderate price. The best houses in the Palais Royal are Vefours, Very or les Trois Frerès Provençaux; the Café de Paris, the Café Anglais, or the Maison Doreé on the Boulevards. The celebrated house of Phillips, in the Rue Montorgeuil, is an excellent Restaurant, and much cheaper than the others. As a general rule, however, it is better for the traveller to dine at his hôtel, if there is a table d'hôte, as these dinners are very good, and the wines better than those to be had at the Restaurants. The Parisians do not sit long over their wine, but adjourn to a Café to partake of a cup of Coffee, with a glass of Cognac. It is indeed a luxury to sit in front of one of the magnificent Cafeés on the Boulevards, in the Palais Royal, or Champs Elyseés, and sip a cup of this delicious and refreshing beverage as they make it in France.

PUBLIC CONVEYANCES.—One of the best features of Paris, is the order, regularity, and civility with which the public conveyance system is arranged. The drivers of all hired carriages are under the strict surveillance of the police; and the penalties of the law are very severe against any who infringe the comfort of a Parisian, either by ill conduct or extortion. In every respect the system in England might be improved by adopting a few of the regulations that effect the French management. To a Londoner the prices will appear very economical. The cab is not taken by the mile, but by the course or by the hour. The course is any distance between the Barrières of Paris, but it should be observed that any stoppage, however slight, completes a course, and a new one is commenced. It will be therefore best for a person having many sights to see, to take a cab by the hour, the difference of which is very trifling. There are two sorts of cabs, those which stand under sheds, and those which stand in the open street. The former will be met with nearly everywhere, not more than two or three together in the same place; they are called *voitures à remise*,—remise signifying a coach-house. The latter remain in long file in some open place or street, and are called *voitures de place*.

FARES.—Voitures à remise, from 6 a.m. to midnight, four-wheeled, the course, 1 franc 75 cents—the hour, 2 francs: two-wheeled, the course, 1 franc 50 cents—the hour, 1 franc 75 cents. From midnight to 6 a.m., four-wheeled, the hour, 2 francs; two-wheeled, the hour, 2 francs 50 cents.

VOITURES DE PLACE.—There are three kinds of *Voiture de Place*, the *cabriolet*, which is an open cab with a head to it; the *coupé* entirely covered, and the *fiacre* a kind of Brougham.

FARES.—From 6 a.m. to midnight, cabriolet, the course, 1 franc 10 cents—the hour, 1 franc 50 cents; coupé, the course, 1 franc 25 cents—the hour, 1 franc 75 cents; fiacre, the course, 1 franc 50 cents—the hour, 2 francs. From midnight to 6 a.m., cabriolet, the course, 1 franc 75 cents—the hour, 2 francs 50 cents; coupé, the course, 1 franc 75 cents—the hour, 2 francs 50 cents; fiacre, the course, 2 francs—the hour, 3 francs.

In visiting places, and going by the hour, it is always cheaper to take a *voiture de remise*, because the horses are kept in better condition and go over the ground faster. The drivers expect always a few sous additional gratuity.

But besides the cabs there are omnibuses by which the visitor may go from one part of Paris to another for six sous (3d). It may be, however, that the omnibus he enters does not go to the place he wishes, he will therefore be obliged to ask for a ticket of correspondence, by which when he leaves the omnibus he is in, which the conductor will indicate, he can get into another going in his direction; you pay immediately after entering.

A few minutes' study of the map of Paris, will give you a very fair idea of the position of the principal streets and places. This will be of great service to you in understanding the following lines of route which the omnibuses take, and a list of which is subjoined to facilitate the knowledge of the visitor as to which to take. There are certain different lines of route which are as follows:—

BATIGNOLLAISES.—These omnibuses run from the Palais Royal to the Batignolles Monceaux.

BEARNAISES.—From Gros-Caillou to the Bastille.

CITADINES.—From Belleville to the Place Dauphine; correspondence to the Versailles railway Place du Havre.

CONSTANTINES.—From the Barrière de Long Champs to the Faubourg St. Martin.

DAMES-REUNIES.—From la Villette, by the Place St. Sulpice to the Champs de Mars and Grenelle.

EXCELLENTES.—From Belleville to the Barrière de l'Etoile, by the outside Boulevards.

FAVOURITES.—From the Chapelle Saint Denis to the Barrière d'Enfer, from the Barrière des Martyrs to the Gobelins, from the Chemin de fer du Nord to the Place St. Sulpice.

GAZELLES.—From the Barrière de la Gare to the Place du Palais Royal.

HIRONDELLES.—From the Chateau Rouge to the Barrière St. Jacques, from the Place Cadet to the Rue Mouffetard.

MONTROUGIENNES.—From the Rue Grenelle St. Honoré to Montrouge.

OMNIBUS.—From the Madeleine to the Bastille along the Boulevards, from the Barrière du Trone to the Place du Carousel, from the Bastille to the Barrière de Monceaux, from the Barrière du Roule to the Boulevards des Filles du Calvaire, from the Barrière Blanche to the Odeon, from Passy to the Place du Carousel, from Neuilly to the Boulevard de la Madeleine, from Bercy to the Bastille, from the Bastille to Père la Chaise, from the Louvre to Bercy, and from Charenton to Saint Lazare.

PARISIENNES.—From Vaugirard to the Chemin de fer de Lyon, from the Pantheon to the Barrière Poissonnière, from the Barrière Montparnasse to the Boulevard du Temple.

TRICYCLES.—From the Porte St. Martin to the Barrière du Maine.

The visitor cannot be too much on his guard against taking the advice of his *Maitre d'hotel* as to the shops where he might wish to make purchases. In most instances the shop-keeper and the hotel-keeper play into one another's hands, and a per centage is allowed for every customer thus introduced. To enable the visitor to rely upon himself as much as possible, and select his own shop for making purchases, we will only subjoin a few of the streets where the best and most reasonable business houses may be found.

First, there are the Boulevards, Rue de la Paix, Rue Castiglione, Rue St. Honoré, Rue du Faubourg St. Honoré, Rue Vivienne, Rue Richelieu.

For those who wish to *change money* they will find several good places in the Palais Royal, or on the Boulevards. Monteaux and Co. transact business with English houses; their offices are in the Boulevards des Italiens and the Palais Royal, 92; also McHenry, almost at the corner of the Rue de la Paix and the Boulevards; and Mr. Delappierre, 70, Rue de Faubourg St. Honoré who transacts business for the gentlemen at the Embassy.

POST OFFICE.—The Grand Post Office is in the Rue Jean Jacques Rousseau. The Office is shut for Foreign Letters at Five o'clock. There is, however, another in the Rue La Fayette, which is open for letters to England until Six o'clock. Letter boxes are distributed about in different parts of Paris, and may easily be found; but if you desire to pay a foreign letter, you must go to the central bureau of the district. The postage of a letter to or from England is now reduced to fourpence.

The following is a Table of French coins. It will be observed that the French use the Decimal system of calculation:—

5 Centimes	1 Sous, equal to about	1 half-penny, English.
20 Sous, or 100 Centimes...	1 Franc ,,	10 pence, ,,
100 Sous	5 Franc-piece ,,	4 shillings, ,,
20 Francs	1 Napoleon ,,	16 ,, ,,

There are also gold pieces valued at forty francs.

Money accounts in France are kept in francs and centimes, or hundredths; the décimes or tenths, which come between, being seldom mentioned.

1 (silver) franc = 10 décimes = 100 (copper) centimes = 20 sous or sols = 10d. English.	£1 = 25¼ or 25½ francs, According to the rate of Exchange.
(1 sou therefore = 5 centimes = ½d.)	1s. = 1¼ franc or 25 sous.
24 francs = 1 Louis d'or (gold) = 19s.	1d. = 10½ centimes or 2 sous.
20 francs = 1 napoleon (gold) = 15s. 10d.	The modern French *gold* coins are pieces of 10 fr., 20 fr., and 40 fr. The *silver* coins are pieces of 20 centimes, 50 cents. or ½ franc, 1 franc, 2 franc, and 5 franc pieces.
100 francs = £4	
The franc exceeds the old livre by 1¼ per cent. (1¼ centimes).	

The above equalities of French and English moneys will vary a little with the rate of exchange; but the prevailing rate has been adopted.

For the benefit of those who may be at a loss how to address themselves to either of the state officers, to obtain an order of admission into the public building they wish to visit, we subjoin the following model, only suggesting that the title of address will require to be changed according to the person addressed. For example: if to a minister, à *Monsieur le Ministre de* ————; if to a general, à *Monsieur le General de* ————

A MONSIEUR LE MINISTRE DE ————

Monsieur le Ministre,

    En ma qualité d'etranger, en passant par cette ville, je prend la liberté de m'addresser à votre Excellence, pour solliciter l'extréme faveur d'une autorisation qui me permette de visiter ———— (name of place) le ————(date).

    En accédant à ma demande vous rendrez une veritable service, à celui qui a l'honneur d'être, avec le plus profonde respect,

Monsieur le Ministre,

Votre très humble et très obeissant,

COMMON FRENCH WORDS AND PHRASES.

A few of the commonest phrases, however ill chosen or arranged they may be, are better than nothing to the inexperienced traveller; and we therefore add a short list for his benefit.

Des Repas. — Of Meals.

Le Déjeuner	Breakfast
Le goûter, le second déjeuner	Luncheon
Le dîner	Dinner
Le thé	Tea
Le Souper	Supper

Le Manger. — Of Eating.

Un pain, du pain	A loaf, bread
Un petit pain	A roll
Du pain blanc	White bread
Du pain de ménage	Household bread
Du pain bis	Brown bread
Du pain frais	New bread
Du pain rassis	Stale bread

La Carte. — The Bill of Fare.

Du bouillon	Broth
Un consommé	Gravy soup
De la Soupe	Soup
Soup à la vermicelle	Vermicelli soup
Soupe au riz	Rice soup
Soupe à la purée	Pease soup
De la viande	Meat
Des côtelettes de mouton	Mutton chops
Un gigot	A leg of mutton
Des rognons	Kidneys
De l'agneau	Lamb
Du lard	Bacon
Du jambon	Ham
Du gibier	Game
Un pâté	A pie
De la volaille	Poultry
Un poulet	A fowl
Un dindon	Turkey
Du poisson	Fish
Des soles	Soles
Des huîtres	Oysters
Des légumes	Vegetables
Un chou	A cabbage
Un choufleur	A cauliflower
Des pommes de terre	Potatoes
Des œufs	Eggs
Un œuf	An egg
Des œufs frais	New laid eggs
Des œufs à la coque	Soft boiled
Une omelette	An omelet
Une salade	A salad
Du Sel	Salt
Du poivre	Pepper
De la moutarde	Mustard
Des biscuits	Biscuits
Des gâteaux	Cakes
Du fruit	Fruit
Du fromage	Cheese
Du beurre frais	Butter
Du sucre	Sugar
Du thé	Tea
Du café	Coffee

De la Boisson. — Of Drink.

De l'eau	Water
De l'eau rougie	Wine and water
Du vin	Wine
Du vin blanc	White wine
Du vin rouge	Red wine
Vin ordinaire, ou vin de Bordeaux	Claret
Du vin de champagne	Champagne
Du vin de Bourgogne	Burgundy
Du vin d'Oporto	Port wine
Du vin de Xéres	Sherry
De la bierre	Beer
De l'eau de vie, de cognac	Brandy — cognac

Un couteau	A knife
Une fourchette	A fork
Une cuiller	A spoon
Une assiette	A plate

LES PLATS QU'ON TROUVE GÉNÉRALEMENT CHEZ LES RESTAURATEURS EN FRANCE. — THE DISHES GENERALLY FOUND AT THE FRENCH RESTAURATEURS.

LA CARTE. — THE BILL OF FARE.

Potages. — Soups.

Au macaroni	Macaroni soup
Au riz	Rice soup
Au vermicelle	Vermicelli soup

A la julienne	Soup with chopped carrots and herbs	Côtelettes au naturel	Chops fried or broiled
A la purée	Peas Soup	Gigot au jus aux haricots	Leg with gravy or French beans
Consommé	Gravy soup	Rognons au vin de champagne	Kidneys done in champagne

Bœuf. — Beef.

Bœuf au naturel	Boiled beef
Bœuf à la sauce tomate	Beef with love-apple sauce
Bœuf à la sauce piquante	Beef with savoury sauce
Bœuf aux choux	Beef with cabbage
Entrecôte	Ribs of beef
Filet sauté	Fillet of beef with gravy
Rosbif aux pommes de terre	Roast beef with potatoes
Aloyau de bœuf	Sirloin of beef
Langue de bœuf	Neats' tongue
Palais de bœuf	Palate of beef
Bifteck à l'Anglaise	Beefsteak in the English manner
Bifteck aux pommes de terre	Beefsteak with potatoes
Bœuf à la mode	Beef larded

Veau. — Veal.

Fricandeau au jus	Larded veal in gravy
Fricandeau aux épinards	Larded veal with spinage
Fricandeau à l'oseille	Larded veal with sorrel
Fricandeau à la chicorée	Larded veal with boiled endive
Côtelette de veau au naturel	Veal chops fried or boiled
Côtelette en papillote	Veal chops broiled in papers with sweet herbs
Cotelette au jambon	Veal chops with ham
Cervelle apprêtée de différentes manières	Calf's brains cooked in different ways
Tête de veau à la vinaigrette	Calf's head with oil and Vinegar
Tête de veau d'autres manières	Calf's head in different ways
Langue à la sauce piquante	Calf's tongue with savoury sauce
Pieds de veau à la vinaigrette	Calf's feet with oil and vinegar
Blanquette de veau	Fricaseed veal with white sauce.
Ris de veau	Calf's sweet bread
Fraise de veau	Calf's fry

Mouton et Agneau — Mutton and Lamb

Côtelettes panées	Chops fried in bread crumbs
Côtelettes en papillottes	Chops broiled in papers with fine herbs

Pieds de mouton à la vinaigrette	Trotters with oil and vinegar
Rognons à la brochette	Kidneys broiled
Rognons aux truffes	Kidneys with truffles

Volaille. — Poultry.

Chapon au gros sel	Capon (boiled)
Chapon au riz, etc	Capon with rice
Poulet sauté	Chicken in gravy
Poulet à la tartarre	Chicken devilled
Cuisse de poulet en papillote	Leg of a chicken in paper with sweet herbs
Dinde truffée	Turkey with truffles
Dindonneau	Young turkey
Poulet aux champignons	Chicken with champignon sauce
Capilotade de poulet	Chicken hashed
Salade de volaille	Cold chicken in slices and vinegar
Galantine de volaille	Brawned fowl
Poulet au truffée	Chicken, with truffles
Filets de poulet	Slices of chicken (breast)
Canard aux navets	Duck and turnips
Canard aux pois	Duck and green peas.
Caneton	Duckling
Pigeon à la crapandine	Broiled pigeon
Fricassée de poulet	Fricasseed chicken

Gibier. — Game.

Côtelette de chevreuil	Venison chops
Filet de chevreuil	Fillet of venison
Perdreaux apprêtées des différentes manières	Partridges dressed in different ways
Perdreaux en salmis	Young partridges jugged
Maurrettes différentes manières	Larks, variously dressed
Gibelotte de lapin	Rabbit smothered
Laperau sauté aux champignons	Young rabbit with champignon sauce
Bécasse	Woodcock dressed in different ways
Bécassine	Snipes
Canard Sauvage	Wild duck
Caille	Quails
Faisan	Pheasant
Ortolans	Ortolans
Grives	Thrushes
Canard sauvage en salmis	Wild duck jugged
Sarcelle en salmis	Teal jugged

Poissons.	Fish.	Dessert.	Dessert.
Saumon	Salmon	Melon	Melon
Turbot	Turbot	Raisin de Fontainebleau	White grapes of Fontainebleau
Raie	Skate	Pêches	Peaches
Morue	Cod	Fraises au sucre	Strawberries with Sugar
Truite	Trout	Ananas	Pines
Soles	Soles	Figues	Figs
Merlans	Whiting	Pruneau cuits au sucre	Prunes cooked with sugar
Maquereau	Mackerel	Quatre mendiants	Raisins, almonds, nuts and figs (four beggars)
Eperlans	Smelts	Cérises à l'eau de vie	Cherries preserved in brandy
Alose	Shad	Prunes de Monsieur	Orleans plums
Carrelet	Flounder	Prunes de reine, Claude	Green gages
Homard	Lobster	Pommes et poires	Apples and pears
Ecrevisse	Cray-fish	Amandes vertes	Green almonds
Huîtres	Oysters	Compotedes differents fruits	Stewed fruits
Brochet	Pike	Gelée des groseilles, etc.	Currant jelly and others
Anguilles	Eels	Meringues	Trifle
		Abricots à l'eau de vie	Apricots with brandy
		Biscuits de Rheims	Sponge cakes
		Macarons	Macaroons

Legumes.	Vegetables.
Asperges	Asparagus
Pointes d'asperges	Heads of asparagus
Choux de Bruxelles	Brussels sprouts
Chou-fleur	Cauliflower
Haricots blancs	French beans (shelled)
Haricots verts	French beans (green)
Chicorée	Endive
Pommes de terre à la maître d'hôtel	Potatoes sliced with parsley and butter
Petits pois	Green peas
Epinards	Spinage
Artichauts	Artichokes
Céleri	Celery

Vins et Liqueurs.	Wines & Liquors.
Bordeau ou Mâcon ordinaire ou vieux	Claret, of Bordeaux, or Burgundy, ordinary or old
Bourgogne, ordinaire ou vieux	Burgundy, ordinary or old
Château Margot	Claret, Chateau Margot
Chablis	Chablis
Grave	Grave
Sauterne	Sauterne
Saint Peray	Saint Peray
Du Rhin	Rhenish
Champagne	Champagne
Volnay	Volnay

Hors D'oeuvre.	Extras.
Omelette aux fines herbes	Omelet with sweet herbs
Omelette au sucre	Omelet with sugar
Omelette au jambon	Omelet fried with ham
Œufs pochés	Poached eggs
Œufs sur le plat	Fried eggs
Beignets de pommes, etc	Apple fritters
Gâteau de riz	Rice pudding or cake
Charlotte russe	Syllabub in light paste
Tourte aux fruits	Tarts of various fruits
Plum pouding	Plum pudding
Fromage (différentes sortes)	Cheese (different sorts)
Beurre frais, salé	Butter, fresh, salt
Petits pâtés	Savoury patties
Truffes au vin de champagne	Truffles done in champagne
Gelée de groseilles ou de framboises	Jellies (currant or raspberry)

Habillements d'Hommes, etc.	Of Men's Clothes, &c.
Une chemise (d'hommes)	A shirt
Un caleçon	Drawers
Une camisole	An under-waistcoat
Une robe de chambre	A morning-gown
Un pantalon	Trowsers
Une cravatte	A neck cloth
Un col	A stock
Un gilet	A waistcoat
Des bas	Stockings
Un cure dents	A tooth pick

Un tire bottes	A boot jack	Le bois de lit	The bedstead
Se raser	To shave	Un lit de plume	A feather bed
Un nécessaire	A dressing case	Un matelas	A mattress
Des chaussons	Socks	Un oreiller	A pillow
Des pantoufles	Slippers	Les draps	The sheets
Des souliers	Shoes	Une couverture de laine	A blanket
Des bottes	Boots	Une courtepointe	A counterpane
Un chausse pieds	A shoe horn	Une bassinoire	A warming pan
		Une table de nuit	A night table

Habillement des Femmes. — Of Women's Clothes.

Une chemise	A chemise	Une chandelle	A candle
Un jupon	A petticoat	Une bougie	A wax candle
Un corset	Stays	Une lampe	A lamp
Un lacet	Stay lace	Une veilleuse	A night lamp
Une pelerine	A tippet	Les mouchettes	The snuffers
Une robe	A gown or dress	Un eteignoir	An extinguisher
Des volants	Flounces	Un bain (chaud)	A bath (warm)
Des manches	Sleeves	Des allumettes	Matches
Un fichu	A neck handkerchief	Du charbon	Coals
Un mouchoir de poche	A pocket handkerchief	Du bois	Wood
Des gants	Gloves	Un acquit	A receipt
Un châle	A shawl	Un billet de banque	A bank note
Une écharpe	A scarf	La cherté—cher	Dearness—dear
Un chapeau	A bonnet	Bon marché	Cheap
Un voile	A veil	La douane	The custom house
Un negligé	A morning gown	Le bureau de la poste	The post office
La coiffure	Head dress	La grande poste	The general post office
Une robe d'enfant	A frock	Le facteur	The postman
Des papellotes	Curl papers	Le poste aux lettres	Postage
		Un banquier	A banker
		Un changeur	A money changer
		Un joallier—un orfévre	A jeweller or goldsmith
		Un marchand de soieries	A silk mercer

Miscellanea. — Miscellaneous.

Du Savon	Soap	Un marchand des nouveautés	A linen draper
Une Eponge	A sponge	Un médecin	A doctor
Une serviette, essuie-mains	A towel	Un pharmacien	An apothecary
Des épingles	Pins	Un dentiste	A dentist
De la soie	Silk	Une marchande de mode	A milliner
Du satin	Satin	Une couturière	A dress maker
Du velour	Velvet	Un coiffeur	A hair dresser
De la dentelle	Lace	Un gantier	A glover
Chambre a coucher	Bed room	Un patissier	A pastry cook
Une petit salon	Sitting room	Chemin de fer	Railway
Un cabinet de toilette	A dressing closet	Voyageur	Traveller
Le salon	The drawing room	Billet ou coupon	Ticket
La salle à manger	The dining room	Bagage	Luggage
Un rez de chaussée	A ground floor	Franchise de port	Luggage allowed
Les appartments	The apartments	Voiture	Carriage
Un poële	A stove	La gare	Station
Un miroir, une glace	A looking glass	Salle d'attente	Waiting room
Un lit	The bed	Facteurs	Porter

Train, *ou* convoi	Train	Ville	Large town or city
Station, *ou* embarcadère	Terminus	Bourg	Walled town
Chevaux	Horses	Boulevards	Site of old walls, or bulwarks
Chien	Dog		
Moitié prix	Half-price	Faubourg	Suburb
Matin (m.)	Morning	Rue	Street
Soir (s.)	Evening	Chaussée	Causeway
1re. cl. (première classe)	1st class	Chemin	Road
2e. cl. (seconde id)	2nd do.	Pont	Bridge
3e. cl. (troisième id)	3rd do.	Bac	Ferry
De grande vitesse, *ou* exp.	Fast train	Porte	Gate
Durée du trajet	Time taken	Hôtel de ville, *ou* mairie	Town-house
Prolongement	Extension	Place	Square
Service d'hiver	Winter service	Eglise	Church
Service d'été	Summer do.	Poste aux lettres	Post-office
Par tête	So much a head	Bibliothèque	Public-library
Administration	Office	Musée	Museum
Billets d'aller et de retour	Return tickets	Jardin des plantes	Botanic garden
Voyage simple	A run one way	Salle de spectacle	Theatre, &c.
Trains mixtes	Mixed trains	Hôpital, *ou* Hôtel Dieu	Infirmary
Trains directs	1st and 2nd class	Hospice	Asylum
		Fonderie	Iron work
		Verrerie	Glass work
Buffet	Refreshment room		
Trains express	1st class only	Dimanche	Sunday
Articles de messageries	Goods, &c, for luggage van	Lundi	Monday
Conducteur, *ou* mécanicien	Engineman, or driver	Mardi	Tuesday
		Mercredi	Wednesday
Chauffeur	Fireman, or stoker	Jeudi	Thursday
		Vendredi	Friday
		Samedi	Saturday
Bateau à vapeur	Steam-boat		
Bateau à vapeur à hélice	Screw steamer	Le printemps	Spring
		Les semailles	Seed-time
Bateau de poste	Post-office packet	L'eté	Summer
Paquebots	Packet boats	L'automne	Autumn
Deux fois par jour	Twice a day	La recolte	The harvest
Deux départs par semaine	Twice a week	Les vendanges	The vintage
		L'hiver	Winter
1re. Chambre	Chief cabin		
2e. do.	Fore cabin		
Navigation à vapeur	Steam navigation	Janvier	January
Pavillon (*in Rhine steamer*)	1st cabin (one half more than saloon)	Février	February
		Mars	March
Salon (do.)	2nd cabin	Avril	April
Chambre de devant (do)	3rd. do. (half of Saloon)	Mai	May
Nourriture	Living, or provisions	Juin	June
Une malle	A trunk	Juillet	July
Un porteur	A porter	Août	August
Télégraphe sous-marin	Submarine telegraph	Septembre	September
Bains de mer	Sea baths	Novembre	November
Un commis de la douane	Custom-house officer	Décembre	December

Une demi-douzaine.	Half a dozen.
Qu'est-ce que cela, Monsieur?	What is that, Sir?
Que dites-vous?	What do you say?
Monsieur, je ne vous ai pas entendu, *ou*, Je ne vous entend pas, monsieur ('Nong tong paw' of the old song).	I do not understand you.
Où allez-vous?	Where are you going?
Que voulez-vous?	What do you want?
Quel est le chemin de Paris? *ou* Ayez la bonté de me montrer le chemin, &c.?	Which is the way to Paris? or, Have the goodness to tell me the way, &c.?
Allez tout droit.	Go straight on.
Tournez à gauche (*ou*, à droite).	Turn to the left (or, to the right).
Merci, *ou*, bien obligé.	Thank you.
Il fait beau.	It is fine weather.
Le temps est couvert; il va pleuvoir; prenez un parapluie.	It is cloudy weather, and going to rain; take a umbrella.
Il fait mauvais temps; nous aurons de l'orage.	It is bad weather; we shall have a storm.
Le soleil luit; il fait bien chaud.	The sun shines; it is very hot.
Le soleil est couché	The sun is set.
Il fait clair de lune.	It is moonlight.
Il fait un brouillard épais.	There is a thick fog.
Le vent est changé.	The wind is changed.
Il fait beaucoup de poussière.	It is very dusty.
Quelle heure est-il, Monsieur?	What o'clock is it, sir?
Il est environ deux heures; *ou*, Deux heures vont sonner.	About two o'clock.
Il est deux heures et un quart.	Quarter-past two.
Il est deux heures et demie.	Half-past two.
Il est deux heures moins un quart.	Quarter to two.
Il est deux heures moins cinq minutes.	Five minutes to two.
Il est midi.	It is twelve (noon).
Aujourd'hui.	To-day,
Ce matin; ce soir.	This morning; this evening.
Demain matin; après demain.	To-morrow morning; day after.
Hier; avant hier.	Yesterday; day before.
Il y a deux jours.	Two days ago.
Dans huit jours; *ou*, D'aujourd'hui en huit.	In a week.
Tous les jours.	Every day.
J'ai faim.	I am hungry.
Que-voulez-vous manger?	What will you eat;
Donnez-moi à boire.	Give me something to drink.
Donnez-moi un verre d'eau de vie.	Give me a glass of brandy.
Apportez le diner.	Bring the dinner.
Donnez-moi des œufs.	Give me some eggs.
Voulez-vous une tasse de café, (du vin, de la viande, du jambon, du thé, de l'eau de vie)?	Will you take a cup of coffee, (some wine, meat ham, tea, brandy)?
Comment vous portez-vous	How do you do?
Fort bien; *ou*, Très bien, je vous remercie.	Very well, I thank you.

Je suis Anglais.	I am English.
Parlez-vous Anglais ?	Do you speak English ?
Soyez le bien-venu, Monsieur.	Sir, you are welcome.
Où demeure Monsieur A ?	Where does Mr. A. live ?
Il demeure Rue B.	He lives in B. street.
Appelez-moi un fiacre (ou cabriolet)	Call a coach (or cab).
Vous pouvez aller par la diligence, ou prendre une chaise de poste.	You may go by the stage coach, or take a post chaise.
A quelle heure la diligence part-elle d'ici ?	When does the coach start ?
Combien prend-on par place ? ou, Combien prenez-vous ?	What is the fare ? or, what do you charge ?
Combien de jours serons nous en route.	How many days will it take ?
Quelle route prenez-vous ?	Which way do you go ?
Quel est le meilleur chemin ?	Which is the best road ?
La route qui passe par B. est la plus courte.	The road through B. is the shortest.
Combien de —— à —— ?	How far from —— to —— ?
A qui est ce château ?	Whose seat is this ?
Quel est le nom de cet endroit ?	What is the name of this place ?
Y-a-t-il des cabinets de tableaux ?	Are there any pictures to be seen ?
Quel magnifique paysage !	What a beautiful country ?
Comment appelle-t-on cette ville ?	What town is this ?
Où nous arrêterons-nous ?	Where shall we stop ?
Quand partirez-vous ?	When do you sail ?
Au point du jour, or, à la marée.	At day break, or, high water.
Nous allons partir.	We are going directly.
Quand nous embarquons-nous ?	When do we go on board ?
Combien de temps serons-nous en mer ?	How long shall we be at sea ?
Je me sens mal, je puis à peine me tenir sur les jambes; la tête me tourne.	I am very sick; I can hardly stand on my legs my head turns round.
Je loge à l'hôtel de C.	I am staying at the Hotel de C.
Quel est le meilleur hôtel; ou, la meilleure auberge ?	Which is the best inn ?
Un dîner à table d'hôte.	A dinner at the ordinary.
Un dîner seul.	Dinner alone.
A quelle heure voulez-vous dîner ?	At what time do you wish to dine ?
On a servi.	Dinner is on the table.
Voulez-vous un peu de soupe ; ou, de potage ?	Will you take soup ?
Non, je vous remercie, je commencerai par du poisson.	No, I thank you, I will take some fish.
Permettez que je vous présente du bœuf.	Allow me to offer you some beef.
De quel vin voulez-vous ?	What wine will you take ?
Garçon, donnez-nous une bouteille de vin de Bourgogne.	Waiter, bring us a bottle of Burgundy.
Vous enverrai-je une tranche de ce gigot ?	Shall I send you a slice of mutton ?
Vous servirai-je des légumes ?	Will you take some vegetables ?
Vous servirai-je des pommes de terre ?	Will you take some potatoes ?
Pas davantage.	Not any more.
Garçon, changez cette assiette.	Waiter, change this plate.
Une cuiller, si vous plaît.	Give me a spoon.

C

Je vous remercie, c'est assez.	Thank you, that's enough.
Mettez les verres sur la table.	Put the glasses on the table.
Apportez-moi un verre d'eau.	Bring me a glass of water.
Garçon, une bouteille de vin ordinaire.	Waiter, a bottle of ordinary claret wine.
Donnez-nous le dessert.	Let us have the dessert.
Voulez-vous avoir la bonté de sonner ?	Be so good as to ring the bell.
Le thé est servi.	Tea is ready.
Combien vous devons-nous ?	What have we to pay?
Je désire avoir mon compte.	I wish to have my bill.
Voici la note Monsieur.	Here is the bill, Sir.
Voici votre argent.	Here is your money.
Pouvons-nous coucher ici ?	Can we sleep here?
J'aimerais mieux une chambre au premier (ou au second, au troisième).	I should like a room on the first floor (or second floor, third floor).
Il me faut du savon.	I want a piece of soap.
Les lits sont-ils bien bassinés ?	Are the beds well warmed?
Les draps sont-ils très secs ?	Are the sheets quite dry?
Apportez-moi encore un oreiller.	Bring me another pillow.
Emportez la chandelle.	Take away the candle.
A quelle heure voulez-vous que je vous appelle ?	When shall I call you?
Monsieur, je vous souhaite une bonne nuit.	I wish you good night, Sir.
Bon jour, Monsieur (ou Madame, ou Mademoiselle).	Good morning, sir.
Apportez-moi de l'eau chaude.	Bring me some hot water.
Apportez-moi mes bottes.	Bring me my boots.
Le déjeûner est il prêt ?	Is breakfast ready?
Je prendrai du café, si vous voulez bien.	I will take coffee, if you please.
Il nous faut encore des tartines.	We want more bread and butter.
Une tasse de thé.	A cup of tea.
Déjeûner à la fourchette.	A meat breakfast.
Voilà de la viande ; voici des saucisses, du jambon, une volaille.	Here is cold meat; here are sausages, ham, fowl.
Avez-vous des chambres à louer	Have you apartments to let?
Meublées ou non meublées ?	Furnished or unfurnished?
Quel est le prix du loyer ?	What are the terms.
Voudriez-vous me donner de la monnaie de France pour ces souverains ?	Will you be so good as to give me French money for these sovereigns?
Banquier.	A banker.
Négociant.	A merchant.
Où est le bureau de poste ?	Where is the post office?
Je voudrais acheter un chapeau.	I want to buy a hat.
Je voudrais acheter des souliers.	I want to buy a pair of shoes.
Je voudrais acheter une robe.	I want to buy a dress (ladies').
Voulez-vous me raser.	Will you shave me.
Voulez-vous me couper les cheveux (chevaux means horses).	Will you cut my hair.
J'ai du linge à laver ; lavez le avec soin.	I have some linen to wash; wash it carefully.
Quand me le rapporterez-vous ?	When will you bring it home?
Il faudra que vous rapportiez la note.	Bring the bill with you.

Voulez-vous que nous allions faire un tour de promenade ?	Shall we take a walk.
De bien bon cœur, ou, très volontiers.	With great pleasure.
Quel est ce joli hameau ?	What pretty place is that ?
Où peut-on lire les journaux ?	Where can we see the newspapers ?
On lit les ouvrages périodiques et les journaux aux cabinets de lecture au Palais Royal.	You may see the periodicals and papers in the reading rooms of the Palais Royal.
Donnez-moi un verre de limonade.	Give me a glass of lemonade.
Je vous suis bien obligé.	I am obliged to you.
J'aime mieux une tasse de café et un verre de liqueur.	I prefer a cup of coffee and a glass of liqueur.
Je suis à vos ordres; allons nous en, ou, partons.	I am ready; let us go.
J'ai besoin d'un cheval de selle.	I want a horse to ride.
Donnez-lui une mesure d'avoine.	Give him a feed of oats.
Il me faut une belle voiture à quatre roues (ou voiture de voyage).	I want a good four-wheel'd carriage (a travelling carriage).
Combien demandez-vous ?	What is the price ? If the reply is not understood, as English figures are used, it is clear if written; therefore say écrivez, s'il vous plaît.
C'est trop cher.	It is too dear.
Bon jour.	Good day.

CARDINAL NUMBERS.

Un, une	1	Neuf	9	Seize	16	Cinquante	50
Deux	2	Dix	10	Dix sept	17	Soixante	60
Trois	3	Onze	11	Dix huit	18	Soixante dix	70
Quatre	4	Douze	12	Dix neuf	19	Quatre-vingt	80
Cinq	5	Treize	13	Vingt	20	Quatre-vingt dix	90
Six	6	Quatorze	14	Trente	30	Cent	100
Sept	7	Quinze	15	Quarante	40	Mille	1000
Huit	8						

ORDINAL NUMBERS.

Le premier, L'unième	the First
Le second, Le deuxième	the Second
Le troisième	the Third
Le quatrième	the Fourth
Le cinquième	the Fifth
Le sixième	the Sixth
Le septième	the Seventh
Le huitième	the Eighth
Le neuvième	the Ninth
Le dixième	the Tenth
L'onzième	the Eleventh
Le douzième	the Twelfth
Le treizième	the Thirteenth
Le quatorzième	the Fourteenth
Le quinzième	the Fifteenth
Le seizième	the Sixteenth
Le dix septième	the Seventeenth
Le dix huitième	the Eighteenth
Le dix neuvième	the Nineteenth
Le vingtième	the Twentieth

ENGLISH DIRECTORY OF FIRST-RATE HOUSES & BEST SHOPS IN PARIS

The First Wholesale and Retail Firm in Paris for Silks, Indian and French Shawls, &c., is unquestionably the Villes de France, 51, Rue Vivienne, and 104, Rue Richelieu. The stock at this house is unrivalled, and our fair readers will be highly gratified by paying it a visit, if only to admire the almost "Eastern gorgeousness," variety, and splendour displayed in this immense and magnificent establishment.

Millinery.—Bonnets, lace caps, head-dresses, &c. We recommend in full confidence for all these articles the establishment of Miss Soller, 45, Rue Neuve, St. Augustine, who has an excellent renommée among the highest classes of society in Paris.

Stays.—For this indispensable article the Parisian makers are known to be eminently superior. We are advisedly directed to recommend Madame Clemencon, 8, Rue Port Mahon, inventor of the "corps pompadour," and the "demi-corps chateleine," which impart so much grace and elegance to the figure.

Silks and made-up Articles for Ladies.—The firm of Gay and Sons, purveyors to her Majesty the Empress, 2, Rue de la Vrillere, is one of the very first in Paris, and deservedly recommended.

Optician.—For all descriptions of Optical glasses and instruments there is comparatively no choice, as those of Mr. Chevallier, 15, Place du Pont Neuf, are reputed all over the world.

Bronzes, Works of Art, Fancy articles and paintings, curiosities, Sevres and Saxon china, marble statues and statuettes, boule, carved oak furniture, and furniture in general in the first style of fashion. Chazaud, 27, Rue and Hotel, Laffette.

Au Regent, 7, Boulevard de la Madeleine. Ready-made articles for ladies in silks and furs, manties, and mantelets, embroidered scarfs, &c. This is a highly respectable house, worthy our highest recommendation.

Bourdin, Watchmaker, 28, Rue de la Paix, Paris. One of the oldest and most respectable establishments of the capital, the only one known for its exquisitely small and useful watches for ladies; its civil chronometers for the use of the nobility, gentry, and men of business. Its travelling clock, for the convenience of the aristocracy, drawing-room clocks, and timepieces for bed-rooms and halls.

The drawing-room clocks are in great variety, and they are most beautifully ornamented with designs in bronze, gilt, or in painted porcelaines.

Perfumer.—The exquisite perfumery of Mr. Guerlain, 15, Rue de la Paix, purveyor to the Empress, is universally acknowledged to be the best in Paris.

Bronzes, Fancy Articles, Paintings, and China, &c.—Chazauds, 27, Rue and Hotel Laffette, is quite an emporium of works of art, and should be visited by every Connoisseur or Amateur of the Fine Arts.

Tailor.—Blay Lafitte, 11, Boulevard des Italiens.—Gentlemen wishing to renew their apparel will find this establishment one of the best in Paris. First-rate style and capital material.

Artificial Flowers for head-dresses, trimmings for dresses, &c. We recommend the best establishment in Paris, that of Mr. Tilman, 104, Rue Richelieu, purveyor to her Majesty the Empress.

Eau de Cologne.—The name of the firm of Jean Marie Farina, 333, Rue St. Honore, is too well known to require commendation.

Artists, Designers, and Jewellers in Hair.—M. Lemonnier, who was awarded the Prize Medal at the London Exhibition, and the Gold Medal at that of Paris, is highly recommended.

Gilt-bronze Manufactory, 15, Rue Vivienne.—The numerous medals and prizes awarded to M. Deniere fully justify our recommending English visitors to this establishment.

Daguerreotypes, Photographs, Stereoscopes, in all styles and sizes. The beautiful specimens produced by Mr. Warren Thompson, 22, Rue de Choiseul, are greatly admired.

Electro-plated Articles.—Thouret, 37, Place de la Bourse.—Mr. Thouret guarantees all the articles he manufactures, and feels confident they cannot be excelled in quality or in price.

Dentist.—Persons requiring a good surgical and mechanical dentist, are recommended to Mr. George, 36, Rue Rivoli, opposite the Tuilleries author of a work on his new system of artificial teeth, inventor of the Baume Dentaire for the instantaneous cure of the toothache.

GENERAL PROVISION WAREHOUSE, Chevillier, 16, Rue de la Paix, Groceries, Wines, &c., as per advertisement.

ROBERTS' LONDON DISPENSARY, 23, Place Vendome, Chemists and Druggists to the British Embassy.

WALKER's ENGLISH MEDICAL HALL, 36, Place Vendôme, English Drugs and Chemicals, Prescriptions accurately prepared.

CHAMPAGNE WINES.— MOËT and Chandon, Boulevard de la Poissonnière.

MARRET AND BAUGRAND, Jewellers to the Emperor, 19, Rue de la Paix, admitted to the Universal Paris Exhibition, where they occupy one of the most conspicuous places.

DAYS AND HOURS FOR VISITING PUBLIC BUILDINGS, PALACES, MUSEUMS, &c.

Admittance to the places marked with a star [*] can only be obtained by a special order or by shewing the passport.

LIST OF THE MOST REMARKABLE BUILDINGS, PALACES, &c.

Open daily during Week Days.	Open to the Public		Observations.
	from	to	
Palace of the Tuilleries	10 a.m	3 p.m.	Can be seen when the Emperor is absent from Paris. Apply to the Ministre d'État.
Imperial Library, Rue Richelieu, 55	10 "	3 "	Except Sundays and Holidays. Vacation from 1st September to 15th October.
Library of Sainte Geneviève, Place du Panthéon	10 "	10 "	Vacation from 1st Sept. to 15th Oct.
Library Mazarine, Palais de l'Institut	10 "	3 "	— from 1st Aug. to 15th Sept.
— of the Arsenal, Rue de Sully	10 "	3 "	— from 15th Sept. to 1st Nov.
*— of the City of Paris, Hôtel-de-Ville	10 "	3 "	
*Museums of the Louvre	10 "	4 "	Public on Sundays and holidays; by passports every day, except Monday.
Imperial Archives, Rue de Paradis du Temple, 20	10 "	4 "	
*Museum and School of the Fine Arts, 16, Rue Bonaparte	10 "	4 "	Apply to the doorkeeper.
*Cabinet of Mineralogy, Rue d'Enfer, 30	11 "	3 "	Sunday excepted.
*Museum Dupuytren, Place de l'Ecole de Médecine	11 "	3 "	Apply to the keeper.
*Museum Orfila, at the School of Medicine	11 "	3 "	Apply to the keeper. Ladies are not admitted.
*Dépôt of War. Rue de l'Université	10 "	4 "	With permission of the director.
*Cabinet of Architecture, Rue Bonaparte,16	10 "	4 "	Apply to the doorkeeper.
*Manufactory of Tobacco, Quai d'Orsay, 63	1 p.m	4 "	
*Museum of the Luxembourg, Rue de Vaugirard, 19	10 a.m	4 "	Mondays excepted. Public admitted with passport or permission.
*Palace of the Bourse, Place de la Bourse	...	...	Sunday excepted.
*Sainte Chapelle, Palais de Justice	9 a.m	4 "	Apply to the keeper.
Column Vendôme, Place Vendôme	...	...	} Permission to ascend to the top grand on payment of a small fee to the keeper.
— of July, Place de la Bastille	...	...	
Triumphal Arch of the Etoile, Barrière de l'Etoile	...	...	
Hotel of the Invalids	12 non	3 "	
SUNDAY.			
Museum of the Louvre, at the Louvre	10 a.m	4 p.m.	
— of the Luxembourg, Rue de Vaugirard, 19	10 "	4 "	
Museum of Cluny, Rue des Mathurins-Saint-Jacques, 14	11 "	4 "	
Conservatory of the Arts et Métiers, Rue Saint-Martin, 292	10 "	4 "	
Hôtel-Dieu, Parvis Notre-Dame	1 p.m	3 "	
MONDAY.			
Museum of Natural History, Jardin des Plantes	2 p.m	5 p.m.	
Tomb of the Emperor Napoleon I., Hotel des Invalides	12 non	3 "	
*Institution des Jeunes Aveugles (Blind School), Boulevard des Invalides, 52	1½ p.m	4 "	
Institution des Sourds-Muets (Deaf and Dumb School), Rue Saint-Jacques, 254	2 "	5 "	With passport or permission of the director.
Academy of Sciences	...	...	

DAYS AND HOURS FOR VISITING PUBLIC BUILDINGS, &c.—Continued.

LIST OF THE MOST REMARKABLE BUILDINGS, PALACES, &c. Open daily during Week Days.	Open to the Public.		REMARKS.
	from	to	
TUESDAY.			
Museum of Coins, Quai Conti, 11	12 non	3 p.m.	
— Natural History, Jardin des Plantes	2 p.m	5 ,,	
Cabinet of Mineralogy, Rue d'Enfer, 30	11 a.m	3 ,,	
Museum of Cluny, Rue des Mathurins-Saint Jacques, 14	11 ,,	4 ,,	
*Manufactory of the Gobelins, Rue Mouffetard, 270	1 p.m	3 ,,	With passport or permission of the director.
WEDNESDAY.			
Tomb of the Emperor Napoleon, Hôtel des Invalides	12 non	3 ,,	
Blind School, Boulevard des Invalides, 54	1½ p.m	4 ,,	
THURSDAY.			
Cabinet of Mineralogy, Rue d'Enfer, 30	11 a.m	3 ,,	
Conservatory of the Arts et Métiers, Rue Saint-Martin, 292	10 ,,	4 ,,	
Museum of Cluny, Rue des Mathurins Saint-Jacques, 14	11 ,,	4 ,,	
Museum of Natural History, Jardin des Plantes	2 p.m	5 ,,	
*Algerian Museum, Rue de Grenelle-Saint-Germain, 107	12 non	4 ,,	With permission of the minister of war.
Foundling Hospital, Rue d'Enfer, 100	12 ,,	4 ,,	
Imperial Printing Office, Rue Vieille du Temple	2 p.m	...	With passport.
FRIDAY.			
Museum of Coins, Quai Conti, 11	12 non	3 ,,	
— of Natural History, Jardin des Plantes	10 a.m	4 ,,	
Museum of Cluny, Rue des Mathurins-Saint-Jacques, 14	11 ,,	4 ,,	
*Institution des Sourds-Muets (Deaf and Dumb School), Rue Saint-Jacques, 254	2 p.m	5 ,,	With passport or permission of the director.
SATURDAY.			
Cabinet of Mineralogy, Rue d'Enfer, 30	2 p.m	5 ,,	
Museum of Natural History, Jardin des Plantes	10 a.m	4 ,,	
*Manufactory of the Gobelins, Rue Mouffetard, 270	1 p.m	3 ,,	With passport or permission of the director.
Tomb of the Emperor Napoleon, Hôtel des Invalides	12 non	3 ,,	

The Park of St Cloud.

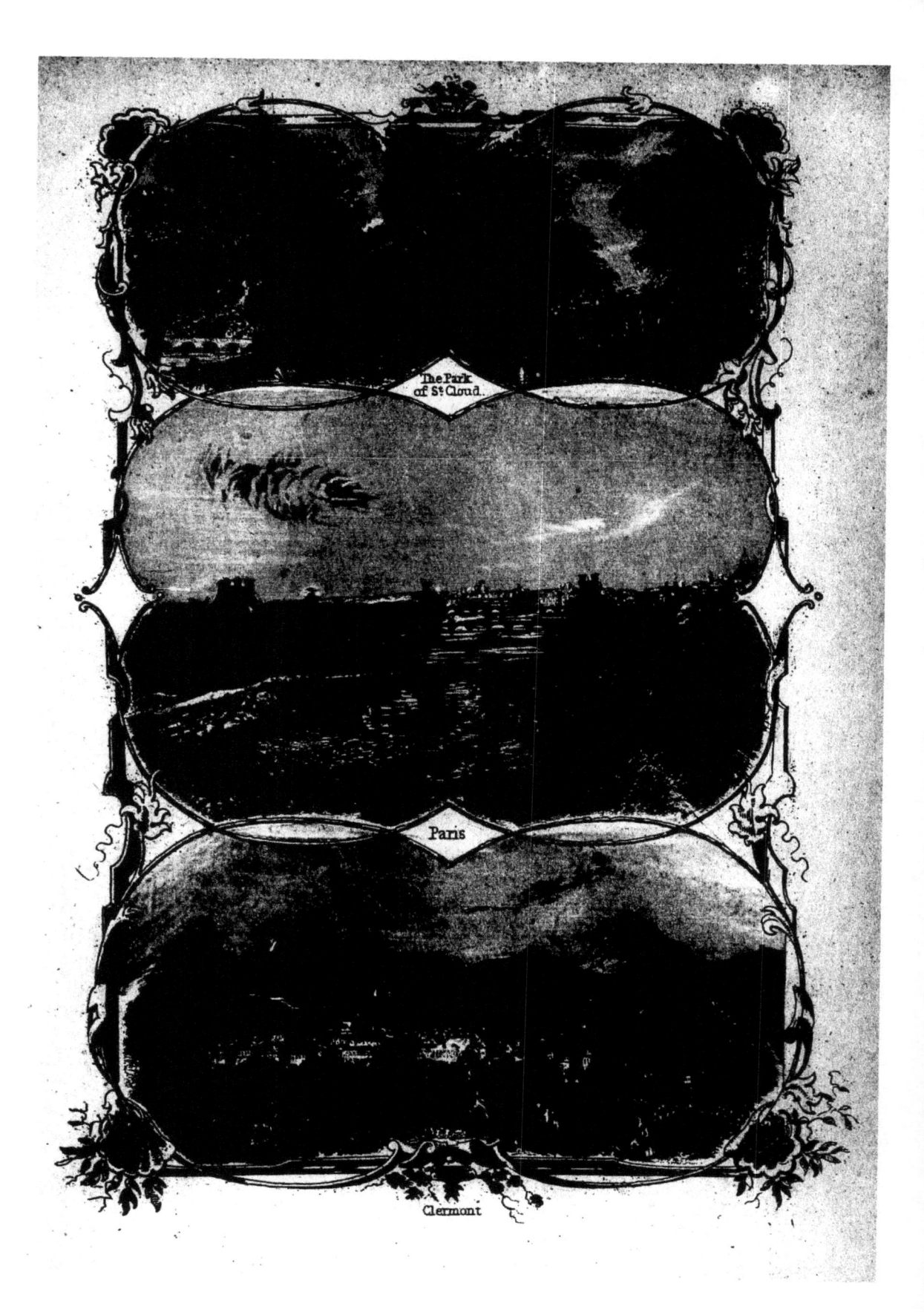

Paris

Clermont

PARIS.

HISTORICAL.

In the time of Julius Cæsar, Paris, to which the name of Lutetia was given by the Romans, was only a collection of mud huts, inhabited by a rude and savage tribe, on a small island, with the Seine for its foss. That island is now the Ile de la Cité. The Latin rule removed, in some degree, the traces of this ancient barbarism. The Roman emperors frequently made the rising city a place of residence, and, under Julian especially, Paris assumed a greater degree of importance, and obtained considerable political privileges.

In 496, Clovis, who had been elected chief of the Franks at the age of fifteen, became king. The wife of Clovis was a christian, and by her influence, a church, dedicated to Sta. Genevieve, the patron saint of Paris, was built. Under the reign of this prince, the city was first securely fortified. For nearly two centuries after, little addition was made, but in the reign of Hugh Capet, the mason and carpenter were again at work. The place had also acquired sufficient dimensions to be divided into four administrative quarters. Under Philip Augustus, A.D. 1180–1222, the streets were first paved; several churches erected; a considerable portion of Notre Dame finished; the tower of the Louvre remodelled and fortified, and a great part of the suburbs enclosed with walls. During the age of Louis XI., Robert Sorbonne founded his schools in the locality still called the Sorbonne. Under Charles V., the faubourgs being much extended and in danger, from the frequent invasions of the English, the fortifications were enlarged, and Paris surrounded with new fosses.

Fresh improvements went on under the reign of Francis I. The old tower of the Louvre was pulled down, and the foundations of a palace laid upon its site. The Hotel de Ville was commenced; better means of communication opened up between different parts of the city, and its defences again enlarged and strengthened. Henry IV. was also a great benefactor to his capital. The Pont Neuf, the building of which had been delayed for want of funds, was completed at his private expense; the hospital of St. Louis founded; many streets, squares, and quays, added to the beauty and importance of the place; the Tuilleries and Louvre continued; and everywhere embellishments vigorously executed.

When Louis XIV. mounted the throne, he lent a great part of his restless energy to the improvement of Paris. In his reign, more than thirty churches, and a corresponding number of streets were built. The Hotel des Invalides, the Observatory, the Colonnade of the Louvre, and the Pont Royal, were undertaken. The Champs Elysée was improved; the Institute de France; and the manufacture of the Gobelin tapestry established. The Portes St. Denis and St. Martin, erected in commemoration of two victories; and the Boulevards became a promenade of general resort. In the two following reigns, magnificent hotels, or private mansions were built in the faubourgs of St. Germain and St. Honoré; the foundations of the Pantheon, St. Sulpice, and the Madeleine laid; the Place de la Concorde beautified, from whence it derived the name of Place de Louis XV.; the manufactory of porcelain removed from Vincennes to Sévres; the Ecole Militaire and College de France instituted, the Jardin des Plantes enlarged; and several theatres and opera houses built. Paris was also encircled by a wall inclosing 8,560 acres.

The political storm which swept over France at the end of the last century, carried away many of the finest of the ancient monuments of the capital. But under the Directory, and the Consular, and Imperial governments, new improvements were pressed forward with vigour; and the city began to assume an aspect of renewed magnificence. The Place du Carrousel was enlarged; the northern gallery of the Louvre, and the Rue de Rivoli commenced; spacious markets were projected; and three handsome bridges thrown over the river. Since 1815, the hand of renovation and embellishment has not been slack. The Place de la Concorde has been remodelled; the Obelisk of Luxor brought from its distant pedestal, where it had rested three thousand years, and reared in the centre, while two magnificent fountains have been constructed on either side of it; the Arc de l'Etoile has been completed; the church of the Madeleine opened for public worship; the Hotel de Ville renewed; the exterior of Notre Dame cleansed; the Palais du Quai d'Orsay, and the Palais des Beaux Arts finished; several new and open streets constructed through the densest and unhealthiest parts of the city; handsome houses and bridges erected; and Paris adorned with an infinity of superb monuments. But nothing can equal the enterprise of the present government; every hour produces some fresh improvement; and Paris, as if by the stroke of a magician's wand, is every day endued with greater splendour.

To finish this historical sketch, we may add that the population of Paris, which, in the fifteenth century, contained only a hundred thousand souls, and under Louis XIV., five hundred thousand souls, now amounts to more than a million.

DESCRIPTIVE.

PARIS.—The metropolis of France, is one of the largest and richest cities of Europe. It is situated in a valley on both banks of the Seine. The river crosses it from east to west, dividing it into two nearly equal parts; it then divides itself into two branches, which again unite after forming three considerable islands. The communication between the banks of the river and the islands is effected by a great number of bridges, many of which are remarkable for the beauty of their construction, and join the quays, which are intended rather for ornament than for business. The environs do not exhibit the same variety as those of London; instead of the gardens, parks, and country seats which surround our great metropolis, Paris, on several sides, presents large tracts of uninclosed corn fields. The stream of life in the great streets, crowed of wagons, carriages, and horsemen, is not so great as in the neighbourhood of our metropolis. Most of the streets, however, are wide, airy, watered by numerous fountains, and full of magnificent hotels and shops. A history of Paris is, to a considerable degree, a history of France, so much has this city, during the last centuries, concentrated in itself all the vital action of France. The preponderance of Paris over all France, not only in a political sense, but in literature, arts, customs, &c., is immense.

Paris is, without doubt, one of the most charming and luxurious capitals in the world. It would be difficult to say whether Pleasure built Paris, or took up her abode within its walls after it was built. There is such a perfect adaptability in its position, and construction to all the ends and purposes of that fascinating goddess, that either suggestion would be equally probable. In its climate, we find that happy medium of temperature, which neither banishes her votaries to the fire side for the greater part of the year, nor enervates them by an intolerable heat, so as to be incapable of exertion in her service. There is, moreover, a charm in the very aspect of Paris, in her boulevards, her gardens, her public promenades, which produces a powerful fascination upon the senses, whilst there are few spots that have not some peculiar grace with which to attract the eye.

Standing on the Pont du Carousel, a picture, rich with beauty, presents itself. Towards the east, and immediately before you, stands out, in bold relief, the Ile de la Cité, with its mass of irregular, tall, white houses; the solemn towers of Notre Dame; the gorgeous pinnacle of the Sainte Chapelle; the solid domes of the Palais de Justice; and the spired turrets of the Conciergerie. The river, descending by two channels, and here uniting, adds a peculiar grace to the scene. Immediately on our left extends the long line of lofty street, abutting on the Quais, the houses of which, gleam in the warm light of the sun and blue azure of the heavens. Sometimes a huge pile of building; sometimes a high Gothic tower; sometimes a colossal statue; sometimes a tiny spire rears itself in the midst. On the other side stands the Institute of France, with its domed centre, and circular wings; and between these two lines of buildings, rolls the swift current of the Seine, animated by the perpetual meeting of boats and the junction of different streams of floating-houses. In continuation of and in pursuance of courses of rows of to this west, on moderate elicious whatof present itself. On the right, the elegant façade of the Louvre, and the thickly-leaved avenue of the Tuilleries. On the left, the Quai de Voltaire and the Palais d'Orsay (behind which the river loses itself by a graceful bend), terminate the view; whilst beyond, the verdurous slopes of Chaillot and Passy, dotted with shining houses, closes a scene of unwonted beauty.

There are few streets in London which will bear comparison with the Boulevards of Paris; they occupy the space originally appropriated to the defence of the city. This space has been converted into wide and magnificent streets, in the centre of which is an unpaved road, and on each side of the road is a row of lofty trees, and between each row of trees and the row of houses are wide gravel walks for the accommodation of the pedestrians. The waving line which these streets assume, adds greatly to the beauty of the Boulevards; the eye cannot reach the end of the prospect, and the uncommon width is productive of no vacuity or dulness; so active are the movements of carriages and passengers, and so lively the scene presented in the shops, the hotels, and the coffee-houses, on either side. The massy stone structures of Paris appear to greater advantage here than in the narrower streets. On the southern side of Paris, the Boulevards extend a still greater length, and are planted with trees, but they are not considered to equal those on the other side of the city.

The banks of the Seine present but few attractions to the visitor, except in the quarter of the Tuilleries, where, on one side are the Louvre and the Tuilleries, with its gardens, and on the other, from the Palais du Corps Legislatif to the Pont Neuf, a succession of fine buildings.

But it is not here that we pause to exhaust the beauties of Paris. If we ascend from the quays to the south, we have the hill crowned by the Pantheon; if to the north, the eye soon meets the steep declivities of Montmartre or Belleville; or, if we stray through the boulevards, those fine, open, planted promenades, that encircle Paris as with a zone of greenery, or enter the Champs Elysées, shaded with stately trees; or stroll through its commercial galleries, and its bazaars, or its public places, embellished with fountains and statues, we shall everywhere find something to attract us, something to admire; so that, whether we consider its palaces, its private edifices, its public monuments, its churches, its casernes, its arcades, or any of its ten thousand places of amusement, we must allow that Paris is unrivalled as a city of beauty, or as a city of pleasure.

FIRST DAY.

THE TUILLERIES—PLACE DU CAROUSEL—LOUVRE—ST. GERMAIN L'AUXERROIS—PALAIS ROYAL—FONTAINE MOLIERE—THEATRE DU PALAIS ROYAL—RUE DU REMPARTS.

THE TUILLERIES.

The Tuilleries and the Louvre, which now form, as it were, but one grand building, will be the primary object of attraction to the visitor, the former as being intimately connected with the modern history, the second with the fine arts, of France. This splendid palace is situated along the side of the river Seine; and fronted on the west by the gardens of the Tuilleries, the Place de la Concorde, and the Champs Elysées. On the spot where it now stands, existed formerly, tile-fields, from whence the name is derived, the word *Tuillerie* signifying a tile-field, or more properly a tile-kiln. These fields were converted into gardens, and laid out in 1665, according to the taste of the age of Louis XIV., by Le Notre, but have since his time undergone considerable alteration. These gardens form a grand paralellogram, containing about 67 acres, and are flanked by the Rue de Rivoli on the north, and the Seine on the south. They consist of flower-beds and public walks in front of the palace, a grove of trees in the centre, and another walk and flower-beds on the

Place of the Carrousel.

The Tuileries.

The Court of the Louvre.

western side of the grove. An elevated avenue of lime trees run parallel with the Rue de Rivoli and the Seine. A deep foss and hedge separate a portion of the flower garden in front of the Tuileries, and this portion is reserved for the private promenade of the family members of the household of the palace. A *Laocoon* and a *Diana* in bronze, amongst other statues, ornament this garden, and on each side of the road-way leading up to the grand entrance may be also seen bronze figures of the *Sicilian Knife Grinder* and *Venus sitting on a Tortoise*. Three circular basins, with jets d'eau, ornament the public gardens; and around the centre one are collected several fine groups of statuary, among which *Æneas rescuing Anchises and leading Ascanius*, the *Death of Lucretia*, and *Atlas changed into a rock*, may easily be distinguished. On the north side, parallel with the Rue de Rivoli, runs the *Allée des Orangiers*, so called from the *orange trees*, which in summer are brought out and arranged along it. At the further extremity is a fine Grecian statue of *Meleager*. The horse-chesnut trees, which form the principal trees in the grove, have long been celebrated for their size and beauty. Beneath them, a most agreeable shade may be obtained; and in the afternoon of a sunny day, crowds of people swarm to it, and paying their two sous for a chair, enjoy an hour or two's recreation. In the evening, between seven and eight o'clock, a military band practises here, when the weather is fine, and adds greatly to the charm of the place. This grove is divided by a broad open avenue, leading from the pavilion de l'Horloge, to the Place de la Concorde, and used on state occasions as a carriage way up to the Tuileries. From this avenue, a fine view of the Obelisk de Luxor, the Avenue de Neuilly, and the Triumphal Arch at the Barrière de l'Etoile may be obtained. The best time, however, for viewing this scene, is the evening, when the sun, being in the west, lights up the whole with a peculiar radiance. On either side of the broad avenue are open spots amongst the trees, converted into small gardens, and decorated with statues. The semicircular banks of white marble nearest the Tuileries, containing the nude figures of a man and a woman, were designed by Robespierre, and intended for the seats of a court of old men, which after the manner of the ancient Greeks, were to preside over the games to be held in honour of the god Germinal. There are also a *Centaur conquered by Cupid*, a *Hercules in his youth*, and a fine *Boar* in marble, beneath the trees. At the eastern extremity, figures of ancient Roman and Greek celebrities are ranged alternately, with some beautifully-executed marble vases. On the west side is the second garden. In the centre is a fine octagonal basin, with a jet d'eau, which, when the waters are in full play, throws up a stream to a height considerably above the level of the trees. *La Petite Provence* is a name given to the parterre on the northern side, from the genial character of its position, which faces the south, and is sheltered from the eastern and northern winds. Here invalids and nurses and old men flock in abundance. The building on the elevated avenue on the south side is the *orangerie*, where the orange trees are kept during the winter months. Allegorical statues of the Seasons, the principal rivers of France, and the Muses, adorn this garden. To the west is the gateway leading into the Place de la Concorde; on either side is a fine group in marble, representing *Victory*, *Mercury*, and *Fame*, on winged steeds. A shady terrace faces the *Place*, from which a good view of it and the river beyond may be had.

PALACE OF THE TUILERIES.

The palace was commenced in 1564, as a residence for Catherine de Medicis, the plans of the building being furnished by Delorme and

MUSÉES DU LOUVRE

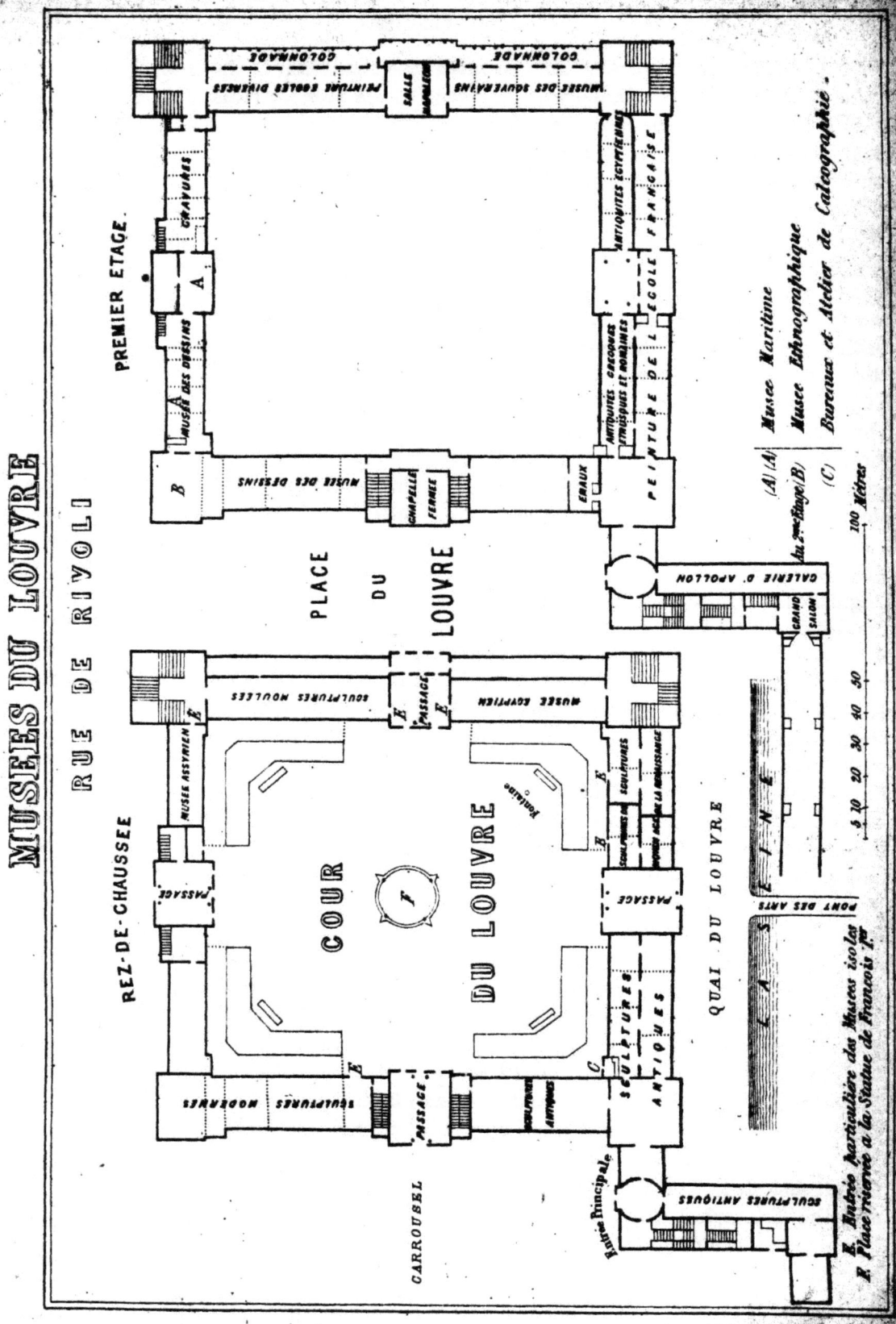

RUE DE RIVOLI

REZ-DE-CHAUSSÉE

PREMIER ÉTAGE

- Carrousel
- Sculptures modernes — Passage — Sculptures antiques
- Musée Assyrien — Passage — Sculptures moulées — Musée Égyptien
- Cour du Louvre (Fontaine F)
- Sculptures antiques — Sculptures — Musée Algérien de la Renaissance
- Entrée Principale
- Sculptures Antiques
- Quai du Louvre
- La Seine — Pont des Arts

- Musée des Dessins — Gravures
- Chapelle Fermée — Musée des Dessins — Émaux
- Musée des Souverains — Peinture Écoles Diverses — Salle Napoléon — Colonnade
- Place du Louvre
- Antiquités Égyptiennes — Antiquités Grecques Étrusques et Romaines — Peinture de l'École Française
- Galerie d'Apollon — Grand Salon

(A)(A₁) Musée Maritime
(B) Musée Ethnographique (du 2ᵐᵉ Étage)
(C) Bureaux et Atelier de Calcographie

Échelle : 0 10 20 30 40 50 100 Mètres

E. Entrée particulière des Musées isolés
F. Place réservée à la Statue de François 1ᵉʳ

rock in the centre of this place, to hide an irreparable architectural defect which exists in the construction of this vast square. This was not however, put into execution, and the late Visconti suggested the construction of two lateral buildings, forming part of the whole. They are now in course of construction. It is intended that the whole of the building shall be finished by the time of the opening of the Exhibition in 1855. At the extreme end of the Carousel is the

Louvre.—On the site of the present palace, stood formerly a castle, far outside the precincts of the ancient Paris. This chateau is said to have been the hunting seat of king Dagobert, and called *Louveterie*, or *wolf hunting establishment*. It was remodelled, fortified, and converted by Philip Augustus in 1200 into a state prison, and by Charles V. into his treasury and library. Francis I. however, demolished the entire building, determined to raise a more handsome one in its stead. Accordingly Pierre Lescot was ordered to supply the design, and the new palace was commenced in 1528. During the reign of Francis and that of his son, the wing now called the *Gallery of Apollo* was finished; under Henry IV. considerable additions also were made, but Louis XIV wishing to complete it, at once appealed to all the architects of Europe, to send in plans. That of the Chevalier Bernini pleased the monarch, and he was sent for from Italy, but the capricious interference of the monarch disgusted the architect, who returned to his native country, after a twelvemonths' sojourn, leaving the physician Perrault, whose designs were afterwards adopted, to carry on the work. The attention of the king, however, was more directed towards the chateau of Versailles, and the works of the Louvre were suffered to relax, so that the present building was not completed until Napoleon lent his energetic hand to it, when it was accomplished by Messrs. Perrault and Fontaine, two hundred and fifty years after the first foundations were laid. The Louvre was used as a place of residence by Charles IX., the persecutor of the Huguenots, Henry III., Henry IV., Louis XIII., and also by Henrietta, widow of Charles I. of England. Since the time of Louis XV., who spent his minority here, it has been given up to the exhibition of works of art, though occasionally it has been used for state ceremonies. On the 28th and 29th of July, 1830, the Louvre was attacked by the people, and obstinately defended by the Swiss guard. Those who fell on the occasion were buried beneath the green sward at the foot of the colonnade next to the Seine. They were, however, subsequently disinterred, and their remains deposited in the vaults beneath the column of July, on the Place de la Bastile, which was erected in commemoration of that event.

The attention of the visitor should be especially directed to the superb colonnade, consisting of twenty-eight double Corinthian pillars, which adorn the western front of the Louvre. This façade, by the beautiful symmetry of its parts, the fine execution of its ornaments, the just economy of their distribution, and by the imposing grandeur of its extent, is justly admired as a chef-d'œuvre in the architecture of the age of Louis XIV. The court of the Louvre is also equally striking. There reign in their construction such a regularity and harmony, that the eye is instantly arrested with delight. The fourth side, however, is of a different date and a different construction, being built before the other parts of the palace, but there is an equal amount of grace in its design; and the sculptured figures which adorn the third storey are the work of the celebrated Jean Goujon. In the centre of this quadrangle stood a statue of the late duke of Orleans. It was removed during the revolution of 1848, and it was proposed to construct a fountain there in its place. This, however, has not yet been put into execution, and a plot of grass only occupies the site.

The entrance to the Musée of the Louvre is at the south-east end of the Place du Carousel. A colossal head of the first Napoleon, encircled by a wreath of bays, adorns a niche above the doorway. On the ground floor on entering is a series of five or six galleries devoted to specimens of ancient and modern sculpture. Some of these specimens are very fine, and though occasionally in a mutilated condition, possess great merit and beauty. On retracing our steps to the entrance, a fine noble staircase leads up to the *Salle Ronde*, by which the superb *Gallerie d'Apollon*, 184 feet long by 28 broad is entered. This splendid room is most elaborately decorated. Opposite each window is a recess in the wall, made to correspond with it, and the ceiling is covered with some very fine paintings. From the saloon, a good view of the Ile de la Cité, the towers of Notre Dame, the Conciergerie, the Sainte Chapelle, and the domes of the Palais de Justice, as well as the quays along the city bank of the Seine may be had. At the further end of this room is the door into the *Salon Carré*, and the *Long Gallery*, where the works of the great Italian, Flemish, Spanish, and French artists are arranged according to their schools. *About half-way down the Long Gallery is a window overlooking the Pont du Carousel. From the balcony of this window, Charles IX. stood to fire upon his Huguenot subjects on the memorable eve of St. Bartholomew.* Returning to the *Salon Carré* we find on the left the *Salle des Bijoux*. This room contains valuable articles of vertu, such as caskets adorned with gems, church utensils, finely cut cameos, silver vases of antique workmanship and curious in the execution, ivory trinkets, jewellery, &c. The casket of Marie de Medicis, which may be seen here, is worth several thousand pounds.

Returning to the *Salle Ronde*, we enter by the right the *Gallerie Française*, containing the works of native deceased artists. Parallel with this gallery is another, containing Egyptian, Grecian, and Roman antiquities. The first include those which have of late years been discovered in and brought from Egypt by the indefatigable exertions of French artists. Etruria and Greece have supplied most of the latter specimens. Many have also come from the excavated ruins of Herculaneum and Pompeii.

A series of galleries runs to the eastward from the *Salle Egyptien* entirely round the building. These galleries are filled with paintings of the best masters, such as Guido Reni, Domenichino, Mignon, for which there was no room in the Long Gallery, miniatures, engravings, maps, sketches by the first artists, &c. They also contain most splendid specimens of art, such as vases of vast and elegant proportions, both of marble and porcelain; tables constructed of variegated stones, stained glass windows. Amongst the rooms of peculiar interest is the *Musée des Souverains*, where may be seen missals elaborately bound, belonging to various queens, and of a very early date; the chair of king Dagobert, a splendid *armorie à bijoux*, once Marie Antoinette's, of beautifully coloured wood, inlaid with pearl and jewels; a curiously-ornamented casket, given by Cardinal Richelieu to Catherine de Medicis; the swords and sceptres of various monarchs, the crown of Charlemagne, the armour of Henry II. and III. and Louis XIV.; the coronation robes of Napoleon and Charles X.; the tent-bed of the former, and some of the clothes he wore at St. Helena; the chapel of the order of the Holy Spirit, and a variety of other very interesting curiosities. The *Musée de la Marine*, which occupies the third storey is also of interest; it contains models of vessels of all descriptions, of forts and guns; plans of the different naval arsenals of France, and everything connected with or relating to the improvement of the marine department. The ground-floor on three sides of the Louvre is taken up with the *Musée des Antiquités Americaines*, and the *Musées de la Sculpture du Moyen Age et de la Renaissance.*

As the visitor will perhaps be perplexed by the multitude of pictures before him, and have but a short time to select those most worthy of his regard, it may be as well to assist him by pointing out a few of the best of the most celebrated masters, who have formed schools and had a host of imitators; though this enumeration must not be taken as anything more than an aid, nor prevent the visitor from studying as many of the others as his time will admit of.

SALON CARRE.

RAPHAEL.—La belle Jardinière (375) estimated at 1,600*l.*

St. Michael treading the Dragon under his feet (382)

MURILLO.—The Immaculate Conception (546.) This picture was bought at the sale of Marshal Soult's collection for 22,000*l.* by the emperor, and given by him to the Louvre.

LEONARDO DI VINCI.—Portrait of Mona Lisa (484) estimated at 3,600*l.*

PAUL VERONESE.—The Marriage Feast at Cana (104) estimated at 40,000*l.*

Magdalene wiping the feet of Jesus with the hair of her head (103), estimated at 6,000*l.*

CORREGGIO.—Sleep of Antiope (28), estimated at 20,000*l.*

Mystic Marriage of St. Catherine (27), estimated at 14,000*l.*

FRANCIA.—A head (318).

VANDYKE.—Charles I. (142), a duplicate of this one is in the royal gallery at Hampton Court.

TITIAN.—Portrait of his mistress (471), estimated at 1,800*l.*

Christ carried to the Tomb (465), 8,000*l.*

RIBERA.—Adoration of the Infant Jesus (553), estimated at 1,600*l.*

GEARRD DOW.—Administering a Cordial to a Sick Lady (121).

THE LONG ROOM.

RAPHAEL.—Portrait of Balthazar Castiglione (385), estimated at 2,000*l.*

MURILLO.—Jesus and his Mother together with John (548).

GUIDO.—The Magdalene (329), estimated at 400*l.*

LEONARDO DE VINCI.—The Virgin amongst Rocks (482), estimated at 16,000*l.*

RUBENS.—Series of Allegories.

TITIAN.—Portrait (462).

RYSDAEL.—Sea View (471).

CUYP.—Meadow Scene with Cows (104).

PAUL POTTER.—Do. do. (400).

REMBRANT.—Tobit and the Angel.

POUSSIN.—Plague Scene (202).

TENIERS.—Interior of an Inn (518).

LORRAIN.—Three Marine Views with Landscape (163-5).

CANALETTO.—Views of Venice.

CARACCI.—The Salutation of the Angel (126). The Nativity (134) estimated at 4,000*l.*

SALVATOR ROSA.—Battle Scene (360), estimated at 2,000*l.*

Landscape and Storm (861).

The Louvre is rich in Italian productions of the highest order, since these rooms contain fifteen paintings by Raphael; twenty-two by Titian; twenty-three by Guido; nine by Leonardo de Vinci; three by Correggio; eleven by Canaletto; twenty-six by Annibal Caracci; and a considerable number by Rubens. Those amongst the French masters, to whose works attention may be drawn, are, *Lebrun, David, Mignard, Jouvenet, Casanova Creuze, Guerin, Leopold Roberts, &c.*

The Louvre is open every day of the week, from ten till four, except *Monday*, which day is reserved for cleansing purposes, and may be seen on shewing a passport.

On leaving the Louvre and traversing the quadrangle, whose symmetrical proportions the visitor has already been admiring, a walk of three minutes will bring him to the gorgeously decorated church of *St. Germain l'Auxerrois*, opposite the eastern façade of the building. A church was erected on this spot so early as the reign of Childeric, but was destroyed by the Normans in 886. A hundred and twelve years after it was rebuilt by king Robert, and dedicated to St. Germain l'Auxerrois. The present church, or part of it, was commenced in the fourteenth century. Owing to its proximity to the Louvre, it enjoyed the royal munificence, and became exceedingly rich. No injury was done to it during the revolution of 1789, but in 1831 an attempt being made to celebrate the anniversary of the death of the duke de Berri in it, the populace rose against it, and everything within was destroyed. The style is showy, and the whole is most elaborately painted and gilded. The porch to the west contains a double row of Gothic arches, five in front and three behind. The glass windows of this church are very richly and beautifully stained. To the protestant this building has a peculiar interest, as it was the bell of this church that tolled the memorable signal for the commencement of the massacre of St. Bartholomew which was responded to on the other side of the water by the tocsin of the *Conciergerie*. In the street close by, the Rue des Fosses, stood formerly the mansion of Admiral Coligny, now demolished to make way for the new improvements, in which he was murdered on that dreadful night.

Returning to the Rue Rivoli, and directing our steps westward, we arrive on the Place, which faces the Palais Royal. The church on the right, the back of which we pass, is the Oratoire, one of the French Protestant places of worship of which we shall speak more at large presently.

The Palais Royal, whose fine façade we have before us, was built by the Cardinal Richelieu, and from him called the Palais Cardinal. Later, however, he made a present of it to his royal master, Louis XIII., on condition that he should use it during his life time, and that after his death the crown should never part with it under any circumstance. Louis XIV., disregarding this stipulation, gave it, in 1692, to the Duke of Orleans and his heirs; and it was here that the orgies of the infamous Regent, and afterwards of Phillip Egalité, were celebrated. As these dukes were devoted to luxury the palace was richly decorated, and contained a chapel where mass was celebrated with pontifical pomp, as well as a theatre, where the productions of the first ducal occupant were exhibited, and strove in vain to compete with the humble-born muse of Corneille. It is also deeply associated with the political intrigues of every reign, from the period of its founder, down to the accession of Louis Philippe. Here those assembled who were working for the destruction or the preservation of the crown; and those who are familiar with the memoirs of Cardinal Retz, will remember how many of the most dramatic scenes of the party of the *Fronde* took place here. In the early part of the first revolution the gardens belonging to the palace became the rendezvous of the most violent politicians of the day. In a circus that now no longer exists, the Jacobins and Thermodarians held their first sittings. Here the tricolor cockade was first assumed, and many of the most extreme measures of the red republicans taken. Camille Demoulins here inflamed the populace by her wild eloquence and in the Café Foy the Dantonists, and in the Café de Chartres the Girondists met. After the death of the Prince Egalité, the property became confiscated to the state, and devoted partly to balls and restaurants, partly to a military commission; here too, the tribunate was established. During the empire it became the residence of Lucien Buonaparte, but in 1814 it was restored to the Orleans family. The Duke continued to reside in it till 1831, when he was called to the throne. In 1848 the Palace again fell a prey to the popular fury, and was thoroughly ransacked; it is now, however, the residence of Prince Napoleon.

The principal entrance is from the Place du Palais Royal, and consists of a triple arched gateway leading into a large court. On either side are two wings which advance to the street; the front of the body facing the court is decorated with Ionic columns supporting a semi circular pediment containing a clock supported by two figures. The façade towards the gardens is still more extended than that facing the Place, and is adorned by eight columns supporting figures. On the right and left are wings which join the building to the *Gallerie d'Orleans*. The interior of this gallery is a fine promenade, three hundred feet in length, covered with a glass roof, and with shops on each side.

Beyond this stretch other galleries, forming with the Gallerie d'Orleans a paralellogram enclosing the pretty and much-frequented gardens of the Palais Royal. The regularity of their structure, and the tastefulness of the style are very imposing. Here is ranged a collection of shops, glittering with articles of jewellery and bijouterie, which of themselves might well attract a stranger to Paris. Every here and there we meet with a Café or a Restaurant, such as those of Véry, Véfour, les frères Provencaux, Foy, de la Rotonde, &c.; and in the midst of the gardens is a small pavilion, at which the journals of the day are sold to persons who eagerly purchase them and sit under the trees devouring their contents.

The garden occupies an extent of 280 yards long by 100 broad, and consists of a long parterre down the centre, with a triple row of elms, limes, &c., which afford a most agreeable shade in warm weather. A pretty fountain plays in the centre. Several marble and bronze figures are arranged in the parterres, and near that of *Eurydice stung by a serpent* at the southern end of the gardens is a cannon fired by the sun at midday. A military band plays here every evening from 7 to 8, after which, till 10 or 11, the place is crowded with men, women, and children lounging about to enjoy the coolness of the air. It is at this time when the galleries are brilliantly lighted up, that the gardens are seen to most advantage, to which we may add, that the merry song of the children who amuse themselves with every variety of game and dance, gives the charm of admiration to the whole scene.

Upwards of £1520 is annually paid to the government for permission to supply the frequenters of these gardens with refreshments.

Passing out of the Palais Royal by one of the passages to the west, we enter the Rue Richelieu, No. 35 of which is the house where Molière died. A tablet erected on the second storey informs the passenger of this fact. Opposite to this is the

Fontaine Molière—A Fountain erected in honour of the father of French Comedy in 1844. It was designed by the late distinguised architect M. Visconti, and is composed of a white marble pedestal resting on a base, surrounded by a stone cistern receiving jets of water issuing from the mouths of three lions. Two allegorical figures by Pradier are placed each side of the pedestal, and the whole is surmounted by a bronze statue of the poet sitting and reading one of his manuscripts. The whole cost of the erection amounted to £6,720. An inscription engraved on the pedestal bears the dates of the birth and death of Molière.

Passing down the street towards the Rue St. Honoré, we pass by the **Theatre Français, ou de la République** as it was formerly called. This Theatre, built in 1787, is a dependence of the Palais Royal, with which several passages on the ground floor connect it. In 1799 it was conceded to the comedians of France, who took possession of it under the title of the Theatre of the Republic, and afterwards under that of *Comedie Française*. From the gallery, which surrounds it, we penetrate into a vestibule, adorned with a marble statue of Voltaire, who is represented sitting in an arm chair. Four staircases lead from the vestibule into the interior of the theatre, which is elegant and commodious, and capable of holding 1,500 persons. Comedy and Tragedy find here their proper sphere; Fleury, Talma, Molé, Larochelle, Monrose, Devienne, Mars, Armand, Damas, are amongst the most celebrated who have illustrated the French Drama on its boards. Messrs. Samsons, Provost, Reynier, &c., to whom must be added Mesdames, Madeleine Broham, Fix, and Mlle. Rachel are amongst the first who now appear there.

The theatre is open all the year.

Price of Places—Avant scène du rez-de-chaussèe, 8 francs; Balconet *loges de la gallerie, †rez-de-chaussèe, 6 frs. 60 cents; 1st loges de face (2nd rang), 6 frs.; 2nd loges (3rd rang), 3 frs. 50 cents; ‡Parterre, 2 frs. 50 cents; 3rd loges (4th range), 2 frs.; 2nd gallerie, 1 fr. 50 cents; Amphitheatre, 1 fr.

Opposite the theatre stood a cluster of houses, recently demolished, which formed the street called la *Rue du Rempart*, which indicates that the ramparts of the city at one time extended so far. The spot has a historical interest to an Englishman; for it was here that Joan of Arc headed an attack when the Duke of Bedford was master of the town, and where she received a serious blow on the head from a stone hurled from a sling. She refused, however, to retire, and continued to fight on with unabated courage.

* Loges signifies Boxes. ‡ Parterre, the Pit.
† Rez-de-chaussee, on a level with the stage.

SECOND DAY.

CHAPELLE EXPIATOIRE—MADELEINE—PLACE DE LA CONCORDE—CHAMPS ELYSEES—CIRQUE DE L'IMPERATRICE—EXHIBITION—PLACE DES CHAMPS ELYSEES—ARC DE L'ETOILE—PONT DES INVALIDES—PONT D'IENA—MANUFACTORY OF TOBACCO—INVALIDES—CHAMPS DE MARS—MINISTERE DES AFFAIRES ETRANGERES—CORPS LEGISLATIF—PONT DE LA CONCORDE—PALAIS DE LA LEGION D'HONNEUR—PALAIS DU QUAI D'ORSAY—BARRACKS—PONT ROYALE—QUAI DE VOLTAIRE.

WE will commence our sight-seeing this morning by a visit to the *Chapelle Expiatoire* (Expiatory Chapel), in the Rue d'Anjou St. Honoré, which may be approached either from the same street, the Rue de la Madeleine, or the Rue de l'Arcade. This chapel was built in memory of the unfortunate Louis XVI. and his wife Marie Antoinette, whose remains were privately deposited here after their execution in 1793 by some zealous royalist. The spot was then an orchard. At the restoration, their remains were disinterred and laid with regal pomp amongst those of their ancestors, in the Abbey of St. Denis, and the present monument erected over their former resting place, that masses might be offered up for their repose. The building is of the Doric order, very elegant and imposing from its simplicity. It is surrounded by a grove of cypresses, and on the pillars that support the railings are sculptured appropriate emblems of mourning. Over the portal is a tablet, recording the reason of its construction; within is a statue of the King, and another of his Queen; on the pedestal of of the first is exhibited his will, on that of the second, extracts of her last letter to Madame Elizabeth. The remains of the Swiss Guards who died so bravely defending their unfortunate sovereigns, are also deposited beneath in the same chapel.

Leaving the Chapelle Expiatoire by the right, and descending the Rue de la Madeleine, we arrive at the

Madeleine.—This beautiful temple is one of the most attractive sights in Paris, and occupies a very fine open position, so that from any point it can be seen to great advantage. Where it now stands, stood formerly the church of the Ville-d'Eveque, but the latter edifice was pulled down in 1764, and the present one commenced by order of Louis XV., after designs by Constant d'Ivry. The works, however, were pushed forward very slowly, and during the revolution entirely suspended. In 1808 Napoleon resolved to finish it, intending to convert it into a Temple of Glory, dedicated to those who had fallen in the Prussian campaign. After his defeat in 1815, the building was again restored to its original purpose, but was not finally completed till the reign of Louis Philippe. It is erected on an elevated platform 328 feet in length, and 138 feet in breadth, and approached by a noble flight of twenty-eight steps; it forms a paralellogram, and is constructed after the model of a Grecian temple. Forty-eight fluted columns of the Corinthian order surround it, 49 feet high, and 16½ feet in circumference; the distance between each column is two diameters, and corresponding with the distances are niches in the walls, containing statues of Saints. The principal façade looks upon the Rue Royale and the Place de la Concorde, and is composed of a portico extending the whole breadth of the building, and supported by ten columns. The tympanum above is adorned with a bas-relief representing the last judgment. The effect of this beautiful façade is very striking; magnificent bronze doors, 33 feet high by 16½ broad, give admission to the principal entrance; the pannels of the doors are adorned with bas-reliefs of scriptural subjects; the roof is of iron, and it is a curious fact, that no wood has been allowed in the construction of the building. It is also lighted internally from above by three domed windows.

The interior of the church is decorated with unusual splendour, gilt and marble being nowhere spared to give full effect to the idea of pomp and magnificence. It consists of a vast body without aisles, but with occasional recesses, which have been converted into chapels. As has been observed, it is lighted from above, and the effect of this upon the decorations is very striking; each chapel contains a statue of the saint to whom it is dedicated. Paintings illustrative of the life of the Magdalene, ornament the tympans of the side arches, whilst sculptures, also representing passages in her career, and executed by the first masters, are distributed here and there. On the ceiling, over the high altar, is a painting exhibiting the principal events that have influenced the Romish Church from its first institution; the last event represented is the coronation of Napoleon by Pius VII. The high altar is very fine, and approached by a flight of marble steps. The Church was consecrated in 1842 by the Archbishop of Paris. The total cost of its building was £523,160.

Descending the flight of steps at the grand entrance, and pursuing our way down the Rue Royale, we arrive upon the *Place de la Concorde*. This *Place* has received various names, having been called successively *Place Louis XV., Place de la Revolution, Place de la Concorde*; it was commenced to be laid out in 1763, and was finished in 1772. It has, however, undergone several alterations since then, and no less than three times within the last year have the plans for its re-arrangement been changed; the last design, however, has been carried into effect, and the works will be completed entirely within a short period. The change, however, has not been for the better; the *Place* consists of a fine open space, the entrances to which, at the four corners, are decorated by eight pavilions, bearing allegorical figures representing the towns of Strasbourg and Lille, Bourdeaux and Nantes, Marseilles and Brest, Rouen and Lyons. In the centre stands the Obelisk de Luxor brought from Egypt in 1833, and placed on its present pedestal in 1836. The mode of raising it to its present elevation, and the machinery employed are engraved on the sides of the base. This monolithe is one of those which were placed in front of the temple of Thebes, so long ago as the reign of Sesostris, 1550 years before the Christian era. The height of this single block of granite is 72 feet; it weighs more than a hundred-and-twenty tons.

On either side of the Obelisk are two elegant fountains, richly embellished with allegorical subjects—the one dedicated to sea, the other to river, navigation. The figures and mouldings which adorn them, represent the Genii of Commerce, Science and Industry. The lower basins, which ought to have been in marble or bronze, stretch fifty feet across, and receive the waters of two superior basins and four jets d'eau, which issue from horns held by marine deities. The Place is also brilliantly embellished by rows of elegant lamp posts, highly gilt; the large ones are forty in number, and bear two lamps each. This fine promenade is surrounded on the north by a line of building separated by the Rue Royale, consisting on the west of the Hotel de Crillon, held by private persons; on the east by the Ministére de la Marine, after which commences the Rue de Rivoli. On the east are the Gardens of the Tuilleries, on the west the Champs Elysées, and on the south the river, the Corps Legislatifs, and several of those noble mansions which stretch along the opposite quay, and once belonged to the nobility of the ancient regime.

In 1770, whilst the people were assembled to view the fêtes, given in honour of the marriage of Louis with Marie Antoinette, a rush was made by the multitude, on an alarm caused by the explosion of some fireworks, by which 1,200 were crushed and trampled to death, and more than 2,000 seriously injured. A collision took place here also between the troops and the people, which proved the signa. for the attack on the Bastile in 1789. In 1793, Louis XVI. and Marie Antoinette were beheaded here. The scaffolds were erected near the site of the present fountains; and in 1848, the proclamation of the late Republic was celebrated here amidst every mark of solemnity and rejoicing.

The Champs Elysées is properly speaking only a continuation of the promenade, which commences with the Gardens of the Tuilleries. Up to the sixteenth century, the space it now occupies, as far as the Barrière de l'Etoile, the Rue du Faubourg St. Honorè, and the river, was but very partially cultivated, and dotted with a few straggling cottages belonging to poor labourers. In 1616, however, Marie de Medicis had a portion of it, stretching along the banks of the Seine, and still called *Cours de la Reine*, laid out as a private promenade. Afterwards Coligny had the whole planted with trees and turfed, when it soon became a place of delightish resort, and received the flattering name it now bears. The Grand Avenue, or Avenue de Neuilly, which rises by a gradual slope to the Arc de Triomph at the summit of the hill, is upwards of a mile and a quarter in length from the Place de la Concorde.

Like every other part of Paris, the Champs Elysées has of late years been considerably improved, and adorned with embellishments of every kind. Beneath the trees are planted some graceful fountains, and, further up, breaking the long perspective of the grand road-way, an extremely elegant one throws out its waters to a considerable height in the form of a bouquet, and enjoys the centre of an open spot called the Place des Champs Elysées. On either side are Cafés and Restaurants, and other places of public divertisement, which, from the tasty manner in which they are constructed, add considerably to the beauty of the picture. To the right is the *Cirque de l'Imperatrice*, a fine open theatre, where the troop of Franconi go through their manoeuvres during the summer months, to the delight of crowded audiences. Behind the Cirque, and separated from the public by a simple balustrade, is the *Palais of the Elysée*, or the *Elysée National*, the garden of which is laid out in the English style, with winding alleys and velvet grass-plots. The Elysée was built in 1718, and became the residence of Madame de Pompadour, and afterwards the Duchess de Bourbon, who for a while gave her name to it. Under the Directory it became national property, and was occupied by officers of state; under the empire, Murat resided there, and Napoleon himself for a time; in 1814 the Emperor of Russia, and in 1815 the Duke of Wellington, took up their quarters here. In 1848 it was given to the President of the Republic. It is now undergoing great alterations, and is intended for the residence of any illustrious personages who may honour Paris with their presence. It was in the palace and the gardens of the Elysée that the Fête given by the Emperor in honour of the visit of the Duke of Cambridge and Lord Raglan, on their way to the East in April, 1854, was celebrated.

From the *Place des Champs Elysées* several avenues branch off—the two on the left, are the Avenue d'Antin and the Avenue des Veuves—here there is the Diorama of M. Langlais, which is well worth seeing. At the entrance of the *Allée des Veuves* is the

Jardin Mobille, where three or four times a week during the course of the summer, open-air balls are given. To these gardens persons are frequently attracted, who do not actually take part in them; and no one should omit to go there who would wish to see Paris life under every variety of aspect; not only is the music and the dancing good, but the gardens are tastefully laid out, and brilliantly illuminated. In the centre is an elegant pavilion, occupied by the orchestra, around which the fair ones and their partners revolve in harmonious confusion. Ladies are admitted free, but the gentlemen have to pay 3 francs. It is open on Tuesdays, Thursdays, Saturdays, and Sundays.

A little further up the Champs Elysées, on the left, is the

Jardin d'Hiver, or Winter Garden, opened in 1845. It is simply a vast green-house, within which are collected a great quantity of rare flowers and even green plants. Concerts, in which the first artists of the day assist, and balls for charitable purposes are often held here. The ordinary price of admission to see the gardens is one franc, but on special occasions, when a ball or a concert is given, the price is increased according to the nature and splendour of the fête.

A little further up the Avenue, still on the left, is the

Chateau des Fleurs, another garden where dancing takes place, and no less elegantly planned than the Jardin Mobille.

Amongst the shrubs and flowers, innumerable jets of light of different colours sparkle, and every where are distributed soft alcoves and quiet nooks; Chinese lanterns also hang from the boughs of the larger trees, and give a picturesque and Oriental appearance to the place. When the lilacs are in full blossom the gardens are very enchanting. A Kiosk in the centre of the grounds contains the orchestra. Fireworks are frequently added to the attractions of this Chateau. A Café and Restaurant supply refreshments. The gardens are open for dancing on Mondays, Wednesdays, and Fridays. Admission—for gentlemen, 3 francs; ladies are admitted free.

Crowning the hill, and just outside the Barrière, is the

Arc-de-Triomph de l'Etoile, a triumphal arch, intended to celebrate the victories which Napoleon had gained over the Austrians and Prussians, and to signalize the entry of Marie Louise, the affianced bride of Napoleon, into Paris. It was commenced in 1806; in 1814 the works had advanced as far as the spring of the arch, when they were arrested until 1823. In that year the government determined to continue them, in honour of the success of the Duke d'Angoulême in Spain; the arch, however, was not completed until 1836.

The total height of the structure is 152 feet, its breadth 137 feet, its depth 68 feet; the foundations which support its enormous weight are laid 25 feet under ground; the total cost has been £47,280. Each of the four principal groups which adorn the four fronts of the building is nearly forty feet high, and the figures twenty feet. On the side facing Paris the group on the right represents the *Departure for the Defence of One's Country;* on the left, *Napoleon, after a Triumph, receiving a crown from the hands of Victory.* On the front, towards Neuilly, the group to the right represents a young man surrounded by his family holding a dead child in his arms, and on the point of rushing out for the defence of his home; that on the left represents *Peace.*

This is one of the monuments of Paris which we would advise the visitor to mount; the ascent is comparatively easy, the stairs well lighted, and the birds' eye view from the summit well worth the trouble. Looking over Paris the Champs Elysées, and the Palace and Gardens of the Tuilleries, with the Place de la Concorde between them, stand in front; to the left is the Madeleine, the Church of the Assumption, with its fine dome, the Column Vendome, the Church of St. Eustache, the Tower of St. Jacques de la Boucherie and the Hotel de Ville, the arches of St. Denis and St. Martin, the Strasbourg Railway Station, Montmartre and Belleville; on the right is the Seine and the Champs de Mars, beyond which the Ecole Militaire, the Hôpital des Invalides, the Observatory, Val de Grace, the Pantheon, St. Sulpice, Notre Dame, the towers of the Palais de Justice, and the Conciergerie, stand out high above a vast mass of buildings; whilst beyond the Church of St. Gervais, the Ecole de Charlemagne, the Column of July, on the the Place de la Bastille, the two Columns at the Barrière du Trone, and the Chateau de Vincennes may easily be distinguished on a clear day. Turning to the west, a long line of hills surrounds the view, to the left of which may be seen Meudon and Mont Valerien, and beneath the Bois de Bologne, to the right, the low towers that rise in dim obscurity in the distance belong to the Abbey of St. Denis. A few sous are demanded by the porter on descending.

Immediately under the Arc de Triomph is *he Hippodrome*, which was opened in 1845 for equestrian evolutions. It is a paralellogram, surrounded inside with circular steps, capable of holding 7 or 8000 spectators; it is a fashionable resort, and attracts great numbers of every class. The theatre is open during fine weather every Tuesday, Thursday, Saturday, and Sunday, from three to half-past five.

When the weather is fine the Champs Elysées presents a most animated appearance; about two or three o'clock in the afternoon the promenaders begin to appear; and from that hour to six or seven, a continual crowd of persons is thronging the principal pathways and alleys, between the Tuilleries and the Barrière de l'Etoile. In the road a perpetual stream of carriages, freighted with the beauty and the fashion of this metropolis of fashion, rolls on towards the Bois de Bologne, where outside the fortifications of the city, and in the midst of its leafy enclosure, or on the banks of its artificial and recently-constructed lakes, a most delightful drive may be enjoyed. Every variety is here, and at this time afforded, to give pleasure to the eye; and no one can look upon the splendid equipages, the fine horses, the elegant dresses, and the cheerfu faces that pass and repass before him, without being struck by the dazzling effect of such a combination of wealth and taste.

In the evening, when the avenues are lighted up, and when the pavilions of the Café-chantants, decorated with flowers and various silken festoons, are brilliant with jets of fire—when the voice of music and singing is heard in every direction, and the fair performers, habited with all taste and elegance, are ranged within the pavilions, the scene becomes still more enchanting and illusory, and can scarcely be realised by one a visitant from the other side of the channel. The pleasure too of sitting out in the open air, breathing a genial atmosphere, drinking coffee at one's ease, and listening at the same time to a melody of pleasing songs, must not be forgotten amongst the influences that enrich the pleasure of the moment.

Returning to the Place des Champs Elysées, and taking the Allée d'Antin, we shall arrive upon the

Pont des Invalides.— This handsome suspension bridge was constructed in 1829, and serves as a communication between the Champs Elysées, le Gros-Caillou, and the Invalides. It is 350 feet long, and 24 broad, and admits of carriages as well as foot-passengers. The next bridge on the right, towards Chaillot, is the *Pont d'Iena*, commenced in 1806, and completed in 1813, after designs by M. Dillon. It consists of five elliptical arches, is 460 feet, and faces the Champs de Mars. It was named after the celebrated battle gained by Napoleon on the plain near Jena. In 1814, the Prussians, who came with the allied armies to Paris, attempted to destroy the bridge; but Wellington sent a corps and prevented this outrage. It was however called Pont des Invalides until 1880, when it re-assumed its original name. A little to the right of it, on the left bank, is the

Manufactory of Tobacco, which for those who are curious to see the process of preparing the various sorts of snuff and tobacco, is well worth a visit.

Proceeding to the left, we arrive at the *Esplanade des Invalides*, a fine open space, facing the river and the Champs Elysées, and measuring 1440 feet in length. It was formerly planted with very fine trees, but owing to the military camps which have been formed here at different times, it has been much injured. At the further end of it, and separated by a deep foss, is the

Hotel des Invalides, one of the chief public monuments of Paris. Until the reign of Henry IV. no provision was made for the soldier wounded and maimed in war: this humane monarch, however, instituted an asylum for them, which the numerous and severe wars Louis XIV. waged, soon proved small in its accommodations. This prince accordingly determined to erect a magnificent edifice, which should be worthy of his reign, and those whom he was pleased to call the participators of his glory. The present building was, accordingly, begun in 1671, after designs by Bruant, and the principal part of it finished in 1706: several additions have since been made. At the Revolution of 1793, it was called the *Temple of Humanity*; under Napoleon, the *Temple of Mars*; at the restoration, however, these inflated titles were annulled, and the institution resumed its original name. The Hotel is entered by a railed court, which precedes a garden, divided into different alleys leading to the different courts. The sides of this court are enclosed by little gardens, left to the care of the invalids, who thus find occupation and amusement in attending to them. In front of the principal entrance, and on each side of the railing, is a battery of 18 cannons, which is fired on the occasion of any great event. These cannons are the spoils of victory, and were taken from the Venetians, Dutch, Austrians, Prussians, Russians, and Algerians. The façade of the Hotel gives the appearance of great solidity. Several pavilions well proportioned attract the eye. A grand Arch, sustained by columns and pedestals, forms the principal entrance; over this entrance is an equestrian statue of Louis XIV.; statues of Prudence and Justice are placed on the right and left, in bas-relief; whilst two fine figures of Mars and Minerva grace the sides of the gateway. The length of the front is 612 feet. There are in the interior, fifteen courts, the principal of which, called the *Cour d'honneur*, is 315 feet long by 192 feet broad.

At the bottom of this court is the porch of the church: this porch, which is of the Composite order, is crowned by a fine statue of the Emperor, executed by M. Seurre. The interior will be seen to consist of two churches, which are now thrown into one; and the high altar, which stands with such fine effect between them, serves for both churches. The first church is adorned with 54 flags, taken from different nations from the time of the Republic down to the present. In the time of Napoleon, 3,000 banners attested the brilliancy of his successes, but on the eve of the entrance of the allied armies, in 1814, the minister of war ordered them to be burnt, and the sword of Frederic the Great, preserved amongst its curiosities, to be broken. Beneath, in the vaults, repose the remains of several of the most celebrated warriors of France. To obtain a view of the Tomb of Napoleon, it is necessary to go round to the opposite entrance, in the Place Vauban; but, before doing so, it will be worth while to view the interior of the building. In the *Library*, the objects most interesting are two candlesticks which belonged to Marshall Turenne, and also the cannon ball by which he was killed. In the *Salle d'attente* and *Council Chamber* are the portraits of the governors of the Hospital, and also models of the different forts and fortresses of France, such as Cherbourg, Dunkerque, Strasbourg, &c. After this the visitor will be shown the dining-rooms, kitchens, and dormitories; a small gratuity is expected by the guide, and by the officer who shews the library. The internal arrangements of this institution are under the direction of a governor, usually a Marshall of France, assisted by a staff. The building is capable of receiving 5,000 persons, and, with its adjoining dependencies, covers sixteen acres of ground; twenty-six sisters of charity and two-hundred-and-sixty servants attend upon the inmates.

Having seen these places, by taking the turning to the right, on crossing the foss, and going round the building, you will find yourself in the Place Vauban, and opposite the principal front of the *Invalides*, the portico of which is exceedingly beautiful; it is composed of two rows of columns, one above the other, of the Doric and Ionic order, supporting a delta, above which rises the magnificent dome decorated by forty columns. This dome, with its campanile, is one of finest chefs d'œuvres of Mansard, who took nearly thirty years in constructing it. It is covered with gilded lead richly sculptured, but the gold has nearly disappeared; it has been proposed to electro-plate it; if this should be done the effect will be astonishing.

The interior of the dome—church however, with its eight arched chapels and painted cupola, is most beautiful. On the left hand repose the remains of Napoleon as they were brought from St. Helena, and the tombs of Turenne and Vauban stand opposite to one another. In the centre is the grand Mausoleum of Napoleon, which is intended to receive his remains; it stands immediately under the centre of the dome, where the ground is open, and galleries of white marble encircle the sarcophagus which is of red Finland granite. Over the doorway leading into the crypt is the inscription taken from the will of Napoleon:—*Je desire que mes cendres reposent sur les bords de la Seine, au milieu de ce peuple Français que j'ai tant aimé.* The altar, which is the work of the late M. Visconti, is surmounted by a canopy supported by four columns of black marble, consisting each of an entire block, and measuring 22 feet in height. The capitals are gilded, but the light, which is admitted through painted windows, is so arranged as to give them the appearance of being of mother of pearl. A beautiful Christ, in white marble on a bronze cross, adorns the altar.

It should be observed that Bertrand, who followed Napoleon in his campaigns, from 1798 to that of Waterloo, and afterwards shared his exile at St. Helena, as well as Duroc, who was his companion in all his battles, from 1797 to 1813, when he was killed in Silesia, lie on each side of the entrance of the crypt that leads to the tomb of their friend and master.

On leaving the Invalides, the visitor should return to the Place Vauban and pass down by the Avenue de Tourelle, by which he will arrive in a few minutes upon *The Champs de Mars*, a large open space three quarters of a mile long, and nearly a quarter of a mile broad. In this arena took place the *Fête de la Federation*, on the 14th July, 1790, when an altar, called the *Autel de la Patrie*, was erected in the centre, around which thousands of people crowded. Opposite the front of the Ecole Militaire stood a pavilion, richly decorated, for the King; and here Louis XVI. swore to observe the new constitution. It was here also that Napoleon held his famous *Champ de Mai*, in 1815, previous to setting on his fatal campaign in Belgium; and in the same month, in the year 1852, Louis Napoleon distributed the eagles to the army. On this field all kinds of military exercises take place every day, and on special occasions, horse racing. Here was held the grand review in honour of the Duke of Cambridge and Lord Raglan, during their short stay in Paris, previous to their departure for the east. The building which we observe at the south end, is the

Ecole Militaire.—It is a plain building, without any architectural pretensions, and was established by Louis XV. for the gratuitous education of five hundred sons of poor noblemen, but more especially for the children of those who had perished in battle. The building was commenced in 1752, and completed in 1762. Ten Corinthian columns, which rise the whole height of the edifice, support an attic adorned with bas-reliefs. In 1788, the school was abolished, and the scholars were drafted off into other colleges, or took their commission at once in the army. In 1799 it was converted into a cavalry barracks,—Napoleon made it his head-quarters for some time;—it is now a barracks for infantry, cavalry, and artillery corps. In the dome of the edifice an observatory was erected, which exists still. Strangers are not admitted into the interior.

Returning in front of the Invalids, the nearest way to which is by the rue *Motte Piquet*, and retracing our steps to the river, we must turn to the right, and thus continue our route along the Quais. The first object of interest will be the *Hotel des Affaires Etrangères*, or the ministry for foreign affairs, which has just been completed at a cost of £200,000. The building consists of a main body, terminated at each extremity by a pavilion, and two wings project on the side facing the rue de Lille, forming a grand court. The lower part is of the Doric, the upper the Ionic order. Marble medallions give a graceful finish to the fine row of windows which range along the highly ornamented front facing the river. Strangers are not admitted into the interior.

As we proceed up the quay, we arrive at the *Pont de la Concorde*, a fine bridge, 470 feet in length and 60 in breadth, consisting of five elliptical stone arches. It was commenced in 1787 and finished in 1790, when it was called the *Pont de Louis XVI*. In 1792 it was called *Pont de la Revolution*, and in 1800 the name was again changed to the name it now bears. The materials of which it is built were taken from the *débris* of the Bastille. Perronet was the architect.

Opposite the bridge is the *Corps Legislatif*, or the *Palais Bourbon*, as it is commonly called. This palace was built by the Duchess Dowager, of Bourbon, in 1722. Eight hundred thousand francs were afterwards expended on it by the Prince de Condé, and the works were still in progress when the first revolution broke out. The mansion was then pillaged, and for some years remained unoccupied; but, in 1795, it was chosen as a place of meeting for the council of the Five Hundred. It reverted after the revolution to the Prince de Condé, and that part of it used formerly by the council was retained for the Chamber of Deputies. On the death of the Prince it became the property of the Duc d'Aumale, when the private apartments were rented by the state for the President of the Assembly. The whole of it was shortly afterwards purchased by the nation. The *National Assembly* sat here during the existence of the republic, and here took place some of the most stormy and uncontrolable debates ever witnessed. It is now occupied by the Corps Legislatif.

The fine peristyle, consisting of twelve Corinthian columns which decorates the river front, was built in 1804. The base of the delta is 95 feet, and its height, 17 feet. A bas-relief representing France standing on a tribune and holding the constitution in her right hand, is by Carlos. On the side of France are Minerva and Themis, the representatives of Force and Justice; on the left an allegorical group, representing Navigation, the Army, Industry, Peace, and Eloquence; on the right, Commerce, Agriculture, the Arts, and the two rivers, the Seine and the Marne. A broad flight of steps leads up to this noble porch, at the foot of which are statues of Justice and Prudence. Statues of Sully, Colbert, L'Hôpital, and D'Aguessau rest upon pillars that strengthen and adorn the iron railing surrounding the building.

The principal entrance, however, is from the Rue de l'Université. The gateway placed in the centre of a Corinthian colonnade, terminated by two pavilions, has a very fine appearance. The court, which is of considerable size, and surrounded by a fine line of buildings, is adorned with a portico of fluted columns, which serves as the entrance into the *Salle des Seances*. This saloon is on a level with the platform of the peristyle, and arranged in the form of an amphitheatre. It is adorned by a colonnade of twenty-four Ionic pillars of white marble, each a single block. A great number of historical pictures, by the best masters, decorate its walls. It was in this saloon that the Duchess of Orleans appeared with her two children to engage the Chamber to acknowledge the Count de Paris as king on the abdication of Louis Philippe. In the *Salle de la Paix*, a Laocoon, a Virginius, a Minerva in bronze, and a ceiling, painted by Horace Vernet, are worthy of notice. In the *Salle de Casimir Perier* are statues of the Republic, by Barre; of Casimir Perier, by Duret; of Bailley and Mirabeau, by Jaley; and bas-reliefs, by Friquette. In the *Salle des Conferences*, besides some paintings illustrating French History, will be observed figures of Prudence, Justice, Vigilance and Power, as well as medallion portraits of Sully, Montesquieu, Colbert and others. The *Library* of the Corps Legislatif contains about 50,000 volumes, consisting of a collection of all the laws passed, and procès-verbal of the legislative assemblies held here, and also of works relating to diplomatic subjects.

The interior of the Palais may be visited every day by foreigners, on applying to the Concierge; but, to visit the library, it is necessary to write to one of the librarians for permission.

Proceeding onward by the *Rue de Lille*, the visitor will arrive in front of the

Palais de la Legion d'Honneur, built in 1786, and designed as a residence for the Prince de Salm—Salm, who was guillotined in 1792. This mansion was then put up to a raffle, and fell to the lot of a barber. In 1804, however, Napoleon gave it to the Chancellor of the Legion of Honour, which institution had recently been established. This building is very rich in sculpture and ornament. The gate at the entrance represents a triumphal arch, decorated with Ionic columns, and bas-reliefs and statues. Two galleries of the same order, placed on the right and left, lead to the principal building, the façade of which is adorned with Corinthian columns, and a fine Ionic portico. A flight of steps leads up to this portico, and on the frieze above is the inscription of the Order Honneur et Patrie. The interior is decorated with taste and elegance. It is open from 2 to 4, and no further application for admission is necessary than a request to that effect to the Concierge.

Opposite the Palais de la Legion d'Honneur is the *Palais du Quai d'Orsay*, one of the finest and most imposing edifices of its kind in Paris. It was commenced in the latter days of the empire by Napoleon, and completed under Louis Philippe. It was intended as an Exhibition of the works of Industry of France, but was under the Republic devoted to the sittings of the Cours des Comptes and the Conseil d'Etat. The building of this splendid palace cost upwards of a half a million sterling. The principal front is towards the Rue de Lille, containing a spacious court, enclosed by an elegant range of buildings; but the façade towards the Quay is very fine. It is formed of a series of windows, separated by nine arches of the Tuscan, Ionic, and Corinthian orders, the extreme regularity of which gives a striking idea of beauty and grandeur. The arrangement of the interior is in keeping with the exterior. On the walls of the staircase are frescoes by M. Chasserian, representing Study, Agriculture, Commerce, War, Peace, &c. In the *Salle du Comité de l'Interieur* are some fine paintings, amongst them *Moses and Justinian*, by Marigny. The *Salle des Seances Administratives* is a very splendid hall, decorated with twenty-four Corinthian columns of white marble, with gilt capitals. Portraits of Turgot, Richelieu, Suger, Cambaceres, Colbert, and others, grace its walls. The interior cannot be visited.

The building next to the Palais is a cavalry barracks, a fine building, formerly the Hotel des Gardes du Corps of Napoleon. It was built under the empire. By the side of this, with a terrace overlooking the Seine, is the Hotel de Praslin, a fine specimen of one of the mansions of the old nobility, and beyond this the *Quai de Voltaire*. In the house at the corner of the quay and the Rue de Beaune died this celebrated philosopher. The bridge opposite is the

Pont Royale.—It has, however, changed names with the change of times, and has been known as the Pont National, and the Pont Imperial. It was built in 1684 by Frère Romain, a Dominican priest, after designs by Mansard. It is of stone, and consists of five semi-circular arches. Its length is 432 feet, and breadth 52. On one of the buttresses to the west is an index marking the height to which the waters of the Seine have risen during different inundations. The highest rise was in 1740, when they rose twenty-five feet. This bridge leads from the Tuilleries to the Quais Voltaire and d'Orsay, and the Rue de Bac.

THIRD DAY.

PLACE VENDOME—FONTAINE DES CAPUCINS—ST. ROCH—ST. JACQUES DE LA BOUCHERIE—PONT NEUF—PLACE DAUPHINE—PALAIS DE JUSTICE—SAINTE CHAPELLE—CONCIERGERIE—LA MORGUE—HOTEL DIEU—NOTRE DAME—PONT DE LA REFORME—HOTEL DE VILLE—CASERNE NAPOLEON—ST. GERVAIS—HENRY IV. ASSASSINATED—HALLES CENTRALES—FONTAINE DES INNOCENTS—ST. EUSTACHE—HALLE AUX BLES—BANK OF FRANCE—PLACE DES VICTOIRES.

This morning's visit shall be directed to some of the older parts of Paris, and especially those monuments which illustrate the ancient city. But first it will be as well to visit the *Place and Column Vendôme*.

This place or square, which forms an irregular octagon, was commenced in 1688, after designs by Mansard, on the spot where formerly a monastery stood. It was intended by Louis XIV., who originated the place, to contain the Mint, the Royal Library, and the Hotels of Special Ambassadors. The project was, however, abandoned, and the property disposed of, to the corporation of Paris, who agreed to carry out so much of the king's intention as related to the formation of a place, which was accordingly done. At this time a colossal equestrian statue of Louis stood in the centre, but this was destroyed in 1792. In 1806, Napoleon ordered the present triumphal column, after the model of Trajan's triumphal pillar at Rome, to be erected in commemoration of the successes of the French armies. The shaft is formed of 276 plates of metal, derived from 1,200 pieces of cannon taken from the Austrians and Prussians, and weighing altogether more than 120 tons. The height of the column is about 140 feet, the pedestal is 22 feet high, and 16 feet wide. It was, after its completion, surmounted by a statue of Napoleon as emperor; in 1814 this statue was melted down to aid in forming the equestrian statue of Henry IV., now on the Pont Neuf; but, during the reign of Louis Philippe, the present statue of the emperor was placed there.

The plates of which the column is formed, are arranged in a spiral manner, and adorned with bas-reliefs, representing the principal events which signalised the campaign of 1805, up to the battle of Austerlitz. The pedestal is ornamented with casts of helmets, cannons, and military instruments of every kind, in good keeping with the rest of the design. In the interior of the column a staircase has been formed of 176 steps, by which the visitor may reach the gallery over the capital; but the ascent is steep and dark, and we would not advise any of our visitors to mount them, as no other object is gained in doing so than the fact of having been at the top of the column. From the Pantheon, the Arc dé l'Etoile, or Nôtre Dame, a better view may be obtained, with a really agreeable ascent.

Descending the rue Castiglione we see at the corner of the rue St. Honoré the *Fontaine des Capucins*, constructed in 1713. It possesses no architectural grace, but over it is a latin couplet by Santeuil:—

> Tot loca inter sacra, pura est quæ labitur unda ;
> Hanc non impuro, quisquis es, ore bibas.

There were formerly six convents in this neighbourhood: *tot loca inter sacra*.

Continuing by the rue St. Honoré eastward, we see on the left the

Church of St. Roch—One of the wealthiest and most privileged churches of Paris. The first stone was laid in 1653, by Louis XIV. and his mother, Anne, of Austria, but the building was not completed until nearly a century afterwards. The plan was furnished by Jacques Mercier. The external architecture is somewhat plain, but the internal, which is of the Doric order, suggests massiveness and strength. The nave, the roof of which is supported by twenty columns, is 160 feet long. Eighteen chapels surround the aisles. At the further end is this *Chapelle du Calvaire*, a very curious chapel. In a large niche, lighted from an invisible opening above, is represented the top of Mount Calvary, our Saviour on the cross and the Magdalene at the foot weeping. To the right of this chapel we see large rocks and the mouth of a cavern, before which are groups of figures representing the burial of Jesus. The Chapel of the Virgin behind the choir is considered a chef-d'œuvre. It is circular, ornamented with Corinthian pilasters, and crowned by a cupola painted in fresco. The subject is the Assumption. There are several pictures of value in this church; amongst them—the Raising the Daughter of Jairus, by Delorme; the Raising of Lazarus, by Vien; Jesus Blessing Children, by the same; Saint Sebastian, by Bellard. The shrine behind the choir is made of the cedar of Lebanon.

Before the revolution of 1848, Louis Philippe and his family used to attend mass in this church; here, in 1720, the famous Law confessed his conversion to the Roman Catholic faith to be made controller-general of the finances, when he made a present to the church of 100,000*l*. Many illustrious persons are buried here; amongst others Pierre Corneille. On the steps of this church many popular tumults have taken place. In 1830 a valiant stand was made here by the people against the soldiers of Charles X., and here an eager multitude thronged to witness the unfortunate Louis XIV., and afterwards the beautiful Marie Antoinette, led on to execution.

At Easter, and on other great festivals, the finest music may be heard here, as this church has the privilege of making the first selection from the opera companies of Paris on those occasions.

Passing down this street, crossing the Place du Palais Royal into the Louvre, and ing on beyond the Louvre some little distance, we arrive opposite one of the purest specimens of Gothic architecture in Paris.

The tower of *St. Jacques de la Boucherie*. The church to which it was attached, and the date of which is lost in antiquity, was destroyed during the revolution of 1789; and the tower, which alone remains to attest its magnificence, sold to a private individual to erect a foundry in. In 1836 it was purchased by the city of Paris, with a view to its preservation and renewal. The height of it measures 160 feet.

Retracing our steps, and turning down on the left by the Rue de la Monnaie, we shall arrive on the *Place du Châtelet* and turning a little to the right the Pont Neuf. The *Place du Châtelet* is so called from a châtelet or fortress which formerly stood there, from the earliest times of the French monarchy to the year 1812, when it was completely pulled down. The fortress contained both a court of justice and a prison. In the centre is a fountain, consisting of a circular basin 21 feet in diameter, and a column 54 feet high. This column, representing a palm-tree, the leaves of which form the capital, was erected in 1807, and is intended to commemorate the victories of the republic and Napoleon. A figure of Fame holding a wreath in each hand, standing on a globe, and borne up by allegorical figures of the four winds, surmounts the column. Four figures representing Prudence, Vigilance, Law, and Force adorn the base.

Passing on to the *Pont Neuf* we have a fine view of the Cité, the quays, the river, and the Pont des Arts. This latter bridge is very light, though constructed of nine iron arches. It is 518 feet long and 31 feet broad, and derives its name from the Palais des Beaux Arts, to which it leads from the Louvre. It was built in 1804, and cost 56,000*l*. To the right, on the Quai de l'Ecole, is the Place de l'Ecole, containing a fountain, surrounded by a basin surmounted by a stone vase and flanked by lions, which cast the water into the cistern.

Immediately below the bridge, to the west, are the elegant Baths of the Samaritan, where every kind of warm and shower bath may be had, from early in the morning to 10 or 11 at night. Opposite are the baths of Henry IV., where swimming is taught. In the summer season this establishment, as well as others lower down on the Seine, are crowded by bathers. It may be as well to observe that the Baths of Henry IV., and the Imperial Baths along the Quai de Voltaire, are the best swimming baths; and that the Samaritan, and the baths opposite the Imperial Swimming Baths, are the best warm baths. There are, however, numerous warm baths in every part of Paris, which are very moderate in their charges.

The Pont Neuf is perhaps the most frequented of all the bridges of Paris. Walk on it and you are sure to meet a white horse, a soldier, and a priest, became of old a proverb, to indicate the crowd of people of every sort and every condition which crossed it. This bridge connects the two banks of the Seine with the island of the city, and opens up a communication between the most populous and busy quarters of Paris. It was commenced in 1578, but, owing to the civil troubles that afflicted France at this period, it was not completed till 1604. Henry IV. was so anxious for its construction that he defrayed the expenses out of his private purse. The entire length of the bridge is 1,008 feet, and its breadth 86 feet. Formerly shops were established along the sides of the parapets; but during the recent improvements, these houses have been taken down. The ground on which the centre of the bridge rests was formerly a separate island, called l'Ile aux Vaches. Here, in 1304, Jacques Molay, grand master of the Templars, was publicly burnt to death. The statue of Henry IV., which fills the open space between the two bridges, was placed there in 1818, and replaces the one erected there by his widow, Marie de Medicis, but which was destroyed in 1793. Opposite the statue is the entrance into the *Place Dauphine*, which was planned by Henry IV. in 1608, and so called in commemoration of the birth of the Dauphin Louis XIII., son of that monarch. In the centre is a statue to the memory of General Desaix, who fell at Marengo.

In this place is one of the principal omnibus bureaus, from which a person can go by correspondence to almost any part of Paris.

Proceeding straight through the Place, we shall arrive by a flight of steps in the passage and courts of the

Palais de Justice—The front of which, however, is on the opposite side, and faces the Place of the same name. This edifice, by the antiquity of parts of it, by its associations, and by the peculiar manner of the people of the law who frequent the quarter, is one of the most curious monuments of the capital. It was here that from the time of Hugh Capet or his son Robert, who is said by some to have built it in 1000, down to the reign of Charles V., who left it in 1354, that all the French kings dwelt. The first edifice was small, but it was successively enlarged by St. Louis, Philippe le Bel, Louis XI., Charles VIII., and Louis XIII. The towers with conical roofs, which face the quays, are referred back to the time of Philippe Augustus; and the square tower, known by the name of the *Tour de l'Horloge*, which forms the angle with the quay and the Marché des Fleurs, belongs also to the same early period. This tower contains the famous clock, made in 1370 by a German, and presented to Charles V. It is the first clock of the kind that the Parisians had seen. In the lantern over this tower formerly hung the *Tocsin*, or clock alarm-bell, which was rung on the occasion of the death of the king, or the birth of the dauphin. It was this bell too that, on the fatal 24th of August, 1572, responded to the death-signal from the bell of St. Germain L'Auxerrois, for the massacre of the Hugenots. It was destroyed, however, in 1789.

Before 1618, in the great hall of the palace, the king was accustomed to receive ambassadors, to give banquets, and celebrate the marriage of the princes or princesses of royal blood. Around it were arranged, in chronological order, statues of the Kings of France, from Pharamond down to the last deceased. At one end stood an immense marble table, it is said, of one block, at which kings and persons of the highest degree were privileged to eat. It afterwards became the stage upon which the first theatrical representations, such as the mysteries, took place. The hall, however, was burnt down early in the seventeenth century, and the *Salle des Perdus* constructed in its place. The entrance into the old building was by no means graceful, but within the last few years great improvements have been made, and the beautiful façade that at present exists constructed. The principal front is towards the Rue de la Barillerie. A spacious court, the *Court de Mai*, enclosed by a magnificent railing and two side buildings, leads up to the main building. This is again approached by a noble flight of steps, the largest in Paris, and adorned by Ionic columns and allegorical figures, representing Justice, Prudence and Force.

The *Salle des Perdus*, to which these steps lead, is a fine hall, 230 feet in length and 86 in breadth. It is divided into two naves by a row of columns and arcades which support the vaulted roof, and ornamented by a monumental statue of Malesherbes, the advocate of Louis XVI., and was constructed by M. Desbrosses in the rennaissant style of architecture. In the old chamber Henry II. of England was received and fêted, when he came to do homage to the King of France for his Norman possessions.

Passages diverging from this grand saloon lead to the different courts of law, and over the entrance of each is inscribed the name of the court. The Court of Cassation is erected on the place of the ancient Salle Saint Louis, which that monarch had repaired and decorated on occasion of his marriage with the Duchess of Suffolk, the beautiful sister of Henry VIII. It is now enriched with bas-reliefs representing Louis XIV. between Justice and Truth. The chambers of the Court of Appeal, as well as those of the *Première Instance*, and simple police are here.

To the curious and the antiquarian in taste, a visit to the *Depot des Archives Judiciares* will be very interesting. It is situated in three long galleries, immediately above the grand salle and next to the roof, and is ascended by a tortuous and difficult staircase. Amongst its undisturbed treasures may be found the form of proceedings on the trial of Ravaillac, the assassin of Henry IV., and others whose crimes have rendered them notorious. In an old box in the same chambers are contained the clothes which Damien, the regicide, wore when led to punishment, and the rope-ladder so ingeniously made by Latude, when he attempted to escape from the Bastille.

On leaving these interesting antiquities and descending into the Cour de Mai, the visitor must next seek out the *Sainte Chapelle*, which is on the south side of the Palais. This is one of the most curious monuments of the thirteenth century, and interesting, not only from its historical associations, but as being one of the most beautiful and pure specimens of Gothic architecture which exists. It was built in 1242 by Saint Louis, as a depository for the *crown of thorns worn by our Saviour during the crucifixion, a piece of the true cross, the spear-head which pierced our Saviour's side*, and other such relics which this superstitious monarch had purchased from the emperor Baldwin for two millions of francs. What is principally admired in this building is the very lightness of its construction, the magnificence of its stained glass windows, and the elegance of the groups of columns which spring up to support the vault and form the mouldings. The chapel was surmounted by a spire, elegant as the rest of the building, but which was unfortunately destroyed by fire in 1620. The architects which Louis XIV. had around him attempted to restore it, but their genius and skill failed to replace it; it has, however, just been replaced by one in beautiful harmony with the edifice, and light and airy as can well be imagined. The height of the present one is 70 feet above the roof. It is superbly gilt. The height of the building from the ground is 110 feet. The interior consists of a single nave and choir. Four beautifully designed windows, illustrating the principal events in the life of St. Louis and his two crusades, adorn each side, while seven narrow pointed ones surround the choir. The whole is gorgeously decorated. At the extremity of the choir is a low chapel, remarkable for its beauty. The roof is supported by seven arches, resting on a cluster of seven small columns. Every part, external and internal, of this chapel, ought to be examined for the delicacy, as well as splendour, of the details of its architecture. A stone marks still the spot of the famous reading desk, which was the subject of the best poem of Boileau, the satirical poet, which was buried here in 1711. The reading desk has been removed to the Abbey of St. Denis.

Forming a part of the Palais de Justice, but at the back of it, is the

Conciergerie, a prison, some of whose cells and dungeons descend many feet below the level of the Seine. It is approached by one of the streets leading out of the Quai des Orfèvres. It was formerly the prison of the Parliament, and at a later period replaced that of the Châtelet. The cell in which Marie Antoinette was confined has been converted

Rue de Rivoli

Entrée du Palais du Luxembourg

Val de Grace

Notre Dame

Chapel of the Palais of Versailles

into a chapel, and several pictures hang around it to illustrate the history of her misfortunes. It was in the same chamber, too, that the Girondists held their last banquet before being led out to execution. In the dungeons of this gloomy edifice, Madame Elizabeth and the terrible Robespierre were also confined; and here several republicans, in the year 1848, condemned for their ultra and dangerous opinions, underwent the execution of their sentence. The entrance facing the quay is flanked, as we have mentioned already, by two round towers with conical roofs. The one to the west is called the *Tour de Cesar*, that to the east the *Tour Bonbec*. The whole of this façade is in keeping with its character, and the eye has only to rest upon it for a moment, for the heart to be penetrated by a gloomy and ominous feeling.

Returning to the *Quai des Orfevres*, and proceeding towards Nôtre Dame, we pass by a small low building on the right, just beyond the Pont St. Michel. This building is the *Morgue*, or Dead-house of Paris. On platforms of stone in the interior are laid the bodies of those who have died by accident or any violent death. They are kept there until claimed by friends or persons connected with the deceased. The number of suicides and deaths by violent means is very great, and sometimes so many as three or four bodies may be seen lying at one time on the platform. It is only a morbid feeling which can induce the great crowds that visit it to enter. Passing on from this and entering the open space, the *Place du Parvis de Nôtre Dame*, we have before us that ancient cathedral and on our right,

The *Hotel Dieu*. This splendid hospital is divided into two by the river, and a large number of wards exist on the left bank of the Seine. So long back as the seventh century, a similar institution was said to have been established on the spot. Philip Augustus was the first king whose generosity prompted him to endow this hospital. Saint Louis after him granted to the institution the tax upon provisions brought to the markets, and subsequently various kings, and nobles, and wealthy men, have enriched it by gifts and legacies, until it has become the richest hospital in Paris. Under the first republic it received the fantastic name of *Hospice d'Humanité*. The building, with the exception of its size, and its object, is unimposing. The entrance is adorned by a portico supported by Doric columns, very simple and neat. Busts and portraits of the most celebrated physicians who have been connected with the institution adorn the vestibule. The interior is divided into twenty-six large and airy chambers, containing upwards of 1,260 beds. The regulations of this establishment are upon the most liberal scale; and nothing is refused to patients which can contribute to their comfort, as well as convalescence.

The hospital may be visited by applying with a passport to the Bureau Central d'Admission dans les Hospitaux, No. 2, Place du Parvis de Nôtre Dame, opposite the Hotel Dieu.

NOTRE DAME.

A temple dedicated to Jupiter, is said to have occupied the spot on which this celebrated metropolitan church is built. When this temple ceased to exist is not known, but, in 522, Childebert, son of Clovis, raised a christian house of worship here. All but the foundations of this structure was destroyed by the Normans, who invaded France, and took Paris in the ninth century. This building remained in a state of ruin till 1160, when Maurice de Saliac, who had risen from a very obscure origin to be Archbishop of Paris, signalised his accession to the archiepiscopal chair by undertaking the reconstruction of the church. The first stone was laid by Pope Alexander the Third, who had taken refuge at the court of Louis le Jeune. Although that part containing the high altar was consecrated twenty-two years after—in 1182—the works went on very slowly, and it was not until 1223, in the reign of Philip Augustus, that the western façade was completed. Even yet it was but partially completed, for the north transept was not built until the year 1312, when Philippe le Bel bestowed a portion of the confiscated property of the Templars upon it, to sanctify his unjust method of suppressing the order; and the *Porte Rouge*, which was so called because it was erected by the Duke of Burgundy in expiation of his crime, the assasination of the Duke of Orleans, was not finished until 1420, so that this magnificent monument of those times took nearly three hundred years in building.

The church is built in the form of a latin cross. Within, it is divided by two rows of pillars and pointed arches, 120 in number, surmounted by galleries decorated by light columns into three naves. The vaulting of the roof, which has nothing particular about it, except its imposing height, rises 102 feet from the pavement. The doors at the side are highly ornamented with scrolls of iron-work, of great elegance. The iron-railing that separates the choir from the nave is also a chef-d'œuvre of its kind. The choir, which is paved with marble, is surrounded by a magnificent wainscoating, containing the twenty-six stalls of the ecclesiastical dignitaries belonging to the church, upon which are engraved scenes in the lives of our Saviour and the Virgin. The high altar, approached by steps of Languedoc marble, with its rich canopy and fine bas-relief, is particularly worthy of remark. Behind is a fine group of sculpture by Coustou, representing the descent from the cross. Around the choir are also arranged some good paintings by Philippe de Champagne, Vanloo, Antoine Coypel, Jouvenet, &c. Four magnificent rose-windows, 36 feet in diameter, highly sculptured, and filled with beautifully stained glass, illustrating scripture history, decorate the windows at the north and south transepts, and east and west ends. The church is surrounded by twenty-four chapels, one of which is dedicated to St. Thomas of Canterbury.

Amongst the curiosities to be seen in the church are the splendid vestments which priests wear on ceremonial occasions.

The exterior of the church of Nôtre Dame is more striking than the interior; and when we contemplate its tout ensemble, we must admit that it is of a solemn and imposing grandeur. The western façade is pierced by three doorways, composed of retiring pointed arches, sumptuously sculptured. The resurrection, and bas-reliefs illustrating the seven cardinal virtues and their opposite vices, decorate the principal porch. The porch to the right is ornamented with a statue of St. Marcel, treading a dragon under his feet, and other subjects, taken from the life of our Saviour and St. Joseph; the porch to the left, by the death and coronation as queen of heaven, of the Virgin Mary. Above the arches runs a gallery extending the whole length of the façade, and called formerly the *Gallerie des rois*, because it contained statues of the kings of Judah. These were destroyed during the revolution of 1793, but are now being restored.

This front is terminated by two large square towers, 280 feet high, mounted by a staircase of 380 steps placed in the north tower. In the south tower is the famous *Bourdon*, a great bell weighing 32,000 lbs., which is only rung on great occasions. It was founded in 1685, and baptised with great ceremony, having Louis XIV. and his wife for sponsors, hence its other name, Emmanuel Louise Thérèse. The clapper weighs nearly a thousand pounds. The portal of the south transept of the church is adorned with sculptures illustrating the life of St. Stephen, and that of the north transept, by sculptures illustrating the story of the Nativity, and the expulsion of evil spirits from those possessed of them.

Passing to the east of Nôtre Dame, we arrive at the *Pont de la Reforme*, or the *Pont Louis Philippe*, which stretches from the Ile de la Cité to the Ile St. Louis; and again from this island to the Quai de la Grève. This bridge consists of two suspensions, supported by cables formed of 250 threads of iron wire. The span of each bridge is 250 feet. It was called the Pont de Louis Philippe, because it was opened in 1834 under the auspices of that monarch, and Pont de la Reforme after the revolution of 1848. It is opposite to this bridge that formerly stood the house in which the unfortunate Abelard and Heloise resided. From the centre a fine view of the river and of the Hotel de Ville may be had.

Crossing this double bridge we arrive upon the Quai de la Grève, and a little further on, at the

Hotel de Ville.—A house called the Maison de Grève, which had been the residence of Charles V. whilst he was dauphin, was purchased by the corporation of Paris in 1357, for 2,880*l*., for the purpose of holding their municipal meetings. In 1533 this mansion, with some others that environed it, were pulled down, and a more spacious one commenced. After a long interruption it was continued from designs by Dominic Certone, and finished in 1605, during the reign of Henry IV. During the revolution of 1793, it suffered greatly from the furious conduct of the populace, but, in 1801, it was rescued from neglect, and made by Napoleon the residence of the Prefect of the Seine. Since that time, however, the whole edifice has been entirely remodelled, and enlarged to nearly four times its original extent. These alterations were completed in 1841, and the result is, the beautiful structure we see before us.

The plan of the Hotel de Ville is that of a regular parallelogram, the four corners of which are crowned by pavilions. The principal façade, which is towards the west, is very fine. Over the principal doorway is an equestrian statue of Henry IV., over which again is an illuminated clock. Besides the two pavilions at the extremities, there are two smaller ones over each entrance, and in the centre a lofty turret, from which a gilded vane springs. The façade fronting the Seine is adorned with twelve allegorical figures representing Commerce, Justice, &c. The whole of the building is in the rennaissant style of architecture.

The apartments of the Prefect of the Seine occupy the ground floor of the right wing; above these are the reception rooms, ornamented with great taste and splendour, and over these again are the archives of the prefecture. In the left wing is the magnificent room known by the name of the *Salle de St. Jean*, where the public festivals of the city take place, besides other fine chambers, in which the sittings of the council general, as well as the meetings of learned and scientific societies, are held. The other rooms of the palace are devoted to offices and residences for the subordinate members of the administration. The staircase leading up to the principal rooms is of great beauty; the sculptures are the work of the celebrated Jean Goujon. In the *Salle du Throne* is a small equestrian statue of Henry IV., of exquisite workmanship, and in the court, which is also decorated with the productions of Jean Goujon, is a statue of Louis XIV. The fine open space which the Hotel de Ville enjoys, as well as the elegance of the houses which are being thrown up around it, enables the visitor to see it to great advantage.

It is hardly to be expected that a place of such municipal importance as the Hotel de Ville should be wanting in historical associations. And in this we are not deceived. The various tumults, civil and religious, that have taken place on the troubled soil of France, have all had some connection with this building. It was here that, in 1358, the bloody insurrection of the Maillotins, so dreadfully suppressed by Charles VI., broke out; it was here that societies of the Fronde met; it was here that Robespierre held his blood-thirsty council, that Louis XVI. appeared wearing the *bonnet rouge* to gratify the people; it was here that Louis Philippe was presented to the French nation by Lafayette in 1830; and here it was that, in 1848, M. Lamartine nobly exposed his safety, and declared to the excited people that, as long as he lived, the *red flag* should never be the *flag of France*.

Immediately behind the Hotel de Ville is one of the principal barracks of Paris. It is large and commodious, and capable of containing a great many soldiers. Since 1851 it has received the name of Caserne Napoleon. To the right of the barracks is the

Church of St. Gervais.—This church was founded in the sixth century, but rebuilt in 1240, and restored and enlarged in 1581. The structure unites three orders of Grecian architecture—the Doric, Ionic, and Corinthian, all in excellent harmony the one with the other; and the approach of the western entrance has long been admired by connoisseurs. In the interior, the style is Gothic, and remarkable for the height of its vaulted roof. The stained glass of the choir, and several of the chapels, are very beautiful. The Chapel of the Virgin in the interior is considered a chef-d'œuvre, and contains a fine statue of Christ, by Cortot. In the Chapel of the Holy Ghost, in the south transept, is a good painting of the Tongues of Fire, and St. Amboise refusing entrance to Theodosius the Great. In another chapel is an Ecce Homo, by Rouget. There are also other fine paintings in the style of the Italian masters, much admired. A monument to Chancellor Letellier has been erected in this church. At the extremity, figures of Religion and Fortitude, life-size, support the dying minister. A plaster Descent from the Cross here is also worth noticing. The street behind this church is the Rue St. Antoine, and leads to the Bastille. It is in this quarter that, during revolutions and popular émeutes, the principal fighting goes on.

It is now necessary that we should retrace our steps. Returning therefore to the Rue de Rivoli, at the north of the Hotel de Ville, we must take the Rue du Temple on the right, and pursue it until we arrive at the Rue Ferronière, a street to the left. Continuing this street we enter the eastern end of the Rue St. Honoré, at No. 3 of which street stood Ravaillac, when he stabbed Henry IV. A bust of the king is placed in a niche between the third and fourth stories, with a latin inscription upon it.

The street opposite leads into the *Halles Centrales* of Paris, where the general marketing for the city takes place. At an early hour of the morning, carts, conveying provisions of all kinds, come in from all parts, and when the wholesale business of bringing is over, about 10 or 11, the retail dealers take their places to carry on their business. On the right, on entering, will be seen a very fine fountain, the

Fontaine des Innocents—One of the finest of the kind in Paris. It stands in the market of the same name. Where it stands was formerly a burial-ground for three parishes, but the accumulation of human remains, after some frightful pest, became so offensive that they were obliged to be exhumed and transported to another place. The spot chosen was some underground quarries, then no longer used, on the other side of the river. The remains were arranged in a regular manner around these caves, which have received the names of *Catacombs*.

On the opposite side of the market is the

Church of St. Eustache—One of the finest and loftiest in Paris. It was begun in 1532 and consecrated in 1637. In 1804 it was visited by Pius VII., when the ceremony of a second consecration was gone through. The interior has recently been cleaned and ornamented. It consists of a nave, two aisles, and deep transept. It is remarkable for the height of its roof, the delicacy of its pillars, and the beautiful effect of its tout ensemble. The length of time which it took in building is no doubt the cause of the defect which exists in its architectural harmony, for we see the Grecian orders blended together with the gothic and the rennaissant style. The roof is supported by ten parallel pillars, which rise a hundred feet from the ground, and which again support half-way up a gallery, running entirely round the church. Above the gallery are twelve windows, ornamented with stained glass, very valuable both as to design and colour. The interior of the choir is also much admired for the beauty of its decorations. The high altar is of pure Parian marble, exquisitely sculptured, and cost upwards of 3,000*l*. The reading-desk is the same which formerly stood in Notre Dame, but which was displaced during the revolution of 1793.

The church is surrounded by chapels, highly ornamented. In that dedicated to the Virgin is a marble statue of the Virgin, executed by Pigal; the sides of the chapel are adorned by some good bas-reliefs. In the same chapel is the tomb of Colbert, by Coysevox. The organ over the doorway has recently been built, and is considered one of the finest in Paris. Either of the streets leading out from the west of the market will lead us to the *Halle aux Blés* and *Fontaine Medicis.*

The Halle aux Blés, or corn market, is a large circular building, 126 feet in diameter, and vaulted by a vast dome. It is built on the spot where anciently stood the Hôtel de Soissons, a palace of Catherine de Médicis. This immense structure, which is divided into a gallery of 28 arches, is capable of holding 30,000 sacks of corn. From the gallery, running round the building above the arches, a curious echo may be heard.

The only relic of the residence of Catherine de Medicis now existing is a Doric pillar, 95 feet high, situated on the south side of the hall. It was erected in 1572 as an observatory for that princess. Two-thirds of the height there is an ingenious sun-dial, constructed by a canon of the Church of St. Geneviève. This dial may be reached by a staircase in the inside. At the base of the column is a fountain. The building may be seen by speaking to the porter.

Passing down by the Rue Coquillière, and turning to the right on entering the Rue Croix des Petits Champs, we shall have opposite to us the

Banque de France.—This building was formerly the Hotel of the Courts of Toulouse. In 1720, it was rebuilt, after designs by Mansard, for the duke of Vrillière, who gave his name to an adjoining street. It was, however, given in 1811, to the administration of the Bank of France, which had been founded in 1803, by Napoleon. The hotel has, however, recently undergone considerable alterations. Passing down the street, fronting the principal entrance, we arrive on the

Place des Victoires.—The houses surrounding this square, are from the designs of Mansard, and have their fronts regularly adorned by Ionic pilasters. In the centre, stood formerly, a statue of Louis XIV., crowned by Victory, surrounded by allegorical figures, in bronze. This monument was destroyed in 1792, and replaced by a pyramid, on which was inscribed the recent achievements of the French arms. In 1806, a colossal bronze statue of General Desaix, was erected in its place, but this was melted down on the Restoration, to form, with the statue of Napoleon, which surmounted the Column Vendome, the statue of Henry IV. on the Pont-Neuf. The present equestrian statue of the

Grand Monarch, habited as a Roman emperor, was erected in 1822. It was erected by Bosio.

A little behind the Place des Victoires, is the church of Notre Dame des Victoires, or des Petits Pères. This church was built by Louis XIII., in 1629, to express his gratitude to Providence for the series of victories he had gained, and which terminated in the taking of Rochelle. It is built in the form of a Roman cross. In the interior, which is very fine, are some admired pictures by Vanloo, embracing the history of St. Augustine. In 1789, this church was converted into the Exchange.

The street to the west, the *Rue Neuve des Petits Champs*, will lead the visitor on to the *Rue de la Paix*, or the *Boulevarde de Madeleine*, when he will arrive at the locality he started from in the morning.

The Boulevards.—Paris is perhaps unique in the plan of its construction. Most cities have their gardens, their parks, their public walks, their parades, their piazzas, or their arcades, in common with the metropolis of France; but those magnificent thoroughfares lined with a verdant fringe of trees, which stretch for miles within the busiest quarters of the city, and constitute the resort of nearly every class of citizen, are altogether peculiar to Paris. It is to these thoroughfares, the Boulevards, that we must go if we would study one of the most prominent phases of French society, and acquire a knowledge of the open air habits of the Parisian. He who has made any stay within this city, and neglected to explore this fine avenue of palatial buildings, from the Place de la Madeleine to the Place de la Bastille, will have lost a splendid opportunity of viewing the French in their real element.

The Boulevards are divided into the internal and external boulevards. The external are those which run round Paris on the outside of the barrier-wall; the internal those that form a magnificent thoroughfare within, though not close to the barriers. They are eighteen in number, of which twelve lie on the north, and six on the south side of the Seine. The principal, or those which are most frequented, numbering eleven, lead from the Madeleine to the Bastille, and are the Boulevards de la Madeleine, des Capucines, des Italiens, de Montmartre, Poissonière, Bonne Nouvelle, St. Denis, St. Martin, du Temple, des Filles du Calvaire, Beaumarchais. The best time for seeing them is in the evening of a fine day, when the wealthy bourgeois and pleasure-seeking *commis* having finished their dinner retire thither to lounge about on its broad pavement, to gaze at its brilliant shops, or to sip their coffee at one of the numerous cafés which abound along the whole extent of these urban promenades. A quiet drive through them on such an occasion is well repaid. The picture of life and animation, of ease and pleasure, of *insouciance* and gaiety here presented to the visitor is truly striking, and scarcely to be met with in any other quarter of the globe. Besides this, there is an air of tranquillity, of softness, of delight that cannot fail to communicate a sense of enjoyment and luxury to his own spirit.

Other objects of attraction than the people, meet him everywhere. The shops splendidly lighted up, and filled with every object that can please the eye tastily arranged, offer themselves to his notice. Cafés beautifully decorated, or like the *Café de la Madeleine*, enclosing bosquets and bowers, fantastically illuminated with variegated lamps, and commanding from its oriental terrace a long view of the boulevards invite him. Noble residences, such as the *Mais on Dorèe* on the Boulevard des Italiens, remarkable for its beautiful architecture, and richly ornamented with gold; or the *Portes St. Denis* and *St. Martin*, erected to commemorate the victories of Louis le Grand; or the *Chateau d' Eau*, with its open space covered with trees, and adorned with a fine fountain, these present themselves to vary and enrich the route through which he passes.

Along these boulevards too lie the principal theatres of Paris. The *Opera Comique* in the Boulevard des Italiens, and the *Opera Francais* on the opposite side in the Rue Pelletier, the *Theatre des Varietés* on the Boulevard Montmartre, *de St. Martin* and *de l'Ambigu* on the Boulevard St. Martin, as well as the cluster of theatres on the Boulevard de Temple, such as the *Gymnase*, *de la Gaîté*, *Cirque Olympique*, *des Folies Dramatiques*, *des Delassements*, *des Funambules*, and lastly, the theatre du Boulevard Beaumarchais.

Such a drive from the Madeleine to the Bastille and back again will have closed a day already well spent.

FOURTH DAY.

VERSAILLES.

HAVING led the visitor to examine and admire many of the finest and most ancient monuments of Paris, it is intended that he should have the opportunity to-day, of inhaling a little of the pure air of the country, and refresh his fatigued sight by a view of the works of art, and the scenery in the neighbourhood of this metropolis. We therefore propose that this day should be devoted to the Chateau and Park of Versailles.

It depends upon the visitor, as to how much time he would like to give to this magnificent place; but the earlier he can arrange his departure the better, as a good day's work is before him. He may leave for Versailles either by the railway, in the *Place du Havre*, called the *Chemin-de-fer de Rive Droite*, or by the railway on the *Boulevard Montparnasse*, called the *Chemin-de-fer de Rive Gauche*. But if he have taken up his abode in the quarter we have recommended, he will find it most convenient to take the former, as the station is within five minutes' walk of the Madeleine. The trains leave at all the half-hours from 7 30 a.m. to 10 30 p.m. The prices are as follows: 1st class, 1f, 50c.; 2nd class, 1f. 25c. On Sundays and Fête days, the fares are increased.

Independently of the purpose which the visitor has in view in making this little excursion, he must be reminded that the trip is one of no ordinary pleasure, and that, were there no Versailles at the end of it, the scenery, and the little pictures of half-urban, half-rural beauty, presented to him as he passes onward, would well repay a visit. The circuit which the railway makes, enables him to have a fine distant view of the city; the windings of the Seine; and the aspect of the country in the immediate neighbourhood of Paris. As he will frequently find himself on a level, high above the river, he will have a panorama stretched before him, full of points of beauty, and objects of interest. To enable him, therefore, to understand this panorama better, we will mark out a few of the spots that stand in most prominent relief on its surface.

On leaving the station, the train passes

through a short tunnel, and then a longer one, bored under a hill, forming a continuation of the rising ground, which, as with a natural barrier, encircles Paris, and of which, Montmartre and Belleville are abrupt eminences. On emerging, he will see the *Docks Napoleon* on the right. These docks are in course of construction, and are intended to form a grand central depôt, whither all the exciseable merchandise of Paris may be collected previous to its general distribution. A little further on, a line branches off to the west, to Passy and Auteuil, for the Bois de Boulogne. After this, the train passes the fortifications, and is fairly out of town. At first, the view is low, flat, and uninteresting, a large plain, extending on every side, which stretches away to the foot of a long line of hills towards the north. In this direction lies the town and abbey of St. Denis. Long strips of imperfectly cultivated land, producing every variety of vegetable and herb that the climate will admit of, gives a good idea to the foreigner, of the general style of husbandry throughout France. To the left, are the western banlieues of Paris, with the Arc de l'Etoile for their crowning point. Small villas, exhibiting the cockney-rustic taste of the citizens, line the sides of the railway. We now cross the Seine, and stop at Asnières. This station is prettily situated near one of the most charming spots in the outskirts of the city. Its proximity to the placid, lake-like river, on which, pleasure boats, on a fine day, are always moving; the clusters of trees that embosom delightful residences, and extend down to the water's edge; the smiling flower-gardens, that peep out from the shade; the verdancy of the country about, all contribute to give this little paradise, a title to the affections of the fête-loving Parisians.

As the train continues rolling on, the scenery changes insensibly. The hills to the north-west being to assume greater shape and boldness. Villages may be discerned dotting their sides; amongst them, Eaubonne, Ermont, and Montmorency: to the left, the dimensions of Paris gradually enlarge themselves. The Arc de l'Etoile, which presents its side to us on leaving the station, now fronts us, and seems to have been acting as the centre to the circumference we have been describing. Montmartre, with its picturesque windmills and conspicuous houses, stands out in bold relief, as well as the minor eminences on which the city is built. An infinite mass of buildings, from which edifice after edifice rises up with majestic proportions, belt the eastern horizon. The Bois de Boulogne, lies at our feet, and becomes a spacious and beautiful foreground; whilst on the right, the villages of Bologne and St. Cloud, lining each bank of the river, seem to blend together into one large town, shaded by the wooded heights of Bellevue and Meudon beyond. Above us rises the high hill on which Fort Valérien is constructed, whose bristling batteries seem to look down on us in defiance, so far are they above our heads.

Passing beyond the station of St. Cloud, a still more lovely picture discloses itself. We there come upon the quiet village of Ville d'Avray, delightfully situated in the bosom of valleys. On every side the slopes are covered with vegetation. Where there are not vineyards, there are woods, lawns, and flower-gardens; and the very look of the villas, all snugly enclosed in some pretty bosquet, cannot fail to inspire the feeling of repose and peace in the heart of one who has forsaken the crowded streets of the city, to visit nature and breathe the balmy atmosphere of the country. With little change in the scenery after this, we enter the terminus at Versailles.

The first object that will strike the visitor on proceeding through the town up to the station, will most probably be, the regularity of the streets, and the uniform grandeur of the houses. Eighty years ago, Versailles was the second place of importance in France. A hundred thousand inhabitants, all in one way or another connected with the most sumptuous court in Europe, contributed to its splendour and its luxury. Dukes, marquises, counts, foreigners as well as natives; all that was considered noble, whether from abroad or at home, was gathered within her walls, and this astonishing elevation was the work of scarcely a century. A small village, surrounded by woods and marshes, existed formerly where Versailles stands. The monarchs of France came here for the diversion of hunting, and left it as soon as the day's sport was finished. Louis XIII., however, fixed his affections a little more strongly upon it, and erected a hunting-box here, whither he might sometimes retire. This hunting-box was the germ of the present magnificent chateau.

In 1660, Louis XIV., tired of the incommodious palace of St. Germain, conceived, in one of his capricious moods, the project of converting this wild district into a beautiful park; and this pretty hunting-box, into a splendid palace, which should contain himself and his numerous court. No expense was spared to carry into effect the king's design; Lenotre laid out the park and the gardens; Mansard furnished the plans for the palace. Upwards of 30,000 soldiers were diverted from their martial occupations, and ordered to assist the workmen in making vast excavations, and raising the immense terraces; and it is estimated that not less than forty millions sterling were exhausted upon the laying out of these vast domains, and the erection of this superb chateau; and such was the extraordinary vigour with which the works were pushed on, that in 1685, hardly twenty-five years after its commencement, the whole was in readiness to receive their royal master. Here the royal family and the court resided until the revolution of 1789. Every part of the interior, as well as the exterior was ornamented with the works of the most eminent masters of the time; but, during the turbulent period that followed the downfall of monarchy in France, the whole was ransacked, and but few of its beautiful treasures preserved. It was even proposed to turn the chateau into a kind of hospital. This, however, was overruled, and the place saved. But the enormous expense necessary for its reparation, has deterred subsequent kings from making it a place of permanent residence; and how long it might have remained in its deserted state, it is impossible to conjecture, had not Louis Philippe conceived the design of converting it into a vast museum, where might be collected whatever illustrated the greatness and splendour of France.

On passing up from the station to the palace, the visitor will not fail to observe the *statue of General Hoche*. Though not a native of the town, General Hoche was educated in it from earliest childhood, and here first displayed those talents that bespoke his future greatness. Turning to the right, we come in front of the palace. The railing which encircles the great court, is a very fine specimen of the kind. On either side of the court are statues of eminent statesmen and warriors of France. To the left, on entering, are: Duguesclin, Sully, Suger, Lannes, Mortier, Suffren, Duquesne, Condé; on the right, Bayard, Colbert, Richelieu, Jourdan, Massena, Tourville, Duguay-Trouin, Turenne; whilst in the middle is placed a fine bronze equestrian statue of Louis XIV. The front of brick, which terminates the court, is the ancient hunting-seat erected by Louis XIII., and which the respect of his son left untouched. The palace is composed of three great divisions. *The main or central* body; *the south wing*; and *the north wing*.

On the eastern front of the left wing may be read the inscription: *A toutes les gloires de la France*, which indicate the present object to which the chateau has been applied.

The central part contains on the ground floor, a hall adorned with busts or statues; four suites of apartments, once royal residences, and several vestibules. On the first floor are the salons, seven in number, that adjoin the entrance to the chapel. They were formerly the grand apartments of Louis XIV.

The *south wing* consists, on the ground floor of twelve rooms, adorned with paintings illustrating the political and military career of Napoleon, from 1796 to 1810, and containing busts of the emperor and his family; and another, the Hall of Marengo, illustrating French history from 1789 to 1814. The busts of generals killed in battle, occupy places in the windows. There is also a gallery of sepulchral monuments. On the first floor, is the hall containing pictures of battles gained by the French, from that of Tolbiac, in the reign of Clovis, down to the battle of Wagram. There is also a gallery of sculpture commencing with productions of the sixteenth century, and embracing those of the eighteenth.

The *North wing* contains, on the ground-floor, a series of pictures representing the most remarkable events anterior to the reign of Louis XVI., and a gallery of busts, statues, and monuments. The first floor contains a continuation of these paintings, from the time of the first republic, down to the reign of Louis Philippe. The second storey contains portraits of eminent persons.

To obtain admission into the chateau, it is necessary for the visitor to shew his passport to the porter, who occupies a bureau on the north wing. This being done, he has only to examine particularly the interior of the great chateau, the outlines of which have just been given.

On entering, then, he will pass through the suite of rooms containing pictures illustrating the history of France, down to 1789, when he will arrive at the *Salle des Croisades*, containing five rooms, embellished by paintings of different battles, fought by the Crusaders in the Holy Land; or which influenced the christian cause in the East. The ceilings are richly decorated with the arms and escutcheons of the principal French chevaliers who went to Palestine. These rooms also contain some beautifully carved doors of cedar wood, belonging formerly to the Knights of Rhodes, and given by the Sultan to Louis Philippe, in 1836.

In the long *Sculpture Gallery* which follows, the visitor must observe the beautiful statue of Joan of Arc, executed by the talented Princess Marie d'Orleans, and the fine statue of the Duke of Orleans in a sitting posture, by Pradier.

Next comes the *Gallery of Louis Philippe*, containing pictures illustrating his career from the time of his presentation to the people in 1830. After this,

The Chapel, consisting of a nave and aisles. The pavement is of rich marble divided into compartments and elaborately wrought in mosaic. The ceiling is eighty-six feet high, and embellished by the pencil of Coypel, Lafosse, and Jouvenet. The high altar is very fine. In the chapel of the virgin, one of the seven which this building contains, Louis XVI. and Marie Antoinette were married.

The Theatre.—During representations the King and his suite occupied seats above the pit; the ambassadors the central compartment of the first tier; and the rest of the guests the different boxes arranged all around. The last representation that took place here was in 1844. The theatre is still left with all the ornaments and decorations which then rendered it so beautiful a place. Ten thousand wax candles are said to have been lighted on one occasion, to give splendour and brilliancy to the scenic representations. The theatre is not shown to the public generally, and, if viewed, a slight gratuity is expected by the attendant.

The *Grands Apartments*, amongst which the visitor will find,

The *Salon d' Hercule*, which was formerly used as a chapel. Here Bossuet and Massillon preached to the court. *Salon d'Appollon* or Throne room where Louis XIV., XV., and XVI. received ambassadors and other great functionaries. The *Grande Gallerie de Louis XIV.*, the most splendid room in the chateau, and, which, notwithstanding its immense size 242 feet long by 35 feet broad, and 43 feet high, was daily crowded with courtiers. The *Salon du Conseil or Cabinet du Roi*, where are the council table and arm chair of the grand monarch, a curious clock that plays a chime when the hour strikes, and is set in motion by a curious machinery by which sentinels are made to advance, a cock flaps his wings, Louis XIV. comes forward, and a figure of Victory or Fame descending from the skies crowns him with a golden chaplet. In this chamber many of the most important designs on which the state of Europe depended, were discussed and planned. The *Œil de Bœuf*, where the courtiers were accustomed to await the King's rising, and many a scandalous intrigue was carried on. The *Salle des Pendules*, so called from a curious clock in it. This clock shews the days of the month, the phases of the moon, the revolutions of the earth and the motions of the planets, besides the hour, the minute, and the second of the day. A meridian traced on the floor by Louis XVI., and a marble table with a plan of the forest of St. Germain engraved upon it should be noticed here. After this, we enter the suite of apartments peculiarly associated with the memory of *Marie Antoinette*, amongst which we may mention the bed chamber where this unfortunate queen slept when the people burst into the palace on the 5th of October, 1789, and from which she escaped by a corridor leading to the Œil de Bœuf. The furniture of these apartments is very chaste, and there is in a recess in one of the rooms a series of mirrors, so planted that the person who looks into either of them shall see everything but his head. The *Escalier de Marbre*, or marble staircase, should be remarked as being one of the finest in France.

The other rooms of the palace are too numerous to be mentioned individually, but we will advise the visitor of the series of portrait galleries that occupies the upper stories. Here may be seen the portraits of the kings and queens of France from the earliest periods, of the princes and dukes of the royal descent, also of the principal personages, military, civil, and ecclesiastic, who have managed the affairs of the kingdom. There are also portraits of foreign princes and high personages, amongst which will be seen those of George IV., the Queen, and Prince Albert, nor should we forget the homage done to foreign genius and learning in this gallery, since we find among the notables of France the portraits of our countrymen Pitt, Fox, Locke, and Newton.

Having thus satisfied ourselves with the beauties and curiosities of the interior of the chateau, we will take a ramble through the park, and admire the magnificent assemblage of works of art, contrasting immediately with those of nature. Immediately in front of the building is a vast terrace, adorned by four statues, representing Antinous, Silenus, Bacchus, and Apollo, by Keller. The gardens which surround it are decorated by fountains issuing from a variety of statuary. To the right, on leaving the chateau, is an avenue leading to the grand fountains called the *Basin of Neptune*. But descending the avenue, directly in front of the palace called the *Tapis Vert*, we come upon a beautiful fountain, the *Basin of Latona*, from which we have a fine view of the *Fountain of Apollo* at the further end of the avenue and the lake beyond. Turning down the alleys to the left, we shall come upon several beautiful fountains and parterres, amongst them is the *Bosquet du roi*, the *Bosquet de la Salle du Bal*, where the court formerly danced on summer evenings, the *Quinconce du Midi* ornamented with eight terminii, and the *Bosquet de la Colonnade*, an enclosed grove with a splendid rotunda composed of thirty-two marble pillars of the Ionic order, with jets d'eau thrown up between each of them. Descending the alleys still further, we arrive upon the *Basin of Apollo*, the largest fountain in the park with the exception of the Basin of Neptune. Apollo is here represented issuing from the water in a chariot drawn by four horses, and surrounded by dolphins, tritons, and sea-monsters.

Pursuing the allé to the left or now facing the palace, we shall find some of the finest fountains. Amongst them we would particularize the *Bains d' Apollon*, a beautiful artificial waterfall issuing from deep caverns, at the entrance of which are groups of nymphs. High rocks are here imitated with a very fine effect, and the delusion is so complete that we cannot but fancy we are looking upon a real and natural waterfall. When we have examined all these we must still reserve ourselves for the most splendid of all the fountains, the *Basin of Neptune*, behind the Parterre du Nord. Twenty-two vases are arranged around the margin. Against the side are three immense groups, representing Neptune and Amphitrite, Proteus and Ocean, whilst two colossal dragons, bearing cupids, repose upon pedestals at the angles. From these groups a flood of water is sent forth, which is further increased by magnificent jets arranged in different parts of this vast basin. The *grand eaux*, or great fountains, play but seldom in the course of the year, and that on Sundays. Should the visitor be fortunate enough to have it in his power to see them, he should follow the stream of people in their examination of the playing waters. They commence to play at 4 o'clock, and continue until 6 o'clock. When all the others are in full play, and the people have had time to inspect them, that is about 5 o'clock, then the magnificent waters of the Basin of Neptune are let forth. The volumes of water they exhaust are so great that they are not allowed to play more than twenty minutes.

Opposite the south wing of the chateau is the *Orangerie*, well worth seeing, where the orange trees and pomegranates are kept during the winter. One of the orange trees is called the *Grand Bourbon*, because it belonged to the constable Bourbon, whose property was confiscated and with it this fruit tree. It is a contemporary of Francis I. The seeds from which it sprang were sown in 1421, by Leonora of Castille, wife of Charles III., King of Navarre, so that this tree has acquired a kind of historical notoriety.

From the avenue d'Apollon, a road leads direct to the *Grand Trianon*, a delightful little residence built by Louis XIV. in 1683, for Madame de Maintenon. It is nearly 400 feet long, contains but a ground floor, and is divided by a pavilion into two parts, united by a peristyle, supported by twenty-two Ionic pillars, eight of green marble, the remainder of red Languedoc marble. Mansard has the credit of being the architect, but he was also assisted in the design by Le Nôtre and Decotte. We remark among the curiosities of the Grand Trianon, a bas-relief presented by the Queen Dowager, of Naples, to the late Madame Adelaide, also portraits of Madame Maintenon, Marie Leczinski, wife of Louis XV., of Marie Thérése, Marie Antoinette, Louis XV. &c., and a circular bason of malachite resting on an ormolu tripod, presented to Napoleon by the Emperor Alexander. The long gallery contains valuable paintings by Roger, Bidault, Johannot, &c. The apartments have been successively used by Louis XIV., XV., and XVI., and Napoleon, and may now be seen left in the same condition as that in which they were arranged for the reception of Queen Victoria, who was expected to make a visit to Paris some time back. The gardens are laid out in the style of the grand gardens, and are decorated with fountains and statues. To the right is the

Petit Trianon, composed of a square pavilion containing a ground floor and two stories. The interior is elegantly fitted up and enriched with paintings by Dejeanne. The Petit Trianon was occupied by the Duchess of Orleans. The gardens are laid out in the English style.

Visitors may view the Trianons every day except Fridays, between 11 and 5.

FIFTH DAY.

MUSEE D'ARTILLERIE—PALAIS DES BEAUX ARTS—PLACE, FOUNTAIN, AND CHURCH OF ST. SULPICE—PALAIS DU LUXEMBOURG—STATUE OF MARSHAL NEY—OBSERVATOIRE—VAL DE GRACE—PANTHEON—BIBLIOTHEQUE—STE GENEVIEVE—ST. ETIENNE DU MONT—ECOLE POLYTECNIQUE—COLLEGE LOUIS LE GRAND—SORBONNE—HOTEL DE CLUNY—THEATRE ODEON—HOTEL DES MONNAIES.

We will devote this day to visiting some of the Museums and Public Monuments of Paris which claim our notice, on the south-side of the river. To take them therefore in the most convenient order, we will commence with the

Musee d'Artillerie, situated in the Place Saint Thomas d'Aquin, Rue de Bac. This museum is amongst the most curious and interesting in Paris, consisting of a fine collection of such arms, offensive and defensive, as have been used in war from the earliest periods. These are distributed in six grand saloons or galleries. In the *Gallerie des Armures* which is divided into three departments by a fine collonade, are arranged chronologically according to the characteristic points of the age to which they belong the defensive armour anciently employed in battle, such as entire suites of armour, coats of mail, cuirasses, casquets, shields, &c. In a gallery parallel with this, is placed a collection of swords and bayonets, ancient and modern. In the three other saloons of the museum is disposed in regular order the collection of protective fire-arms, and extends back as far as the arquebus, with its quaint and impracticable fire-lock, and comes down to the most finished improvement on the system of percussion locks. Enclosed in glass frames will be found everything of the kind that is valuable and curious by the beauty of its workmanship, by the richness of its ornament, by the singularity of its forms, or by its historical importance.

Opposite the stand of arms is a suite of tables upon which are placed models of machines and instruments, used in the artillery service, and models of machines, instruments, and tools, necessary for the construction of weapons of war, and to the different trades which form branches of it. On the walls, between the windows of the third and fourth galleries, are hung assortments of instruments, either for making or proving weapons of destruction, an enumeration of which would take up too much space.

The museum is open every Thursday, from 12 to 4.

Returning to the Rue de l'Université, which crosses the Rue du Bac, near the Musée, and continuing along it and the Rue Jacob, until he arrive at the Rue Bonaparte, the visitor must turn to the left, when he will come to the

Palais des Beaux Arts. In 1791 the Convent des Petits Augustins suffered the same spoliation which befel most of the buildings belonging to the religious orders at this period. But, more fortunate than the others, it was converted into a depository of the different works of art, taken from prescribed churches and chateaus. At the restauration, restitution was made to the proprietors of the different objects that had been collected here. However, in 1819, it was ordered, that on this spot a suitable building should be erected, devoted to the teaching of the fine arts, to replace the old academies founded by Louis XIV.

The first stone was laid in 1820, and the edifice finished in 1832, after designs by Debret. Two courts, separated by the *Arc Gaillon*, a relic of the Chateau d'Amboise, and enclosed by a superb iron railing, front the palace. In the first is the elegant portal, brought from the chateau d' Anet, which was built for Diana of Poitiers in 1548. Round the walls of the inner court, are sculptured the names of the most famous artists of all countries.

The façade of the palace is 240 feet long and 60 feet high.

The ground floor is of the Tuscan order of architecture, the floor above this of the Ionic, whilst the attic which surmounts it is of the rennaissant style. A vestibule adorned with arches and marble columns leads to a double staircase, richly decorated, conducting to the first floor. Those of the pupils belonging to the school of the palace who obtain the first prize, are sent to Rome for three years, at the public expense, and an exhibition of the works they send home is annually held here. The galleries to the north are devoted to paintings, that to the south to architecture. On the second floor are kept all the pictures which have gained the highest prizes. In the *Salle des Models* are models of the most celebrated Greek, Roman, Egyptian, and Indian monuments. The semicircle of the great amphitheatre is adorned with frescoes, by Paul Delaroche.

The Palais des Beaux Arts is opened every Tuesday, Thursday, and Sunday, from 12 to 4 p.m.

On leaving the Palais, the visitor must continue down the Rue Bonaparte when he will come upon

The Place St. Sulpice. In this place which has recently been planted with trees, a flower market is held three times a week. A very elegant fountain erected by order of the first Napoleon after the designs of the late Visconti stands in the centre. It is constructed of stone, and presents the form of a pavilion with four angles, crowned by a dome. Around it are three basins placed one above the other, and flanked by lions. The water escapes from four vases, and falls into a cascade into the basins. In the niches which adorn the pavilion, are figures of Fenelon, Bossuet, Flechier, and Massillon. On the south-side of the place is the great seminary for Roman Catholic priests; to the right is an elegant building serving as a barracks, and opposite is the *Church of St. Sulpice*. This church is founded on the remains of an ancient chapel, dedicated to St. Peter. The first stone of the present edifice was laid in 1646, by Anne of Austria, mother of Louis XIV., but owing to several interruptions and especially the want of money, it was not finished until 1745. The expense of the building was finally defrayed by a lottery. The façade of this church is very fine. Twelve Doric columns, forty-two feet high, supporting an entablature of thirteen feet in height, form the portico, over which is a gallery supported by a corresponding number of Ionic pillars. Two towers partly square, partly octangular, partly circular terminate the front. These were erected at different periods. That to the south begun so late as 1777, is still left in an unfinished state. The height of this tower measures 210 feet.

The building is in the form of a Latin cross, at the further end of which is the choir. In the interior the position of the high altar, which is between the nave and the choir, and surrounded by statues of the twelve apostles, produces a fine effect. Two large shells, a present from the Venetian Republic to Francis I., contain the holy water at the entrances. Behind the choir is a chapel to the Virgin, lighted very artistically, so as to produce a mysterious effect. The statue of the virgin, which is of white marble, is beautifully executed. Most of the chapels are embellished by good frescoes. The pulpit, it should be observed, has no other support than the stairs; and the visitor will be pleased to remark the meridian line at the bottom of the lateral aisle on the north side. This meridian marks the spring equinox, and winter solstice.

On leaving the church, the visitor must take the street immediately to the left, the *Rue Ferou*. This will bring him in two or three minutes to the *Palais de Luxembourg*.

Palais de Luxembourg, or du Senat.

A palace was begun on this site so early as the end of the fifteenth century, by Robert de Sancy, but was not completed until 1583, when it was enlarged and finished by the Duke Epinay de Luxembourg. Marie de Medicis, whilst regent of France, purchased it for 20,000*l.*; and requiring some adjacent land, had it demolished, and a more magnificent one built, after designs by Jacques Desbrosses. After passing through several ducal hands, it was sold in 1692, to Louis XIV., and lastly, became the residence of the *Count of Provence*, who was driven from it in 1791, just ninety-nine years later. During the early part of the revolution, the palace was converted into a prison, in which Josephine Beauhernais, after the empress Josephine, was confined with her husband. In 1795, the Directory used it as a place of assembly. Bonaparte made it the *Palais du Consulat et du Senat*. From 1814 to 1848, the peers of the kingdom legislated there: since the restoration of the empire, the senate once more hold their deliberations there, and the president of the senate occupies it as a place of residence.

The plan of the building is that of a square; the court of the principal entrance, which measures 360 feet by 210, is enclosed on the side next the street by a façade which forms a terrace, in the middle of which is a pavilion, highly ornamented, and containing some fine sculpture. The beauty and richness of the architecture of this palace is much admired in all its deetals. At the extremities of the terrace, are two other pavilions, joined to the main body of the building by two connecting wings. The façade towards the garden, differs little from that towards the street. The pavilion de l'Horloge, in the middle, is embellished by allegorical figures.

In the various salons of the palace, are some fine sculpture; amongst them, figures of Aristides, Cincinnatus, Leonidas, Solon, Pericles, Cicero, &c.. In the *Salle de Messages*, a painting by Caminade, representing Charles IX. receiving the keys of Paris; St. Louis, by Flandrin; and the Duc de Guise, by Vinchon, should be observed; and in the *Salle des Conferences*, some beautiful Gobelin tapestry. The *Salle des Seances* was opened for the reception of the peers of France in 1844. It is a semicircular chamber, covered by a hemispherical vault, supported by eighteen composite columns, and richly decorated. The vault is embellished with allegorical paintings, by Pujol, representing Law and Justice. The *library* of the palace contains upwards of 15,000 volumes, most of them of great value.

On the ground floor is the *Chapelle de Marie de Medicis*, a small quadrangular chamber of the Doric order, and highly decorated. Four pictures, representing the apostle Philip, St. Louis in Palestine, St. Louis pardoning traitors, and the Marriage of the Virgin, grace the walls opposite the windows; and behind the high altar, is a large fresco, the subject of which is taken from chapter IV. of the Revelations. Samuel White, an American artist, has supplied the *Adoration of the Shepherds*, which forms the altar-piece. The *Chambre à Coucher* of Marie de Medicis, is a splendid room, containing paintings by Rubens, Philip de Champagne, and Nicolas Poussin. The arm-chairs we see here, were used at the ceremonial of the coronation of the first Napoleon.

After having seen these apartments, the private apartments of the palace, we will visit the *Musée des Tableaux*, or Picture Gallery. The entrance is on the eastern side of the building, and at the angle nearest the street. This gallery was commenced by Catherine de Medicis, and consisted principally of four and twenty pictures by Rubens. This collection was afterwards increased by various additions. It is now devoted to the works of living French artists, who have produced a work considered sufficiently excellent to be purchased for the nation: but, owing to the rule, that on the decease of such artist, the pictures placed in the Luxembourg, shall be removed to the Louvre, a constant alteration is taking place in the arrangements. Amongst the present collection, those most worthy of inspection are:—

45. The Death of Elizabeth, by PAUL DE LA ROCHE.
22. Landscape and Animals, by BRASCASSAT.
66. Evening, by CHARLES GLEYRE.
75. Cain after the murder of Abel, by PAULIN GUERIN.
75. The Malaria, by AUGUST HEBERT.
76. Subject taken from the History of the Jews. HEIM.
90. Shepherds and view of the deserted port of Ambleteuse, near Boulogne. PHILIPPE AUGUSTE JEANRON.
104. Desolation of the Oceanides, at the foot of the rock where Prometheus is bound. LEHMANN.
115. Lady Macbeth. CHARLES LOUIS MULLER.
116. Reading the list of names of the last victims of the Reign of Terror. MULLER.
131. Scene taken from the Coast of Normandy. CAMILLA ROQUEPLAN.
141. Charlotte Corday, when she had just assassinated Marat. HENRI SCHEFFER.
152. Massacre of the Mamelukes, in the castle of Cairo, by order of Mehemet Ali. HORACE VERNET.
153. Judith and Holophernes. HORACE VERNET.
154. Raphael at the Vatican. HORACE VERNET.
156. Landscape in Savoy. LOUIS ETIENNE WATELET.

The Jardin de Luxembourg, the most beautifully arranged garden in Paris, and the constant resort of the students of the Sarbonne, and the families of the middling classes of the neighbourhood. It was at first planted after the plans of Desbrosses, but during the period of the early revolution, it was much defaced, to make way for cafés, &c. During the empire, it was again restored to something of its original beauty, and has since been considerably embellished. To the west is a fine grove of trees, beneath which, immense numbers of children sport on summer evenings. Immediately in front of the southern façade of the palace, is a delightful flower-garden, stocked with the most beautiful flowers, and adorned with a fountain and basin, and several marble statues. A stone balustrade which is reached by a flight of steps, separate the flower-garden from the grove of trees, which encircle it almost entirely, leaving only space for the grand avenue facing the palace. Statues of the queens and heroines of France, from the time of Pharemond, down to the seventeenth century, are ranged round the outskirts of the trees, amongst which should be noticed, those of *Joan of Arc* and *Marie Stuart*, on the eastern side.

Having walked through the gardens, we will proceed down the grand avenue, and leaving the gardens by the iron-gateway at the southern extremity, we shall pass out into the Avenue of the Observatory. On the left, about halfway down, is the statue recently erected to the memory of *Marshal Ney*, exactly on the spot where nearly forty years ago, he was shot as a traitor. He is represented leading on his men to action, and encouraging them by his voice and example. The building at the further end of the avenue is

The Observatoire Imperiale. — This building was begun in 1667, in connection with the Academy of Sciences, then recently established, and finished in 1672. It was found, however, inconvenient for astronomical purposes, and a small building to the east of it was accordingly erected. It is a curious fact that neither wood nor iron enters into the construction of the building. The Observatoire contains a good collection of telescopes, magnetic instruments, globes, &c. In a room on the second storey, is a meridian traced on the floor; and two instruments fixed here, give an account of how much rain has fallen in Paris during the year. The *Bureau des Longitudes* holds its sittings here; and in one of the wings of the building, is an amphitheatre, capable of holding eight hundred persons, where lectures are given to young students. Marble statues of Casini, Laplace, and other illustrious astronomers, adorn the rooms of the interior. The late M. Arrago had his residence here. On leaving the Observatoire, the visitor, having his back upon it, must take the first turning to the right, the *Rue Cassini*, and pursue it until he come to the *Rue St. Jacques*. Turning to the left, and descending it for a short distance, he will see before him

The Hopital Militaire and Church of Val-de-Grace, built by Anne of Austria, after designs by Mansard. After being married twenty-two years to Louis XIII., and having no children, this queen made vows in several chapels, amongst others in that of Val-de-Grace, and promised to build a church if she had an heir. Shortly after this Louis XIV. was born to her, and, to perform her vow, laid the first stone of the present edifice shortly after. In the court is a monument to Larry the celebrated surgeon who served in the armies of Napoleon. The exterior and the interior of this church, the plan of which is that of a Latin cross, is very fine. The front is ornamented with a portico of Corinthian columns; the nave is intersected at the transept by four lofty arches. Above the arches are figures of the Virtues in high relief; the ceiling is also divided into compartments, highly decorated, and filled with figures of saints. Behind the altars are chapels, separated by iron railings from the body of the building, where the nuns and superiors of the convent attend mass. The remains of Henrietta Maria, wife of Charles 1st, were placed in the vault beneath this church.

Descending the Rue St. Jacques until it crosses the *Rue Soufflot*, we have to the right of us

The Pantheon, with its lofty porch and magnificent dome. On this site stood formerly a church, built by Clovis at the intercession of St. Geneviéve and Clotilda his wife; but this church having fallen into decay, Louis XV. determined to erect a grand and magnificent one in its place. Soufflot furnished the plans, and on the 6th of September, 1764, the foundation stone of the new structure was laid by the king, in great pomp and solemnity, all his court attending. A lottery was also established to defray the expenses. The proportions of this building are truly noble. The tympanum of the portico, which is supported by twenty-two fluted Corinthian pillars, is 121 feet in breadth and 22 feet in height. Allegorical figures grace this tympanum, representing *Genius* and *Science* on either side of *France*. On the right of her are those amongst her sons who have illustrated their country by their pen, as Voltaire, Rousseau, Fenelon, Mirabeau, Lafayette, Canot, &c.; on the left are grouped her military heroes, at the head of whom is placed Napoleon. *History* and *Liberty* are also represented at the feet of France, writing down the names of her great men, and weaving garlands for their brows. By a decree of the *Assembleé Constituante*, in 1791, the building was converted into a temple, where were to repose the ashes of the great men of the country. The inscription, *Aux grands hommes la Patrie reconnaissante*, written in characters of gold over the portico that still remains, attests this purpose. To Mirabau, who died the same year, the first honours of this sepulture was decreed. The plan of the church is that of a Greek cross. The interior is devoid of much ornament, but the vastness of its size and sublimity of its tripple dome, give it an imposing air, which would be destroyed were there introduced those details which so well embellish smaller edifices. The length of the building is 302 feet, its width 255 at the transept. The top of the cupola is 268 feet above the pavement, and reached by a flight of 475 steps. In the south transept is an altar to St. Genevieve, to whom the church is dedicated, and in the north another to the Virgin, both of them very elegant. Copies by M. Balze, of the frescoes of Michael Angelo and Raphael in the Vatican, adorn the walls; and on the spandrils of the arches which support the dome are four allegorical paintings, representing Death, Justice, France, and Napoleon. The cupola is painted by Legros, and consists of four groups, each containing a monarch of France whose reign is supposed to form an epoch in her history. The four are Clovis, Charlemagne, St. Louis, and Louis XVIII. They each pay homage to St. Genevieve, who descends from the heavens in clouds to greet them. Louis XVI., Marie Antoinette, Louis XIV., and Madame Elizabeth are conspicuous personages in this high drama. The painting covers 3,721 square yards; the artist received £4000 for his work, and was created a baron.

The Lantern that crowns the summit of the dome is very high, being not less than 450 feet above the level of the Seine. The ascent to it is very easy, and, from the gallery on the outside, a magnificent bird's eye view of Paris and the vicinity around may be obtained. The visitor by this time we presume is pretty familiar with the aspect of most of the buildings and prominent objects of Paris, to determine many of the edifices for himself. However, as there are some places he has not seen, and therefore will not be able to recognize for himself, we will point them out. In front of the church are the Palais and Gardens of the Luxembourg, and beyond the Invalides, to the left, Val de Grace and the Observatoire. Inclining to the right, the visitor will observe the Sorbonne, the towers of St. Sulpice, the Tuilleries, the church of the Assomption, recognized by its magnificent dome rising beyond the trees, and the Column Vendome. To the east may be seen the Jardin des Plants, the Wine Market, the Column of Juillet, with its gilded figure of victory, the twin-pillars at the Barrière du Trone, and away still further, emerging from the woods, the lofty and substantial towers of the Fortress of Vincennes. On the hills to the left, the long range of building that may be seen there is the prison of the Bicêtre; to the north the eye ranges over a variety of buildings, and sees stretched out the greater part of Paris. Crossing the river, the most prominent objects are the Hotel de Ville, St. Gervais, and, further to the right, the *Ecole de Charlemagne*; to the left the tower of St. Jacques de la Boucherie, behind which rise St. Eustache, the Bourse, the Portes St. Denis and St. Martin, and the Station of the Strasbourg railway, whilst the heights of Montmartre and Belleville bound this beautiful panorama. The river, which may be descried dividing the city into two unequal parts, may be traced towards the east, until its windings are lost far beyond St. Mandé and Charenton, in the distant vine-covered valley. Immediately beneath the Pantheon will be perceived the Marie of the 12th Arondissement, the Ecole de Droit, the Bibliotheque de St. Geneviève, St. Etiénne du Mont, and the Lycie Napoleon, an old building, with a church tower and cloisters. This college was formerly called the College of Henry IV.; in 1848 it received the name of Lycie Corneille, since 1851 it is known as the Lycie Napoleon. It was here that the sons of Louis Philippe were first educated.

In the vaults of the Pantheon are the tombs of Voltaire and Rousseau. The remains of Mirabeau were removed shortly after their interment by one of those capricious freaks which drive the people into a sudden determination, however unjust or absurd it may be. The remains of several distinguished marshalls and generals of Napoleon's army repose here, also those of Soufflot, the architect of the edifice.

During the insurrection of June, 1848, the Pantheon was the scene of a sanguinary conflict. The insurgents had taken possession of the building, and it was necessary to bring heavy pieces of artillery to bear upon them, to dislodge them; the marks of the firing might still be seen some time after on the walls of the church, and the bronze doors, but since the building has been converted into a church, the damage then done has been repaired. However, traces of the conflict may be seen, in the holes pierced in the pictures that line the south and north walls, caused by bullets fired from muskets. On the 2nd December, 1851, the edifice was given to the Roman Catholic Church by the present Emperor, as a place for divine worship.

To descend into the vaults of this church a fee of four sous is demanded; but when this is paid, nothing further is required, to ascend to the lantern. The ascent is comparatively easy and very well lighted. Opposite the north side of the Pantheon is the *Bibliotheque de St. Geneviève*, which used to form part of the College of Henry IV., but which has recently been transferred to the present building. It contains 250,000 volumes and 30,000 MSS., besides busts and portraits of celebrated men. It is open every day, except Sundays and Fête-days, from 10 to 3, and from 6 to 10. On the south side are inscribed the names of those who have distinguished themselves in the walks of science and literature, not only in France but in foreign countries.

To the right of the library is the *Church of St. Etiénne du Mont*, the date of whose erection goes back so far as the early part of the eleventh century, when the square tower and turret we now see were probably built. The portal was constructed in 1610. The interior of this church is very beautiful; a gallery consisting of a low elliptical arch, with two spiral staircases of exquisite detail leading up to it, traverses the body of the building in the middle. On the right is the tomb of St. Geneviève, the patroness of Paris, enclosed by railings, upon which tapers are always lighted. The painted glass which adorns the windows is very fine, and belongs to the 16th century. Several valuable pictures may be seen here; amongst them, the *Preaching of Stephen*, by Pujol; *St. Geneviève praying to Heaven to appease a Storm*, by Grenier; and *St. Peter curing the Sick*, by Jouvenet. The *Jews collecting manna*, and *St. Bernard praying*, are also good paintings. On the wall, near the chapel of St. Geneviève, is an epitaph written on Racine, by Boileau, and another on Pascal, who was buried in this church.

Behind this church, in the Rue Descartes, is situated the *Ecole Polytecnique*.

Retracing our steps by the Rue Soufflot, as far as the *Rue de Cluny*, and descending it, we pass by first the *College of Henri IV.* which stands back a little way, and the *Sorbonne*, then the

College Louis le Grande, or Lycie Descartes as it has since been called. It was founded by the Jesuites in 1563, and reconstructed in 1682. It has, since the revolution, received several names; that of Lycie Descartes was given it in 1848. The building is of a very quaint style. The dead and Eastern languages as well as the elements of science are taught here.

The Sorbonne.—This university derives its name from Robert Sorbon, confessor to St. Louis, who founded the schools here about the middle of the 13th century. In 1629 the old building was restored by Cardinal Richelieu, who had graduated there, and still retained a feeling of filial veneration for the place. In the chapel attached to the Institution is the tomb of the Cardinal—a chef d'œuvre, by Girardon. Religion is represented as supporting the dying man, who is left in a recumbent position; two genii support his arms, and a woman, emblematical of science, is weeping over him as though at the loss of her patron. The two figures, Science and Religion, are said to be portraits of the Duchesses of Guyon and Fronsacneices of the Cardinal's.

The three faculties of Belles Lettres, Science, and Theology are taught here gratuitously, the professors being paid by the government. Descending the street, we arrive in front of

The Hotel de Cluny and **Palais des Thermes,** one of the most interesting public places of Paris. The *Palais des Thermes*, of which the ruins are still to be seen, in conjunction with the Hotel de Cluny, is supposed to have been built by the emperor Julian, though others assert that Constantius Chlorus was the founder of it. Whatever may be the truth of these two assertions, there can be no doubt that the origin of the palace mounts up to a very early period. In the year 365, Valentinian and Valence resided in it; and the same was occupied by Gratian, Maximus, and several others of the Cæsars. After them it became the residence of the early kings of France; it was, however, pillaged by the Normans during their devastating invasions, and finally sold by Philippe Agustus to his chamberlain. The palace was then divided into several distinct residences. In 1334 an Abbé of Cluny bought a part of it, to which he gave the name of the

Maison, or Hotel de Cluny, whose history we will pursue a little further. The present building was erected in 1490. A hundred years later it was in the hands of a body of comedians who acted their plays there, and gained such a reputation that it was jocularly said—The four best preachers in Paris put together, failed to obtain so goodly an audience as the players. In 1625 it was bought by the Abbess of Port Royal, and continued in the hands of the sisterhood until the revolution, when the horrible Marat held his meetings there. After this epoch it passed into the hands of several proprietors, and lastly into those of M. Dusommerard, the distinguished savant and virtuoso, who spent large sums of money in forming a collection of the most rare and precious objects of art, of furniture utensils, and curiosities of the middle age, and which he distributed in different apartments of his hotel. The museum became at length so fine, that the government thought it ought to become national property. It accordingly purchased the hotel and its valuable contents from its possessor.

In this palace Mary, sister of Henry VIII. of England, and widow of Louis XII., resided after the death of her husband; and the bedroom in which she slept is still known as the *Chamber of the White Queen*, it being the custom of the queens of France to wear white for their mourning. Here also James V. of Scotland celebrated his marriage with the daughter of Francis I.

The architecture of this building is admired for the grace, the finish, and the lightness of its sculptures. It partakes of the Gothic and rennaissant style, and is in a state of perfect preservation. The visitor enters by a court, on the left of which is a bureau, where he has to show his passport and write his name in a book. He then proceeds to the interior; the first room he passes through contains mosaics, reliefs, and plaster models, well worth examining. The other rooms, retaining their ancient character, are adorned with magnificent fire-places, vast marble chimney pieces, beautifully stained glass windows, and all the decorations of the mediæval period. In the *Chambre de la Reine Blanche*, amongst a variety of other objects of art, such as ivory cabinets, curiously-painted vases, and all the paraphernalia of a lady's toilet in those days, are to be seen several fine bas-reliefs and paintings, of which we may enumerate the *Diana Venetrix*, by Primaticcio, and *Mary Magdalene at Marseilles*, painted by King René of Provence. The *Chapel* is considered a chef-d'œuvre for the airiness and delicacy of its decorations. A stone staircase leads down from the chapel into the garden, and from thence into the *Palais des Thermes*, of which only the cold baths remain; they are sixty feet in length, and thirty five in width. The passages by which the water was conducted may easily be seen. The hotel is open Wednesdays, Thursdays, and Fridays, from 12 to 4.

The streets about this quarter of Paris are rather complicated, but if, on leaving the Hotel de Cluny, the visitor descends by the

Rue de l'Ecole de Medicine, he will pass by the Institution devoted to the education of the students of medicine. This edifice which consists of four divisions enclosing a spacious court, was commenced in 1769, and finished in 1786. The peristyle is formed of four rows of pillars; another peristyle is surmounted by a triangular tympanum, upon which allegorical figures are sculptured. The interior is decorated with appropriate paintings and busts of the most celebrated physicians and surgeons of France. The amphitheatre is capable of holding 1,200 persons. Twenty-three professors are attached to the Institution, who treat all branches of the art.

Pursuing the same street we shall arrive at the *Carrefour de l'Odeon*, or a place where several streets meet. Glancing up the centre one to our left, we see the front of the *Odeon Theatre*. A theatre was erected on this spot in 1779, but was burnt down in 1818. It is frequented by the students of the Latin Quarter, and for the quality of its performance only ranks second to the Theatre Français; it is capable of containing 1,700 persons. The prices range from 1 to 5 francs; the Stalls de Balcon, and the Stalls d'Orchestra are 4 francs.; the Parterre, or Pit 1 franc, 50 cents. This theatre is closed during a part of the summer.

Descending by the Rues Ancienne Comedie and Dauphine, we shall arrive on the *Quai Conti*. To the left, hardly fifty yards, is the handsome building of the

Hotel des Monnaies (or the Mint), built

in 1771. The principal entrance is by the richly-decorated gate in the centre of the façade. In the interior, which is beautifully adorned with pillars and galleries, is a cabinet of mineralogy, containing a vast number of specimens of minerals, collected with the greatest care by the late Lesage. The *Salon des Medailles* possesses a complete collection of medals struck from the time of Francis 1st: the collection of medals and coins in this establishment is said to be one of the richest and most curious in Europe. There are other saloons devoted to their special object in the coinage of money. These cannot be visited without a special permission from the director. The cabinets of mineralogy and medals are open every day from ten to two.

SIXTH DAY.

BOIS DE BOLOGNE, ST. CLOUD, SEVRES, MEUDON.

It is proposed that the visitor should pass this, the sixth day, in enjoying the fresh air of the country, and visiting the *Chateau of St. Cloud, the Porcelain manufactory at Sèvres, and the beautiful terraces of Bellevue and Meudon.* There are two ways to get to St. Cloud; one by the railway to Versailles, which, as the visitor knows, makes a considerable detour around Paris: and the other by the railway to Auteuil. We think that the latter course will be the best, as it is by far the shortest, will diversify the trip, and enable the visitor to see the wood and lakes of Bologne.

The trains start from the railway-station, *Place-du-Havre*, the same station as we go to for Versailles, every twenty minutes. The office for the Bois de Bologne is on the left. Having got two tickets, which costs five sous, second class, or ten sous first class, the visitor takes his place and proceeds the whole distance to Auteuil. As the road is cut considerably under the level of the ground, there is no opportunity afforded of seeing the country until we arrive at Passy, when the green trees and grass burst upon us. The next station is Auteuil.

On descending from the train, the *Bois de Bologne* is on the right. Having crossed the fortifications, the visitor will do well to penetrate into the wood by one of the avenues to the right, and he will then shortly arrive upon the lakes. These lakes have only recently been dug, and are intended to afford another source of recreation to the gay Parisians, who habitually make the Bois de Bologne the course of their promenades. The wood derives its name from a considerable village which lies to the west of it, and through which the visitor will pass. Before the year 1790, the trees were of small growth, or decaying, from their great age. They were, during the revolution, cleared away in a great measure; and what was not then destroyed, was afterwards cut down in the year 1814, for the defence of Paris against the approach of the allied forces. The English encamped here under Wellington in the following year. From that time the greater part of it has been planted, new walks made, and a variety of improvements taken place. To the north-west of the wood are the remains of the abbey of Longchamp, celebrated towards the middle of the seventeenth century for its choir of nuns, and whither, on the Wednesday and Thursday in Passion Week, the elite of Paris flocked to hear the music and singing. From this circumstance has sprung up the Fête de Longchamps, when the wealthy display their fine equipages, and the fair their fine habiliments, by driving out to the wood and back. In fact, it is considered the time for commencing to wear the new fashions for the spring season.

On retracing our steps to Auteuil, we shall find at the station, an omnibus, which will take us on to St. Cloud, for the small sum of two sous. The drive between St. Cloud and Auteuil is by one of the avenues of the wood, and, until you emerge into the village of Boulogne, very agreeable. On the other side of the village flows the Seine, which you cross by a fine bridge, and enter St. Cloud by the gates of the park.

St. Cloud derives its name from Cleodald, grandson of Clovis, who escaped assassination when his two brothers were murdered by their uncles Clotaire and Childebert, and hid himself in a hermitage in the wood that covered the hill. A village sprang up here, which has been the theatre of bloody conflicts. In 1358, it was pillaged and sacked by the English; again in 1411, by a party of Armagnacs; and during the wars of the League, became frequently taken and burnt. It was here that Henry III. was assassinated, and in a house near the palace, Henry IV., his successor, resided after the event. During the minority of Louis, the park had already become celebrated for the beauty of its gardens and its mansion; and the fine view, with the Seine winding along at its feet, was universally admired. The king, who was desirous of possessing himself of the estate, to make a residence of it for his brother, the duke of Orleans, deputed Cardinal Mazarin to negociate the purchase of it. This he did, and by chicanery and force, wrested it from its proprietor, M. Fouquet, for the sum of 300,000*l*., although it had cost the latter upwards of a million in erecting the chateau, and laying out the grounds. No sooner was it in regal hands, than three of the principal architects of the time were employed in harmonising the old, and erecting new buildings; whilst Lenôtre, taking advantage of the natural position of the grounds, designed the park, the admiration of all visitors. St. Cloud then became the residence of the dukes of Orleans, until the revolution, when it was made part of the national property. During the empire, Napoleon frequently resided here with Josephine, and from this palace Charles X. issued those celebrated ordonnances suggested by Prince Polignac, which led to his banishment in July, 1830. Louis Philippe subsequently inhabited the chateau, and rested there a few moments in February, 1848, during his flight from Paris. It is now the residence of the present emperor.

The chateau is built on the southern slope of the hill to the left of the town from the river. The principal building is after the designs of Mansard, and adorned with Corinthian pillars and bas-reliefs. The front faces the grand avenue of the park, whilst on the left are the cascades and jets d'eau, and on the right, the private walks and flower-gardens.

The interior of the chateau consists of suites of apartments, to which the visitor approaches by a very richly-ornamented vestibule, in which is a fine statue of Mars recumbent. The first room to be remarked is the

Salon de Mars, decorated with marble pillars of the Ionic order. Amongst the different subjects to be noticed is the ceiling, the compartments of which are embellished by the pencil of Mignard. The Forges of Vulcan, Mars, and Venus, accompanied by Cupid and the Graces, Jealousy and Discord may be particularised amongst these paintings. We then enter the

Gallerie d'Appollon, which is adorned by paintings by the same artist, representing Apollo in most of his mythological forms. Paintings by Canaletti Van Oels and Van Spaendonk also grace the walls. In this apartment, Pius VII. baptised the eldest son of the king of Holland, now the emperor Louis Napoleon Bonaparte, and here also in 1810, the civil contract of marriage between Maria Louise and Napoleon was celebrated. After this we enter the

Salon de Diane. This saloon is ornamented with some very fine specimens of Gobelin tapestry. The ceiling, painted by Mignard, relates the mythological history of Diana, and is thus in conformity with the *Gallerie d'Apollon*, which records that of her brother. Adjoining to this is the *Chapelle*, an elegant chapel adorned with Tuscan pillars. The altar-piece is a chef-d'œuvre by Lusueur, who has chosen for his subject the *Presentation in the Temple*. Returning to the *Salon de Mars*, we enter the *Salon de Venus*, which, like the other Salles de Diane, &c., is called from the subjects on the ceiling by which it is embellished. *Juno borrowing the girdle of Venus* is the principal painting, and is by Lemoine. This fine apartment is now used as a billiard-room. The table, which stands in the centre of it, is very splendidly ornamented. We now come to the *Salon de Jeu*. The principal object of interest in it is a table in mosaic, given by Leo XII. There is also some fine tapestry here, illustrating scenes in history. Adjoining this is the *Library*, consisting of 12,000 volumes. The other apartments belonging to the grand suite, are the *Salon de Mercurie* and the *Salon de l'Aurore*. In the former, the compartments of the ceiling tell the story of Mercury and Pandora: the paintings are by Aleaux, and in the latter they are embellished by the history of that goddess. The painting is by Loir. There is also some fine Gobelin tapestry in the former. We now enter the

Petits Apartments, or those devoted to the comfort and domesticity of the royal households who have occupied the chateau. It is here that Marie Antoinette, Josephine, Marie Louise, and the family of Louis Philippe reposed after the fatigues of state duties. The rooms to be particularly noticed are these; the *Salle du Consul*, formerly the bed-chamber of Marie Antoinette; the *Cabinet du Travail*, where Louis Philippe rested a few moments during his flight from the Tuilleries, the 24th February, 1848: the *Salon de la reception de la reine*, where may be seen a curious clock, with twelve dials, marking the hours of as many capitals of Europe. All these apartments are beautifully decorated, and ornamented with superb vases and some fine pictures.

The park lies on the road between St. Cloud and Sèvres, and is about ten miles in circumference.

The fountains and disposition of the waters in this park have for a long time been celebrated, and next to those at Versailles, merit an especial visit. The *Haute Cascade*, from which the water is first seen issuing, is adorned by a group of statues representing the Seine and Marne, and was designed by Lepantre. The second fall, called the *Basse Cascade*, receives the waters of the *Haute Cascade*, and ejects them in a grand sheet into a canal, along which twelve jets d'eau are ranged. The effect of the waters issuing from urns and dolphins, and other emblematical figures, and falling after a graceful rise, into the different sculptured cisterns intended to receive them, is very magnificent. To the right of the *Cascade*, is the *Grand Jet*, also called *le jet giant*, which throws its waters one hundred and thirty feet above the level of the basin, and as it is situated on high ground, may be seen at a considerable distance sparkling in the sun, high above the green foliage of the trees. The rainbows, which the falling spray forms, are very beautiful. Other basins and fountains of extreme elegance are distributed about the grounds.

The part of the park now to be sought out, is the high terrace in front of the river, from which a fine view of Paris and the surrounding country may be had. It is at the top of the grand avenue, facing the western front of the chateau, and may be distinguished by a kind of watch-tower, called the *Lantern of Diogenes*, or by others, of *Demosthenes*, which is built on an open space here. This monument was erected by order of Napoleon, and is designed after the original one by Lysicrates at Athens.

The waters play at St. Cloud every alternate Sunday during the summer. To see the interior of the chateau, application must be made to M. le Colonel Thienon, Governeur de St. Cloud.

Continuing our route by the avenue facing that we ascended from the palace, and taking a pathway to the left, we shall, on arriving at the bottom of the hill, find ourselves at the town, and shortly after at the porcelain manufactory of

Sevres. The town of Sèvres is situated on the left bank of the Seine, on the high road between Paris and Versailles. In the rocks that environ it, are immense cellars or underground streets, divided into thirty compartments, where the wine is kept until it has attained a superior quality from age. These cellars are capable of containing upwards of fifteen thousand pieces of wine. But that for which Sèvres is chiefly celebrated, is its porcelain manufactory. This manufactory was established originally at Vincennes, in the year 1738, under the superintendence of the Marquis de Fulvy, but was transferred to Sèvres in 1759, by order of Louis XV., and was made a government establishment. This manufactory contains a fine museum of porcelains of every kind, foreign as well as French; modern as well as antique. The workshops where the vases, &c., are fabricated, are very difficult to be seen, but the rest of the establishment may be seen on shewing a passport.

At a short distance beyond Sèvres is the *Terrace of Bellevue* and the *Chateau of Meudon*. This chateau stands at the end of a grand avenue, having before it a fine terrace, one thousand seven hundred and thirty feet in length, and five hundred and fifty in breadth; constructed by Henri de Guise, in 1660. During the revolution, the estate was seized by the government, and the grounds converted into a park for artillery practice. Shortly after this, a part of the chateau was burnt down, when Napoleon ordered the remaining portion to be repaired and enlarged, and the grounds to be laid out in gardens. At the restoration, it was made crown property, and subsequently used by the duke of Bourdeaux until 1831, when it was given as a residence to the duke of Orleans. It is now occupied by Prince Jerome Bonaparte.

The interior of the building is beautifully fitted up with rich silk and Gobelin tapestry, and contains many works of high eminence, by the first artists of the time. Amongst them may be mentioned the *Group of Cupid and Psyche*, in marble, in the vestibule; and the paintings by Teniers, Schnetz, Vergnaud, which are all chef-d'œuvres. The chateau may be visited any day except Fridays, from twelve to four.

From the terrace that lines the ground to the east, a most beautiful prospect may be had. Immediately beneath, in the valley, is the prettily situated village of Meudon. It is worth remarking that the satirist and wit Rabelais, was formerly pastor in this village.

On the opposite slope of the hill is Fleury; its cottages and summer houses gracefully embosomed in the fine wood that covers the whole rise. To the left, the landscape is cut as it were by the railway viaduct, consisting of seven beautiful arches, rising upwards of one hundred feet, whilst, beyond the plain of the river, and the busy houses of the city stretch away into the far horizon. On a fine day, this is perhaps one of the finest and most enlivening prospects in the neighbourhood of Paris.

When the visitor has sufficiently admired this view, he may return to Paris by taking an omnibus at Sèvres, or by the railway at Bellevue, which is half way down the hill. If by the latter means, he will enter by the *rive gauche* into Paris, at the Boulevard Mont Parnasse, where he will find omnibuses waiting to take him to any part of the city.

SEVENTH DAY.

BIBLIOTHEQUE IMPERIALE—PLACE RICHELIEU—BOURSE—CONSERVATOIRE DES ARTS ET METIERS—ST. DENIS—ENGHIEN—MONTMORENCY AND ST. VINCENT DE PAUL.

The short trip into the country of the previous day will, we trust, dispose the visitor to accompany us to-day to some of the remaining monuments and public places of Paris which he has not already seen. We will therefore take our start from the *Bibliotheque Imperiale*, in the Rue de Richelieu. This building presents to the street only a large unsightly wall, with blank windows; but on entering the gateway, the visitor finds himself in a vast court, five hundred and forty feet long, in the centre of which is a statue of Charles IX. During the regency of the Duke of Orleans, the royal library proving too extensive for the number of volumes which had accumulated in it, the books were transferred to the present building, a mansion that formerly belonged to the Cardinal Mazarin. This library had been formed at an early period, and gradually augmented by successive monarchs, who collected valuable books and manuscripts from different parts of the world. In the reign of Henry II., a decree was issued that a copy of every book printed within the jurisdiction of the king's censor should be placed in it. Its value was also considerably increased by the confiscation of the property of the Constable Bourbon, and a collection of medals and MSS. bequeathed to it by Catherine de Medicis. At the death of Louis XIV., it is computed that there were no less than seventy thousand volumes in the royal library. During the revolution of 1789, the number was rapidly increased, by the confiscation of all the printed volumes and MSS. belonging to the monasteries and other religious establishments which were then suppressed. It is supposed that the Bibliotheque Imperiale now contains upwards of a million and a half of volumes, including duplicates and pamphlets.

In the different salons of the library may be seen specimens of bookbinding and printing, from the earliest time of its invention. An apocalypse, printed from solid blocks of wood; a bible printed by Guttenburg; and a translation of the *Ars Moriendi*, printed by Caxton, are among the chief curiosities. In one of the rooms, two colossal metal globes, nearly twelve feet in diameter, made at Venice, by order of Cardinal d'Estrèes, may be seen. The other salons well worth noticing, are the *Cabinets of Medals and Antiquities*; the *Gallery of Ancient Sculpture*, where is the Egyptian zodiac of Dendarah, and the *Salledes Ancêtres*, a room fitted up after the Egyptian original, and representing the ancestors of Thoutmes III.

There is in the building a spacious hall for reading, to which the public are admitted from ten to three, every day except Sundays and fete days, without any order or impediment. To the other parts of the library, visitors are only admitted on Tuesdays and Fridays, from ten to three o'clock.

The open space in front of the Bibliotheque Imperiale is the *Place de Richelieu*, where formerly stood the French opera house. It was at the entrance of this theatre that the duke de Berri was assassinated in 1820, and the event made such an impression on the king, that he ordered the building to be demolished, and another erected elsewhere. The *Theatre Lyrique* was accordingly transferred to the spot behind the Boulevard des Italiens, where the present spacious establishment was erected in the short space of a year. In the centre of the *Place*, an elegant fountain has been erected. The principal figures represent the four principal rivers of France, the Loire, the Rhone, the Garonne, and the Seine. It was placed there in 1835, and cost 4,000*l*. The design is by the late M. Visconti.

A little further on, towards the boulevards, and turning to the right is the

Bourse, one of the finest pieces of architecture in Paris. It occupies the space once occupied by the convent of the *Daughters of St. Thomas*, and was commenced in 1808, after the designs of Brongniard, the architect. It was not finished until 1826. It consists of a parallelogram two hundred and twelve feet long, by one hundred and twenty-six feet wide. The whole is surrounded by a gallery supported by sixty-six Corinthian columns, beneath which the merchants walk and discuss their business. A fine flight of steps, running the whole front of the palace, gives it a majestic appearance. At each corner of the building is placed a statue emblematic of Commerce, Consular Justice, Industry, and Agriculture.

The interior consists of a vast hall, one hundred and sixteen feet long, by seventy-six feet wide, capable of containing two thousand persons, where the principal business of the exchange is carried on. The ceiling is divided into compartments, and embellished with fresco paintings by Abel de Pujol and Meynier, having the effect of bas-reliefs. The subjects are all allegorical, and consonant with the purpose of the building. To the right we see the *Union of the Arts and Commerce giving prosperity to the State; on the left, France receiving the products of the four quarters of the world;* in front, *Paris delivering the Keys to the Genius of Commerce, and inviting Commercial Justice to enter her gates.* A library, called the Bibliothèque du Commerce, principally containing works on commercial subjects, is in connection with the Bourse, and may be seen any day from twelve to four. The hall is always open.

Opposite to the Bourse is the *Theatre du Vaudeville*, established in 1827. It is capable of containing one thousand three hundred persons. Light dialogues and comedies, relieved by singing, characterise the performances at this theatre. The prices range from one franc up to six francs. Performances commence at half-past six.

The next object of interest we will visit is

the *Conservatoire des Arts et Métiers*. It will therefore be necessary to proceed on to the boulevards by the Rue Vivienne, which runs in front of the Bourse, and pass down by the Boulevard Poissonnière, Bonne Nouvelle, and St. Denis, to the Rue St. Martin. In the Rue St. Martin, before arriving at our destination, we shall observe on our left the *Fontaine St. Martin*, a curious fountain, built against a round and spired tower, which once formed part of the outer walls of the abbey of St. Martin des Champs. A few steps more will take us to the

Conservatoire. This institution was founded on the site of the above-mentioned abbey, by the Convention, under the management of Gregory, Bishop of Blois, in 1794. The object of the institution is the improvement of machinery of every kind, by exhibiting models of the best and most recent inventions, for the purpose of stimulating the creative faculty in the minds of other artists and mechanics. Previous to 1798, three repositories of machines existed in Paris, but in this year they were amalgamated into one. In 1810, a gratuitous school of arts was originated, which was re-organised and enlarged several times, until in 1838 it was finally established under its present regulations. No patent for any sort of improvement in machines, or the invention of new ones, is granted until a model of the same has been deposited in this museum; so that instruments from the simplest tool to the most complicated piece of mechanism, are collected and classified in the salons of this building.

The principal entrance to the Conservatoire is on the west, under a solid archway, richly sculptured, under the pediment of which, is inscribed, *Conservatoire Imperiale des Arts et Métiérs*. The edifice consists of a part of the old abbey of St. Martin des Champs, and of the chapel belonging to it erected by Pierre de Montereau, the architect of the Sainte Chapelle. The style is Gothic. The museums are held in spacious saloons, communicating with lecture rooms of modern construction. The library, which contains upwards of twenty thousand volumes, on mechanical and mathematical subjects, is most elegantly fitted up. It is divided by seven lofty pillars, from each of which spring ribs, expanding along the groins of the roof. The bases and capitals are gilt. There are also fresco figures of Chemistry, Natural Philosophy, Painting, and the Plastic Art.

On the *ground floor*, are arranged in beautiful order, weighing machines, looms, spinning machines, printing presses, screw-making machines, agricultural implements, such as ploughs, harrows, mills, crushing and winnowing machines, &c. There are also specimens of porcelain, silk, glue, &c. In the vestibule is a bas-relief of Dedalus and Icarus, by Ruxtheil, and, in an adjoining out-house, Tuxford's locomobile engine, which gained the chief medal, at the Great Exhibition of 1851, may be seen.

On the *upper storey* are exhibited steam and fire-engines, apparatuses for lighting and heating, turning lathes, and amongst them one that belonged to Louis XIV.; cranes, pulleys, musical instruments, large mirrors, and a collection of optical instruments. There are, moreover, rooms devoted to geometrical illustrations; to carpentry; to the making of compasses; to specimens of stereotype; furnaces, &c. Also to instruments belonging to the science of natural philosophy or physics; as air-pumps, electric machines, &c., and to clocks and chronometers.

The museum is open to strangers on Thursdays and Sundays, from ten to four.

Having seen all that is to be seen here, there will be time to spend the rest of the afternoon in a short trip to the *Abbey of St. Denis*. The town itself, which contains about fifteen thousand inhabitants, offers nothing of striking interest, if we except its antiquity—its historical associations—and its beautiful abbey, which enclose the ashes of nearly all the kings of France, from the time of Clovis to that of Louis XVIII. It is situated about three miles and a half from Paris, on the right bank of the Seine, and may be reached either by omnibus or railway. The railway, however, is the best, being more easily attained, and also more expeditious. The station is that of the *Chemin de Fer du Nord*, rue La Fayette. The trains start at all the half-hours. The first class is seventy cents, or fourteen sous; the second, fifty-five cents, or eleven sous. A run of a few minutes takes you to the station at St. Denis. The abbey is a few minutes' walk from the station.

The foundation of this abbey is almost coeval with the establishment of christianity in France. It is said that St. Denis, who was beheaded on Montmartre, the Mount of Martyrs, walked, after his execution, with his head under his arm as far as this spot, angels celebrating the miracle in songs as he passed along, where he stopped and gave up the ghost after requesting that he might be buried there. A tomb and then a chapel successively rose above his ashes. Ste. Geneviéve, the patroness of Paris in 496, was the means of having the chapel enlarged, and in the following century it became the abode of a company of Benedictine Monks. Chilperic, the youngest son of Dagobert, was the first who was laid within its vaults, whilst his father was the first king who shared the same fate. In 754 Pepin le Bref was consecrated in the church, and, as a mark of his gratitude, pulled down the old edifice, and commenced another on a scale of greater magnificence. This building was finished and consecrated in 775, in the reign of Charlemagne. Only the crypt of this church now remains. It was demolished by Suger, Abbot of St. Denis, in 1140; and in the course of five years another was erected, of which the towers and porch remain. The other parts of the present building were constructed between the years 1231 and 1281, a period of half a century. In the erection of this edifice, not only the most celebrated architects were employed, but the most skilful makers and stainers of glass were sent for, even from distant countries. During the revolution of 1793, this church, the work of so much skill and labour, the mirror of so much beauty and elegance, excited the fury of the people, for containing the tombs of the Kings of France, and suffered accordingly. The richly stained glass was broken, the lead of the roofs melted down to make bullets, the splendid monumental tombs of the kings broken open, and their ashes, which had been quietly inurned there for centuries, scattered to the winds, the *Oriflamme*, the consecrated banner of France, torn to pieces, and a decree was even passed for the entire demolition of the abbey. In 1806, however, Napoleon, who had given back the church to the empire, ordered the restoration of the church, and especially the vault of the Bourbon, which he intended henceforth to be the resting-place of his own dynasty.

The *tout ensemble* of this church is pure Gothic, and is one of the finest specimens of the style of the period in which it was built. The façade, which is the part erected by Suger, is very fine, and contains three portals, consisting of retiring arches, ornamented with angels, &c. Bas-reliefs of *Jesus in the Midst of the Saints*, and the *General Resurrection*, grace the centre porch. The bas-reliefs on the north porch represent *St. Denis and his companions led to execution*.

The form of the church is that of a regular cross, and consists of a nave and two aisles. The nave is very splendid, and exhibits those light and elegant forms, which particularly distinguished the architecture of this period. The chapels which surround it are in admirable keeping, and produce the most striking effect.

The choir is separated from the nave by a railing of beautiful workmanship. The church is also enriched by paintings of some of the first masters—that over the high altar is by Krayer, a pupil of Rubens, and represents the martyrdom of St. Denis. In the chamfering of the second window is a statue of the Virgini and Child in white marble, the robes of which are interspersed with precious stones. In the Sacristie are ten paintings, illustrating the principal events connected with the history of the Abbey. Amongst them are *Charles V. and Francis the First visiting the Abbey*, by Gros; *St. Louis receiving the Oriflamme*, by Barbier; *the Preaching of St. Denis in Gaul*, by Monsiau, &c.

But that which will now particularly interest the spectator is the tombs of the different monarchs; and that which first claims his attention as being the most ancient, is the tomb of Dagobert, a work of the thirteenth century. It is a mausoleum with pinnacles, and a richly ornamented canopy, representing the dream of a monk, who dreamed that he saw the king carried off by a legion of devils. The tombs of Louis XII and Anne of Brittany, beautifully executed in white marble, by Paolo Poncio, and of Henry II. and Catherine de Medicis, should be noticed. The tomb of the last is adorned with twelve columns of deep blue marble, and twelve of white marble. The two sovereigns are reposing on a couch. Next to this is the tomb of Francis I. and Claude, of France, erected in 1550. Bas-reliefs, representing the battles of Marignan and Cerisolles, ornament the pedestal, which support figures of the king and queen.

In one of the transepts we see a spiral column, raised to the memory of Henry III., who was murdered at St. Cloud by Jacques Clement. Opposite, is a marble pillar raised by the unfortunate Mary Queen of Scots, to the memory of her husband, Francis II. Two other columns, one of marble, to the memory of the Cardinal Bourbon, and the other of porphyry, to the memory of Henry IV., should be noticed. The tombs of Du Guesclin, Sancerre, and La Rivière are to be seen in the first chapel, on ascending the south steps of the choir.

After the visitor has examined these monuments, he will be conducted by a guide to the tombs of the kings of the first, second, and third races. In one of the chapels are the tombs of Henri II. and Catherine de Medicis, a bust of Henry IV., Diana of France, in a kneeling posture, and Charles de Valois. An urn in front contains the heart of Francis I. Not far from this is a statue of Marie Antoinette kneeling, which is considered to be a most perfect likeness. There are also two colossal figures. This monument is intended as an expiatory souvenir of the memory of the Duke de Berri, who was assassinated in 1820. Between these two is the mausoleum of Louis XVIII. It would, however, be impossible to enumerate more out of so many sepulchral objects of interest. We have only pointed out the above as, we think, possessing more interest, either from their historical associations, or the beauty of their execution.

Having examined these monuments, the visitor should endeavour to regain the station, in order to meet the trains for Paris. But, should he have time, he could not do better than meet one of the trains leaving Paris, and proceed a little further on to *Enghien* and *Montmorency*.

Enghien is situated about 9 miles from Paris, on the borders of a lake, since 1766 celebrated for its sulphurous waters, which, as well as the prettiness of the situation, has given rise to several thermal establishments, and the construction of several private country villas. To this spot the Parisians frequently retire after the heat of the day, to enjoy a cool evening in its green bosquets, or a quiet ride on its enchanting lake. On the hill above Enghien, to the right, is the ancient town of

Montmorency.—Containing upwards of two thousand inhabitants. It owes its principal importance to the beauty of its position, being seated high amongst the hills, and enjoying a magnificent prospect of the country below, and the woods by which it is surrounded. A multitude of country seats may be seen dotting the valley, over which the eye runs, whilst to the left the majestic form of Paris may be traced in the distance. The air here is pure and fresh, and the fruits that grow on the sides of the hills early ripen, and acquire an exquisite flavour. But Montmorency owes its principal attractions for the visitor to its *Hermitage*, which was formerly the residence of Jean Jacques Rousseau, and the spot where he composed his *Emile* and finished his *Heloise*.

Returning to the railway station, half-an-hour's run will bring us again into Paris, and the Rue la Fayette. In this street is the fine church of

St. Vincent de Paul, which is well worthy of inspection, and may be almost said to rival the Madeleine in the gorgeousness of its decorations. It is of modern construction, being commenced in 1824, and finished in 1844. A graceful flight of steps, bordered by a carriage drive, leads from the Rue la Fayette up to its elegant portico. Two lofty square towers containing two clocks, one for telling the hour of the day, the other the days of the month, flank the façade. The interior of the church consists of a nave and four aisles, separated by rows of Ionic pillars. Richly gilt bronze railings divide the aisles into chapels, whilst a semi-circle of fourteen columns of the same order, supporting a semi-cupola, enclose the choir. Over the altar is a bas-relief of the Last Supper. The church contains fine specimens of stained glass, and the windows where St. Vincent de Paul is represented, surrounded by the Sisters of Charity, is remarkably beautiful. A splendid organ surmounts the southern portal.

The visitor may descend to the Boulevards, either by taking the Rue Hauteville, which is opposite the church, or by the Rue du Faubourg Poissonière, which is at the end of the Rue la Fayette.

EIGHTH DAY.

LE TEMPLE—ARCHIVES IMPÉRIALES—IMPRIMERIE IMPÉRIALE—PLACE DES VOSGES—BASTILLE—PERE LA CHAISE—PLACE DU TRONE—VINCENNES.

As we visited yesterday some of the most interesting places in the northern arrondissement of Paris, so to-day we will visit some of those lying eastward, even as far as Pere la Chaise and Vincennes. But, before we leave the town we will go to some of those places which are most remarkable for their historical associations or peculiar attractions, as they lie in our route. It will therefore be best to hasten on as far as the Boulevard du Temple, where, descending the street of that name, we shall see the market and the ruins of the palace of that name.

The *Temple*, as its name implies, formerly belonged to the order of the Knights Templar, who possessed extensive domains in this quarter of the city. All that exists of it at present is the Palais du Prior, which, in 1814 was converted into a convent, and dedicated to the Dames Benedictines de l'Adoration du Saint Sacrement, under the direction of Madame la Princesse de Condé, formerly abbess of Remiremont. The façade fronting the court of the Temple is composed of eight Ionic columns, above which are placed allegorical figures of Justice, by Dumont; Hope, by Lecomte; Abundance, by Foucon; and Prudence, by Boichot. The portico is composed of six Doric pillars. The façade fronting the street is adorned by two statues representing the Marne and the Seine.

There stood formerly in the Temple a high quadrangular tower, 150 feet in length, which was built in 1222 or perhaps earlier, and flanked by smaller towers. This was the doujon or fortress of the knights, and sometimes it was even inhabited by the kings of France. The earlier souvenirs of this tower fade away before the immediate interest of more recent events. During the first revolution it became the prison of the unfortunate Louis XVI., and it was here that he made his will and bade his last adieu to his family before being conducted to the scaffold. Here also were confined Sir Sidney Smith, Pichegru, Moreau, and Toussaint Louverture. It was demolished, however, in 1810, and no vestige of it remains.

In what was anciently the grand enclosure of the Temple has been established a market, where old clothes, furniture, &c. are sold. It is worth entering, for though there is no danger of being lost amongst its labyrinths of narrow alleys, there is sufficient to afford amusement in looking at its quaint shambles and shops. Proceeding down the Rue du Temple until we arrive at the Rue de Brague, which is on the left of us, we shall have at the further end of the street the

Archives Imperiales, the principal entrance of which is from the Rue Paradise. Until 1697 this property belonged to the Dukes of Guise, but in this year it was purchased by François de Rohan, Prince de Soubise, who, in 1706, had the place rebuilt after designs by Lemaire, and gave it the name of Hotel de Soubise. The principal entrance is adorned by corinthian columns, trophies, the arms of Rohan and Soubise, and some fine sculpture by Coustou. The vestibule and staircase are painted by Brunetti. At the period when this fine edifice was erected, this quarter was the fashionable part of Paris; and this, as well as several other mansions in the neighbourhood, attest the splendour of the nobles of the early part of the eighteenth century. This splendour, however, has been greatly dimmed by the uses to which these hotels have been put, and, in the present instance, it is not very easy, amidst the masses and heaps of papers that fill every part of it, to realise altogether the stories of its former sumptuousness.

Before 1789 the national documents were scattered about amongst various public offices and religious establishments; but in 1793, by a decree of the Convention, they were collected together and placed in the palace of the Tuileries, where they were separated into two classes, the *Archives Judiciaires* and the *Archives Domaniales*, under the direction of the antiquarian Camus. The latter were, in 1798, transferred by order of Napoleon to the Palais Bourbon, from whence they were subsequently transferred to the Hotel de Soubise. These archives are divided into six sections, viz.: the ancient *Tresor des Chartes*, or collection of titles and charters from the twelfth century down to the first revolution; eighty volumes of manuscript, containing different acts passed from the time of Philip Augustus to that of Louis XVI.; of an infinitude of documents, belonging either to Paris or the provinces; of a topographical collection, and an excellent library of 14,000 volumes relating to the history of France, as well as a variety of curiosities and souvenirs, illustrative of the progress of civilisation in France.

The public is admitted every day from 9 till 4, to visit the establishment, but a written order is required from the Minister of the Interior to use the manuscripts.

Close by the *Archives Imperiales* is the *Imprimerie Imperiale*, where all the government papers, and papers referring to state matters, are printed. The entrance to it is in the *Rue Vielle du Temple*. This building, which possesses no great architectural beauty, was formerly called the *Palais Cardinal*, because it belonged to the Cardinal Rohan, whose intriguing spirit made him so conspicuous a figure during the reigns of Louis XV. and XVI. The national printing office was established first at the Louvre by François I., but in 1793 it was transferred to the Hotel de Thoulouse, since the Bank of France, and from thence, in 1809, to the place it now occupies.

This establishment, as we have said, is principally devoted to the printing of the acts of government and of the legislature. It is one of the most complete in the world, and contains several steam presses, as well as a great number of hand presses. It possesses also fifty-six founts of letters, comprising all the known languages of the nations of Asia, and even the Assyrian cuneiform characters. The kings, queens, and knaves, as well as the ace of clubs, in a pack of cards, are printed here, this being a government monopoly, but the rest of the pack are printed by the card manufacturers themselves. The weight of type in use at this establishment amounts to 7,142 cwt. Besides the printing department, the various operations of binding are done here. When Pius VII. visited the office, the Lord's Prayer in 150 different languages was presented to him, and before he left, the same, bound up in a splendid volume, was placed in his hands.

The public is admitted to view the Imprimerie Imperiale from 1 to 3 on Thursdays, but this must be under an order of M. le Directeur de l'Imprimiérie Imperiale.

At the corner of the Rue Franc Bourgeois may be seen an elegant turret, near which the Duke of Orleans was murdered in 1407, by the Duke of Burgundy. This murder acquired a greater degree of importance from the long and bloody feuds which it gave rise to, and which disturbed France for several years, and finally led to the capture of Paris by the English.

Pursuing the Rues Franc Bourgeois and Neuve St. Catherine, we shall arrive on the **Place des Vosges**, or, as it is sometimes called, the *Place Royale*. This place, surrounded with buildings of a uniform character, containing galleries of arcades, was built by Henry IV., on the place of the ancient Palais des Tournelles, or Palace of Turrets, so called from the numerous turrets that decorated it. This famous palace was occupied by Louis XII. and Francis I., but was destroyed in 1565 by order of Catherine de Medicis, in consequence of her husband, Henry II., having been killed whilst tilting with the Count of Montgomery, in a tournament held in the great court. The present houses were commenced in 1602. The part that is separated by an iron railing from the street is planted with trees, and adorned with four fine fountains, encircled by prettily arranged flower gardens. In 1639 a bronze equestrian statue of Louis XIII. was erected here by the Cardinal Richelieu, but this, like that of Henry IV. on the Pont Neuf, was destroyed in 1792. During the empire a splendid fountain occupied its site, but, in 1825, the present statue in white marble was placed there.

The *Place des Vosges* derives its name from the circumstance that the government, during the first revolution, to stimulate the payment of taxes throughout the country, decreed that that Department which first paid up its assessments should be honoured by having its name given to one of the public places of Paris. The Department of the Vosges won that honour, and the *Place Royale* was changed into the *Place des Vosges*.

During the late revolution of 1848, this place was the scene of several severe conflicts between the troops and the insurgents. The latter, however, gained the day, and a batallion of the line were forced to lay down its arms. This batallion was afterwards disbanded by order of General Lamoricière, but a young lieutenant, of the name of Mahler, rather than deliver up his sword, allowed himself to be killed in a neighbouring street, received the name of this young hero, to commemorate the action.

Passing out on the south side by the Rue des Vosges, we enter the eastern end of the Rue St. Antoine, celebrated in every revolution, and see on the left the *Place de la Bastille* and the *Column of July*. On this spot stood formerly the Bastille, the grounds of which ran back as far as the river. On the 14th of July, 1789, the old fortress of the Bastille was taken by the people, and in the following year entirely demolished, when part of its materials were carried off, to assist in the construction of the Pont de la Concorde. Several propositions were put forward for embellishing the vacant space after the destruction of the building, but little was done, until Napoleon ordered the foundations of an enormous fountain to be laid. The entire design, however, was never completed. Nothing further was executed until 1831, when it was agreed to erect a monument to the memory of those who had fallen during the Three Days, and the present column was begun. It is erected on an archway built over the canal St. Martin, and rests upon a basement of white marble, supported by blocks of granite. The column itself is of bronze, and of the composite order. It is 154 feet high and 12 in diameter. The weight of the metal employed amounts to 1,458 cwt.; the whole cost of erection, to 48,000l. Upon the shaft are inscribed the names of 615 of those, who fell in the memorable conflict of July. Over the capital is a gilt globe, surmounted by a figure, also gilt, of the Genius of Liberty. It is represented standing, with one foot on the globe, whilst his wings are outspread, as if ready for flight. The statue is by Dumont, the medallions on the basement by Marbeuf. During the sanguinary days of June 1848, the *Place de la Bastille* was the theatre of some of the most desperate struggles between the insurgents and the soldiers. At this end of the Rue St. Antoine the largest barricade was thrown up, and in attacking it, it was, that General Negrier was killed. It was at this barricade also, that the Archbishop of Paris, who had come on his errand of peace, was struck down by a stray shot. The houses on either side of the Place suffered greatly on the occasion, and were dreadfully riddled with balls. One of them, the *Belle Fermière*, which stood alone at the entrance of the Rue de la Roquette, was reduced to ashes by cannon balls and howitzers.

Taking an omnibus from the Place de la Bastille for the Barrière du Mont Louis, we shall arrive opposite the entrance of

Père la Chaise, or the Cemetery of the East, so-called from its being laid out on a piece of ground where formerly stood the house of Père la Chaise, the confessor of Louis XIV. who is notorious as having persuaded that monarch to revoke the Edict of Nantes. Before his time, however, this spot was called *Champs l'Evêque*, because it belonged to the Bishop of Paris. It afterwards became the property of a wealthy grocer, who built a magnificent mansion on the hill, which was afterwards given to the Jesuits of the Rue St. Antoine, in whose possession it continued until the reign of Louis XIV. It then received the name of Mont Louis, and Père la Chaise was made superintendent of the institution. It was subsequently purchased and repurchased passing through several hands, until M. Frochot, prefect of the Seine, bought it for the purpose of converting it into a cemetery which

Chapelle Des Invalides.

Eglise De Ste Geneviève

Fontaine Des Innocens

Donjon Du Chateau Vincennes

Porte D'entrée Chateau de Vincennes

CIMETIÈRE DU PÈRE LACHAISE.

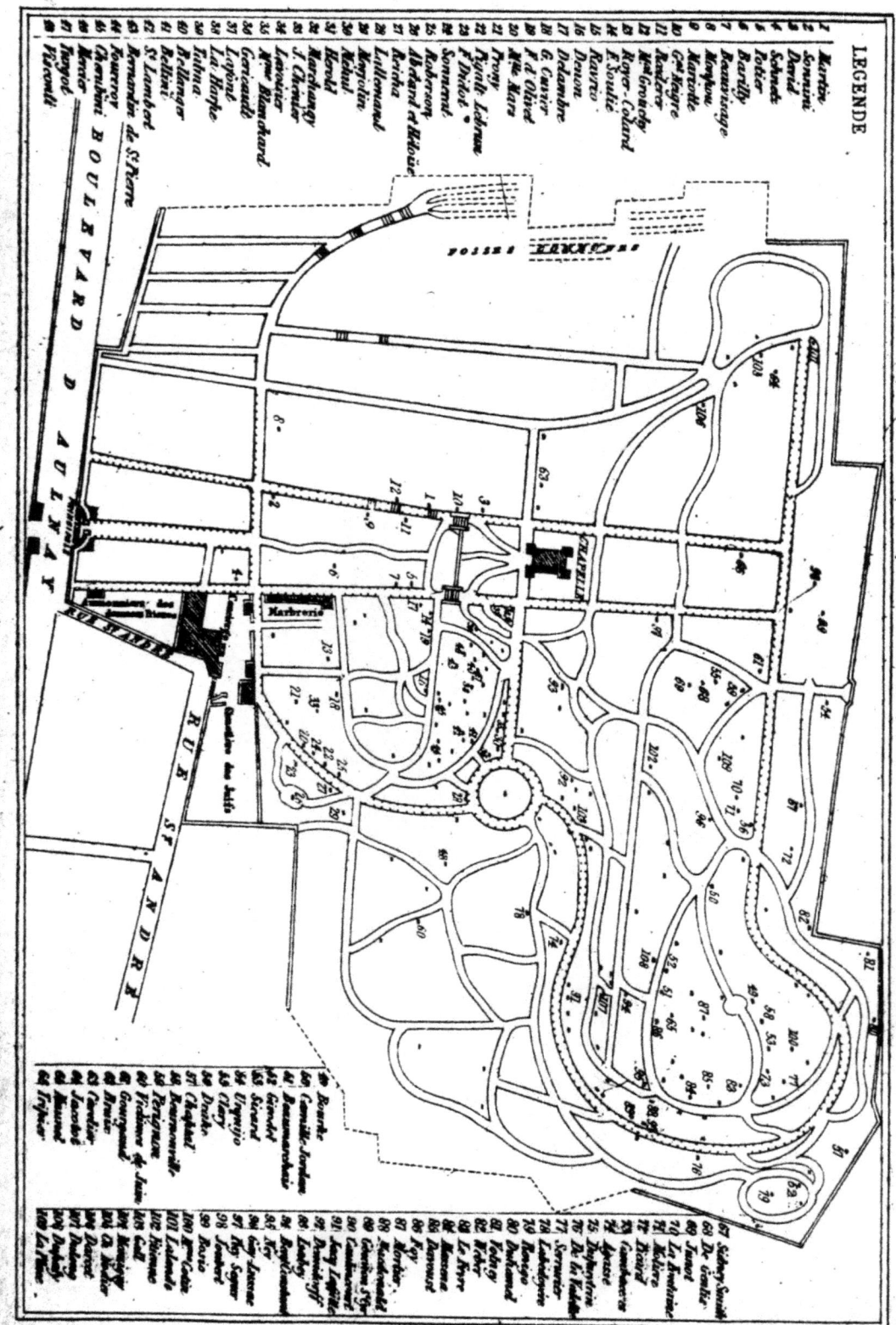

LÉGENDE

1. Martin
2. Souzini
3. David
4. Schrok
5. Potsa
6. Raritty
7. Boursirage
8. Morghen
9. Marielle
10. Gal-Negre
11. Grétry
12. Mélingnés
13. Royer-Colard
14. F. Souté
15. Reurio
16. Denon
17. Delambre
18. G. Cuvier
19. J. A. Olivier
20. Mlle. Mars
21. Preny
22. Rigaille Lebrun
23. F. Piclot
24. Sonnerat
25. Robinson
26. Abélard et Héloïse
27. Reicha
28. Lillemand
29. Bergolèse
30. Méhul
31. Herlé
32. Marchangy
33. J. Chenier
34. Mme. Blanchard
35. Lavoisier
36. Garizendo
37. Lajont
38. La Harpe
39. Rollinger
40. Tetina
41. Rebini
42. St. Lambert
43. Boscardin de St. Pierre
44. Tourreil
45. Cherubini
46. Morin
47. Turgot
48. Florville

49. Boïte
50. Camille Jordan
51. Beaumarchais
52. Gérard
53. Girard
54. Urquyo
55. Oksy
56. Deschu
57. Chaptal
58. Parmentier
59. Villars de Jancigny
60. Rose
61. Georguaul
62. Jacobi
63. Lucchesi
64. Manuel
65. Trogier
66. Sidney Smith
67. De Galles
68. Tanci
69. La Fontaine
70. Wolcy
71. Bichat
72. Lafrénière
73. De la Lallée
74. Robertson
75. Severgin
76. Boyer
77. Reiuma
78. La Pierre
79. Bernard
80. Falay
81. Kollin
82. Kyla
83. Kohner
84. Guiborg
85. Aug. Lafont
86. Rothschild
87. Laiby
88. Rossini
89. Ney
90. Lesseps
91. Ney Cigne
92. Treilard
93. Baria
94. Ducrow
95. E. Coste
96. Libault
97. Mme. Blême
98. Ney. Cid
99. Cordin
100. Ney. Moscova
101. Delatre
102. Ney. La Flèche

was accordingly effected. In 1804 the ground was consecrated, and on the 21st of May of that year the first grave made in it. It then contained 42 acres, but it has since been so considerably augmented that it covers upwards of 150 acres.

The hill on which Père la Chaise has been formed commands a fine view of Paris and the country beyond, and being tastily arranged and laid out, has become a place of universal attraction. The tombs and monumental chapels possess, many of them, great beauty, and architectural elegance. The principal to be seen are the tombs of *Heloise and Abelard*, the *Princess Demidorf, Casimir Perier, Massena, Ney, Lavalette, La Place, La Fontaine, Molière, Boileau*, &c., although the Cemetery is said to contain already 50,000 funereal monuments.

The tomb of *Heloise and Abelard* lies to the right on entering. It consists of a rectangular chapel, built of materials brought from the Abbey of the Holy Ghost, which Abelard founded in the twelfth century, and of which Heloise was abbess. The length of it is fourteen feet, the breadth eleven, and the height twenty-four. Fourteen columns, with rich foliaged capitals, support trifoliate arches, surmounted by cornices wrought in flowers. The whole is Gothic. In the chapel is the original tomb built for Abelard by Pierre le Venerable.

The monument to *Casimir Perier* is erected on a piece of ground given gratuitously by the city, as a mark of respect for their illustrious citizen, and consists of an excellent statue of that statesman placed on a high and profusely decorated pedestal.

The tomb of the *Princess Demidorf* is a beautiful structure of white marble, elegantly ornamented, and adorned with ten Corinthian pillars, which support the entablature.

A pyramid of white marble, twenty-one feet high, and a bas-relief portrait of the marshal, point out the resting-place of *Massena*, and a little further on is an iron railing, which encloses the remains of his comrade-in-arms, Marshal Ney. No other sign indicates the spot. Some passing hand has rudely traced the words, *vir victor, herōem calcas*, on the railing.

It would be impossible to enumerate or point out in these pages the various objects of interest, historical, &c., to be seen in this cemetery. We would advise the visitor therefore to hire a guide, as it will save much time and labour. A guide may be had for a small gratuity, as there are several in attendance, and will be able to conduct him at once to the monuments possessing the chief attraction. We would only warn the visitor from not losing too much time on the ground, as he has to go to the *Barrière du Trône* and the *Château de Vincennes*. The Barrière du Trône must be reached by passing down by the external boulevards. This Barrière constitutes the eastern entrance of Paris, as the Barrière de l'Étoile forms the western entrance. Two handsome Doric columns, nearly two hundred feet high, stand on either side of the gateway, and form a prominent object from any part of Paris. They were commenced in 1788, but remained unfinished until 1847. On the summits of these pillars, two statues, one of *Philippe le Bel*, by Dumont, and the other of *St. Louis*, by Etex, have been raised. Allegorical figures representing Peace and Victory, Industry and Commerce, adorn the pedestal of the columns. The Barrière derives its name from the fact that, in the August of 1660, a throne was placed there, on which Louis XIV. sat whilst he received the homage of the Parisians. Winding staircases lead to the galleries at the top of the shafts, from which a good view may be had.

About three quarters of a mile down the avenue is the

Chateau de Vincennes, a fine old feudal fortress, which is well worth the effort of a visit. It owes its origin to Philip Augustus who surrounded the wood of Vincennes with thick walls, and built at this extremity a hunting seat. Louis IX. often visited this manor, and, at the foot of an oak close by, used to administer justice to those who brought complaints to him. Philip the Bold enlarged the forest by taking in several estates, and defended it by new enclosures. In 1337, however, Philippe de Valois ordered the hunting-seat to be destroyed, and the donjon, or high tower, now standing, to be erected. Charles V., who frequently made this place his residence, built the Sainte Chapelle within its walls; Louis XI., ever suspicious, jealous, and cruel, turned it into a state prison, where he could delight himself in tormenting his victims, with the additional pleasure of the assurance that they could not easily escape from his hands. From this time till the reign of Charles IX., who came to die there terror stricken with remorse, for the massacre of St. Bartholomew's Day, it was little frequented by the kings. Marie de Medicis ordered considerable embellishments to be made there, and her son, Louis XIII., continued new constructions at the southern extremity, which, however, were not finished until the reign of Louis XIV.

The chateau may be considered as a specimen of the means of defence during the middle ages, as it is constructed on the best principles then known. Unfortunately, however, the nine square towers which flanked the fortress were destroyed in 1818, to place the buildings on the more advanced principles of modern fortification, so that the only one that remains intact is the Donjon. The chateau is constructed in the form of a parallelogram, of which the length is about a thousand feet, and its breadth six hundred. The donjon is surrounded by a thick wall, and a ditch 40 feet in depth. It is flanked by four turrets, which, at each storey, forms a chamber with a fire-place in it. There are five stories, and on the fourth an external gallery, from which a splendid view of the wood, the hills to the east of Paris, and Paris itself, may be enjoyed. The walls are 16 feet in thickness, and shew not the least sign of decay.

As we have said, the Donjon early became a state-prison, and from that time many illustrious victims have been immured within its walls. Amongst the most illustrious we may mention the Prince de Condé, whom Marie de Medicis seized and placed there, with the hope of thus prolonging her regency; the Marshal Ornano, who died there in 1621; the Duke de Vendôme, who was confined here for some time; Mirabeau, a considerable part of whose unhappy existence was passed here; the Prince Polignac; and lastly, the Duke d'Enghien, whose impolitic seizure and murder will leave a lasting stain on the character of Napoleon. In the chapel is a monument, erected to the memory of the noble duke, and in the eastern foss is a cypress tree, planted on the place where he was shot.

But what perhaps will interest the English visitor, especially to learn, is, that it was in this donjon that the brave and heroic Henry V., after being crowned King of France, died in 1420, and where, in 1431, his unfortunate son resided until 1434. The chateau is now one of the principal arsenals of France, and in a gallery on the eastern side is a fine collection of small arms. The visitor may obtain admission to see the chateau by applying to the *M. le Ministre de la Guerre.*

An omnibus, leaving Vincennes, will take the visitor into the heart of Paris after he has examined the fortress.

PERE LA CHAISE

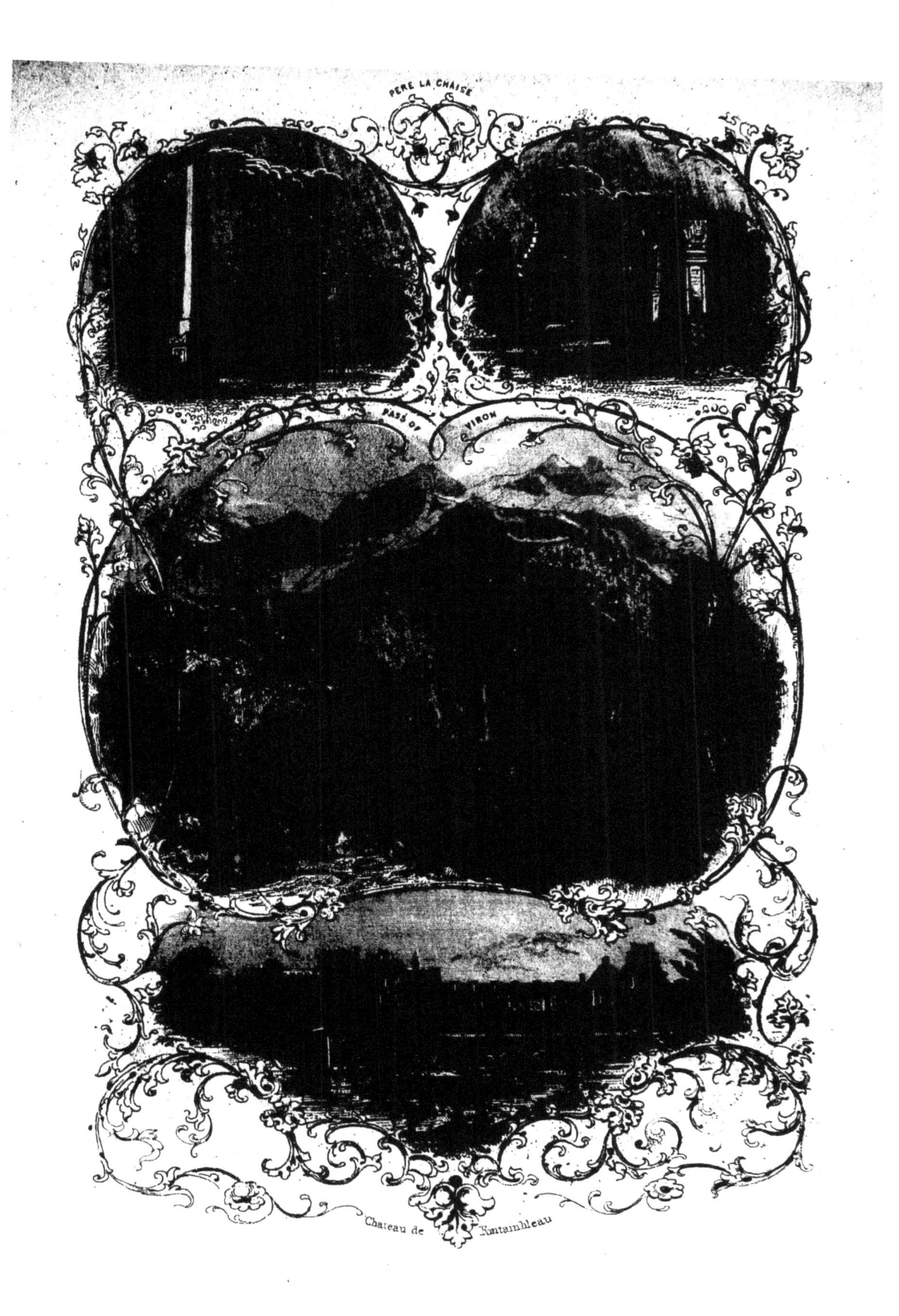

PAYS DE VIRON

Chateau de Fontainbleau

NINTH DAY.

FONTAINEBLEAU.

Station.—Chemin de Fer de Lyon, Boulevard Mazas. **Hours of Departure.**—6 5, 9 5, and 10 8 a.m.

One of the richest treats, either for the travail-worn Parisian or the travel-worn visitor, is an excursion to Fontainebleau; and well does it repay the little fatigue which the journeying of the day causes by the variety and beauty of the objects it presents. The town itself, prettily situated in the midst of the forest, is regularly built, with broad and fine streets, and from any point affords a striking picture of neatness and cleanliness. It contains between 8,000 and 9,000 inhabitants, and is distant about 40 miles from Paris. It possesses a public library of upwards of 30,000 volumes, and an obelisque, erected in 1786, in commemoration of the birth of the children of Louis XVI. It is a subject of dispute from whence the place derives its name, but it is supposed that it comes from *Fontaine Belle Eau*, which was given to the spot as early as the tenth century, on account of the abundance of good water then found there.

The Chateau. The present palace rose at different epochs, and we shall therefore not be surprised to find that it is in some respects irregular and heterageneneous. Louis VII. and Philippe Auguste were amongst the first who took up their abode here, and after them Louis IX. and his successors. The latter greatly enlarged and embellished the palace, but, by the time of Francis I., a part of the primitive building had fallen to ruin. This prince, however, who loved the site, had the chateau nearly entirely reconstructed by the first architects of the age, who were even sent for from Italy. Henry IV. is said to have laid out more than two millions pounds upon it, whilst Louis XIII. and Louis XIV. made considerable additions. Their successors, down to Napoleon and Louis Philippe, have also left traces of their affection for the spot, by various improvements and decorations.

The chateau is full of historical associations, and some tragical events. In 1259, Francis I. received the emperor, Charles V., on his visit to France in this palace, when great fêtes and rejoicings were given. In 1602 the Marshal Biron was arrested here, and sent to the Bastille to be executed. In 1657, Christina, queen of Sweden, had the Marquis of Monaldeschi assassinated in one of the apartments. Here, in 1685, Louis XIV. signed the Revocation of the Edict of Nantes, and in the following year the great Condé died at the age of sixty-six. Nearly eighty years afterwards died also, in this chateau, the Dauphin, the only son of Louis XV., and father of Louis XVI., Louis XVIII., and Charles X., of an illness supposed to have been caused by poison. In 1808, Charles IV., of Spain, who had been kidnapped by Napoleon, was confined here 24 days, and, in 1812, Pope Pius VII. suffered the same fate here for nearly two years. In 1809 was pronounced here the declaration of divorce between the emperor and Josephine; and on the 6th of April, 1814, Napoleon, in presence of the remnants of his favourite Garde Impériale signed his abdication in the Court du Cheval Blanc, which, from that circumstance, has received the name of *Cour des Adieux*.

The chateau of Fontainebleau covers nearly thirteen acres of land, without including the external dependencies, the garden, or the park. It is composed of five courts, the *Cour du Cheval Blanc*, the *Cour de la Fontaine*, the *Cour du Donjon*, the *Cour des Princes*, and the *Cour des Cuisines*, or *de Henry IV.*, besides several buildings in different styles. The principal entrance is by the *Cour du Cheval Blanc*, or *des Adieux*, which is 300 feet in length by 100 feet in depth. On the right rises the wing of Louis XV., a long building four stories high; to the left extends the wing of Francis I., only one story in height, formerly appropriated by the ministers of the court. At the bottom is the grand façade, the work of the architects, Vignole and Serlio. In the centre is the celebrated staircase, known as the *Escalier en fer à cheval*, consisting of two flights of steps, and so called because it is in the form of a horse-shoe. It is also called the *Escalier d'Honneur*, and was built by Lemercier in the reign of Louis XIII. It was on these steps that the Emperor Napoleon stood, when he bade adieu to his faithful soldiers in 1814; and it was in this court that, in the March of the following year, he passed in review the troops he was about to lead to Paris and Waterloo.

The court derives its name of *du Cheval Blanc* from an equestrian statue in plaster, a copy of the horse of Marcus Aurelius, which was cast at Rome, and brought to this spot in 1650.

Behind the principal body of the building lies the *Cour de la Fontaine*, surrounded on three sides by the beautiful structures of Serlio, and containing a double staircase leading up to the *Salle de Spectacle*. In the middle is a basin, into which four grotesque heads pour water. From this court the visitor enters into the gardens, from which he sees the beautiful pavilion of Louis XIV. The *Cour du Donjon* follows immediately after, and is so called from the heavy and massive donjon built by Louis IX., which stands at one extremity of the court. Forty-five columns of grey freestone, with capitals quaintly sculptured, support the external balcony. The court is enclosed by a peristyle, pierced by a gateway, designed by Vignole, and surmounted by the graceful baptistery of Louis XIII., by Debrosses. Crossing the foss on the other side, we arrive at the *Cour des Cuisines*, a vast and regular area of buildings, constructed in 1590 by Jamin, for the offices of Henry IV. The *Cour des Princes* is the smallest of the courts, and abutting upon it are the apartments occupied by the Queen Christine.

Having given a description of the plan of the chateau, we will now enter its principal saloons, and point out whatever may be most interesting and curious for the visitor to notice. Entering then the *Wing of Louis XV.* from the *Cour du Cheval Blanc*, the visitor passes through a suite of apartments formerly occupied by the sister of Napoleon, and afterwards by the Duchess de Nemours, and arrives at the *Gallerie des Assiettes* or *des Fresques*, so called from 88 beautiful plates of Sèvres porcelain, representing the principal objects connected with the history of Fontainebleau. It is also celebrated for the fine frescoes painted by Ambroise Dubois, which adorn its ceilings and wainscot. From this gallery, a passage leads to the *Appartements de la Duchesse d'Orléans*, the first salon of which was fitted up as an oratory by Pius VII., during his imprisonment in the palace; a porcelain cabinet in a small room belonging to the suite represents the arrival, reception, and marriage, of the duchess with the late duke. Adjoining is the *Appartement d'Anne d'Autriche*, composed of seven rooms richly decorated. On the ceiling of one of them, the gods of Olympus are represented in relief on gilt wood. In it Charles V. slept during his visit to Francis I., in 1539. The

...salon is admirable for the profusion of architectural ornament with which it is decorated. Passing by the *Salle du Billard*, we arrive at the vestibule, at the foot of the horse-shoe staircase, from which a door leads into the *Chapelle de la Sainte Trinité*, in which the marriage of Louis XV. and the late Duke of Orleans were celebrated. It was built after the designs of Vignola, in the reign of Francis I., on the site of the chapel erected there by St. Louis; but the decorations were not finished till the reign of Louis XIII. The fine paintings on the vault are by Freminet. The high altar is by Bourdonne. The six statues are by Germain Pilon; the Descent from the Cross by Jean Dubois.

Gallerie de François I.—The gallery was embellished by order of the prince, whose name it bears, in 1530, and displays the richness of his taste. It is situated on the first floor, at the bottom of the Cour de la Fontaine. The ceilings and wainscots are of oak and walnut, profusely sculptured and gilded. Fourteen large frescoes by Rosso and Primaticcio, surrounded by bas-reliefs in stucco, adorn the walls. The apartments occupied by Napoleon, and where he signed his abdication the 5th of April, 1814, are entered from the landing-place of the chapel by a staircase. There also is kept a *fac-simile* of the document, and the table on which it was signed. The bed-room of the emperor is in nearly the same condition as he left it. Passing through the *Salle du Conseil* and the *Grande Chambre du Roi*, the visitor is ushered into the *Appartement de la Reine*, consisting of four rooms facing the garden of Diana. The *Chambre de la Reine* is most beautifully decorated, and was successively occupied by Marie de Medicis, Anne d'Autriche, Marie Thérèse, Marie Antoinette, Marie Louise, and the ex-queen of the French, Marie Amélie.

The visitor will now be ushered into the *Gallerie de Diane*, built by Henry IV., and decorated with some fine frescoes by Ambroise Dubois. It was nearly destroyed by the fall of the roof at the beginning of the present century, but in 1807 the rebuilding of it was commenced, after designs by Heurtant, and completed during the reign of Louis XVIII. The paintings on the ceilings are by Abel de Pujol and Blondel. From this gallery we pass on into the *Salons de Reception*, which are nine in number, decorated with a profusion of gilding and painting. These rooms are in the donjon or keep of the chateau, and form the oldest part of the building. It will be impossible to give a detailed description of them all: the principal of them to be observed are the *Salon des Tapisseries*, containing some fine old Flanders tapestry; the three *Salons de François I.*, with a beautiful chimney-piece attributed to Benevuto Cellini; the *Chambre de Henri IV.*, decorated by Ambroise Dubois and Paul Bril; and the *Salle de Louis XIII.*, once occupied by that monarch, but since that time greatly altered. The ceiling is one of the most beautiful specimens of the kind. Adjoining this *appartement* is the *Salle de Spectacle*, established as a theatre by Louis XV., and capable of containing 600 spectators. It is sometimes used for concerts given by the garrison.

Returning to the *Escalier du Roi*, we shall enter the *Appartement de Madame de Maintenon*, fitted up for that celebrated personage by Louis XIV. In one of them, the *Grand Cabinet*, the king signed the Revocation of the Edict of Nantes, and accepted the crown of Spain for his grandson from the Spanish deputies, an act which caused the long and bloody war of the Succession. After this comes the *Gallerie de Henry II.*, built by Francis I., but decorated by Henry II., with great magnificence. This gallery, which is the most splendid room in the chateau, is 120 feet long by 30 in width, and as many in height. It serves as a ball-room. The chamfering of the windows is nine feet in thickness. The walls are painted in frescoes by Primaticcio and Nicolo, which were restored in 1835 by Alaux. Its beautiful chimney-piece is the work of the sculptor, Rondelet. This room, from the luxurious splendour of its fittings up, may be regarded as the finest in the palace.

Having visited the *Library*, formerly the *Haute Chapelle*, we descend to the *Chapelle de St. Saturnin*, between the Donjon and the gardens, which has a peculiar interest for the English visitor, as having been consecrated by Thomas à Becket during his temporary exile in France. It has, however, been frequently restored and ornamented since its consecration in 1169. The subjects of the stained glass windows were proposed by the late Princess Marie, daughter of Louis Philippe. From this we pass on to the *Gallerie des Colonnes*, a vast salon built under the Gallerie de Henri II., and corresponding with it. It is so called from the enormous columns of stucco by which it is ornamented. It was here that the religious part of the ceremony of the marriage of the Duchess of Orleans, according to the Protestant ritual, took place in 1837. Passing through the *Porte Dorée*, a gateway richly ornamented by Rosso and Primaticcio, we arrive at the *Vestibule de St. Louis*, which contains statues of the monarchs, who mainly contributed to embellish or enlarge the chateau, from Louis VII. down to Henri IV., from which we enter twelve rooms called the *Petits Appartements*, in one of which is a painting representing the murder of Monaldeschi. An inscription under the window records the deed as having taken place near the spot. The visitor will now find himself, after quitting these apartments, in the *Vestibule de la Sainte Trinité*, with the *Cour du Cheval Blanc* once more before him.

Having made the round of the interior of the chateau, it will be expedient to lose no time in visiting the gardens. The *Jardin Anglais*, designed and planted by Heurtant, extends along the front of the chateau. There is also another garden laid out by Lenotre, in the old fashioned style of gardening. Across the sward winds a little stream, which takes its source at the Fontaine Belle Eau, and falls into a pond, covering an area of eight acres, to the south of the Cour de la Fontaine. Beyond this is the *park*, containing a great number of pleasant alleys and walks, and a magnificent cascade, which feeds a canal upwards of a mile in length. In the waters of the garden are some fine fish, especially carp, which are kept until they become of an enormous size. But that which the visitor will probably be most anxious to see is the magnificent

Foret-de-Fontainebleau.—The surest and most expeditious way is to hire a vehicle, a number of which are always ready, and to penetrate, under the guidance of the driver, into the heart of the forest. However, to those who would prefer it, there are always saddled horses at hand, and the advantage of these is, that paths may be pursued which it is impossible to follow on wheels. Whichever course the visitor adopts, expedition is necessary. The spots most frequented are the *Hermitage de Franchard*, where was formerly a large monastery, and near which is the *Roche qui pleure*, the waters of which were supposed to have miraculous powers of healing; the *Gorge de Franchard*, a wild and romantic place, consisting of a huge amphitheatre, covered with woods and rocks; the *Gorge d'Apremont*, more magnificent still, inasmuch as it is more extensive, and commands a fine view; the *Caverne des Brigands*, which is situated at the top of the gorge, and was dug about a century and a half ago by robbers, who infested the country, and made this place, then almost inaccessible, their retreat; and the *Valley of the Solle*, near which is the *Cliff of St. Germain*. The view from this spot is very beautiful, and of a softer character than that on the other side of the forest. Standing on the head of the valley, the eye ranges over a fine amphitheatre, covered with oaks and beech, and enclosing a plain, dotted with picturesque villages. The landscape is bounded by a long line of hills, far away beyond the hills that form this beautiful amphitheatre. At the *Cliff of St. Germain*, the stones are nearly all crystalised. There are other places of great beauty to be seen, but as it would be impossible to traverse every part of a forest containing nearly thirty thousand acres in one day, we have pointed out those spots which the visitor may request his guide to take him to. Half way between Fontainebleau and the Gorge of Apremont, is a *carrefour* in the wood, from which several alleys branch off. It is remarkable for the height of the trees that surround it. There is one oak there, especially worth noticing. It rises nearly eighty feet before throwing off a branch.

We will now suppose the visitor returned to Fontainebleau, and will only warn him that the last train leaves at 8 13 p.m. for Paris.

TENTH DAY.

RUE ST. ANTOINE—ST. PIERRE ET ST. PAUL—FONTAINE ST. ANTOINE—HOTEL DE SULLY—TEMPLE PROTESTANTE—ARSENAL—GRENIER DE RESERVE—PONT D'AUSTERLITZ—JARDIN DES PLANTES—HALLE AUX VINS—MANUFACTURE DES GOBELINS.

We wish this day, the tenth and last that we shall have, especially to direct his steps, to guide the visitor to a part of the city he has not yet visited, and to two objects of considerable interest, the *Jardin des Plantes*, and the *Manufacture des Tapisseries des Gobelins*, which he has not yet seen. It will, therefore, be advisable for him to make his way to the Hotel de Ville, behind which and the Caserne Napoleone, is the rue St. Antoine. This street, besides possessing some fine specimens of domestic architecture of the middle ages, acquires great interest, from the political events of which it has been the theatre. It is also the centre of the protestant quarter of Paris, and contains a large number both of Lutherans and Calvinists.

On the right, as he descends, the visitor will see the Lycée Charlemagne, a college established on the site of an old Jesuit college, which was founded in 1582, and suppressed during the first revolution. Next to this is the church of *St. Paul and St. Louis*, began in 1627, and finished in 1641, in which year Cardinal Richelieu consecrated it in presence of Louis XIII. and his court. It is one of the finest in Paris, and built on an elevated platform, approached by a flight of steps. The façade is decorated with three orders of architecture, placed one above the other, of which, the two lowest are Corinthian, and the upper composite. The interior is richly embellished with architectural ornaments and sculpture. The chapel of the Virgin is entirely ornamented with marble. This church suffered greatly during the revolution of 1789, when several of its finest decorations were destroyed; it has, however, in some measure recovered the injury it then received. Opposite the church is the Fontaine St. Antoine, consisting of a sexagonal pavi-

..., surmounted with a dome, and crowned by a campanile. An inscription on the south side intimates that it was erected by the prefect and town council, to give fresh water to the inhabitants.

Further on, at No. 148, is the *Hotel de Sully*, the mansion occupied formerly by that celebrated minister. It is a fine specimen of the time in which it was built, as it is still in good preservation. Proceeding further up the street, the visitor will come upon the *Temple Protestante*, or chapel belonging to the French protestants, of the Calvinistic persuasion. It was built formerly by Mansard, for the Dames de la Visitation, whose convent was destroyed in 1789. Service is performed here every Sunday, in French, at half-past Twelve.

Passing down the Rue Petit Musc, which is the first to the west of the *Temple Protestante*, we shall arrive at the *Rue de Sully*, in which is

The Arsenal.—On this site, the city of Paris established a depôt for artillery and munitions of war, in 1396, which afterwards became national property; but a fearful explosion having taken place in 1563, the building was reconstructed on a larger scale. Henri IV. also had it enlarged, and added a garden, and created the office of grand-master of the artillery, which he bestowed on Sully. Louis XIV. transferred the casting of cannon to the frontiers of his kingdom, so that the only use to which the present establishment was put, was that of casting statues for the gardens of Versailles, &c.

It possesses, however, a very rich library, called the *Bibliothèque de l'Arsenal*, to which the public is admitted every day (Sundays and fête days excepted), from ten to three. It contains about two hundred thousand printed volumes, and six thousand three hundred manuscripts. The works are chiefly on history, foreign literature, and poetry. It is especially valuable for its collection of Italian authors. It was formerly called Bibliothèque de Paulmy, being originally formed by the Marquis de Paulmy. It was afterwards named *Bibliothèque de Monsieur*, having been purchased by Charles X., whilst count of Artois, but since 1830 it has received the name of Bibliothèque de l'Arsenal.

The rooms in which Sully was accustomed to receive Henry IV. are still shewn. Apply with passport, to the director, at the bureau.

Passing down the Rue Morny, we arrive at the *Grenier de Reserve*, a building commenced by Napoleon, in 1807. His object in constructing this immense building, which is two thousand one hundred and sixty feet in length, was to have collected there, a sufficient quantity of grain and flour, to provide Paris for four months against the contingency of want. It was to have had five stories, besides cellars and attics. However, only the ground floor was finished when he abdicated in 1814, and the original plan being abandoned, what had been built was roofed in, and divided into three stories. Four water channels, for turning mills, were also cut underneath the cellars. The government requires every baker to keep constantly twenty full-sized sacks of flour in this storehouse, and he can add to this, any quantity he likes, on payment of a small charge, as the building is capable of containing one hundred thousand sacks. The cellarage is sometimes used as a supplementary depôt for wine. Application for admission must be made at the bureau, in the *Place de l'Arsenal*. Continuing down the Rue Crillon, towards the river, and taking the left, we arrive at

The Pont d'Austerlitz.—A fine cast-iron bridge, consisting of five arches, supported by piers and butments of stone, placed on piles. It was begun in 1801, and finished in 1807 at a cost of one hundred and twenty thousand pounds. It is four hundred feet in length, and fifty-six in breadth. It was undertaken

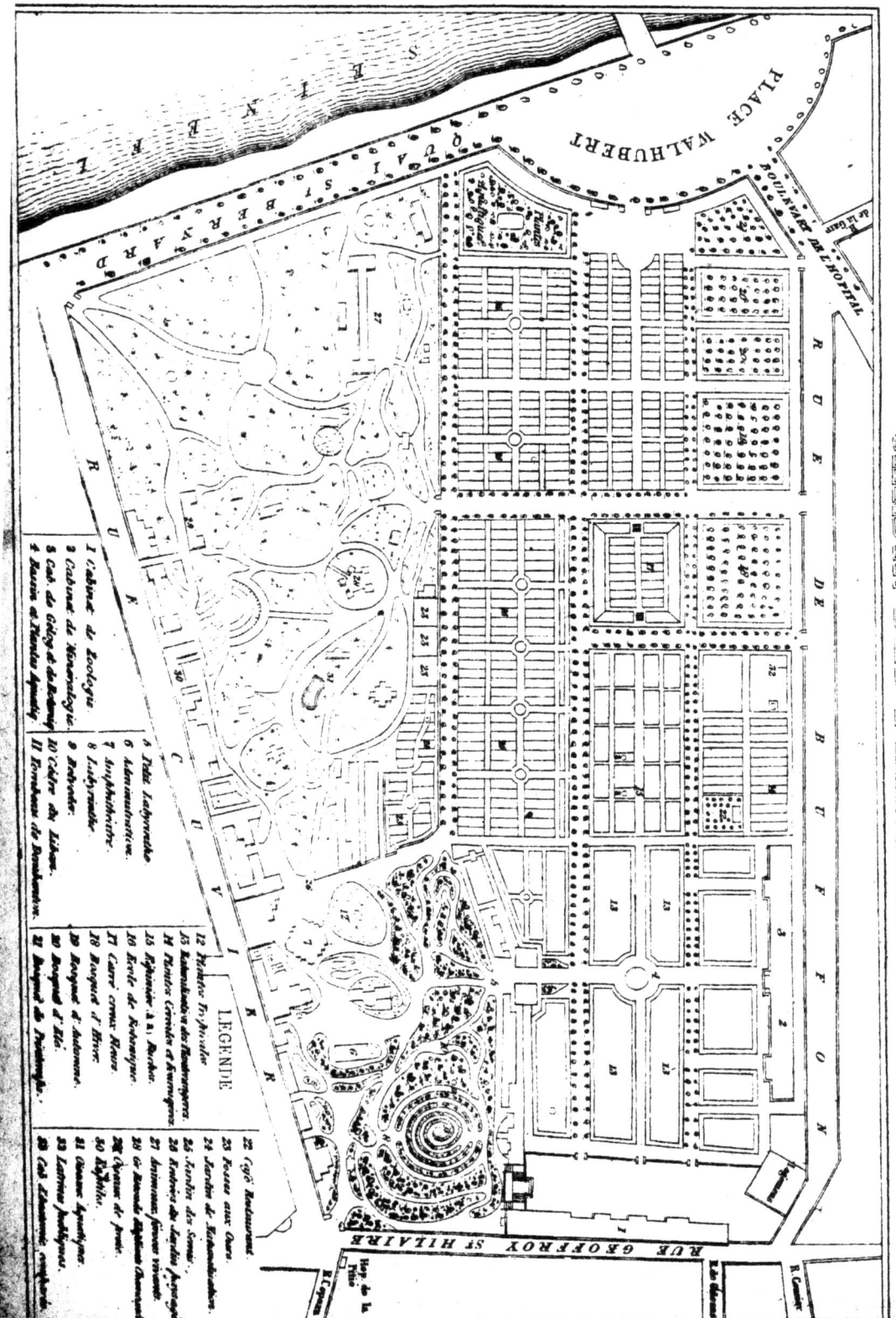

JARDIN DES PLANTES.

LÉGENDE

1 Cabinet de Zoologie
2 Cabinet de Minéralogie
3 Cab. de Géol. et de Botaniq.
4 Bassin et Plantes Aquatiques
5 Petit Labyrinthe
6 Administration
7 Amphithéâtre
8 Labyrinthe
9 Belvédère
10 Cèdre du Liban
11 Fontaine de Pradicrou
12 Rotonde Impériale
13 Éducation des Mûriers
14 Plantes Céréales et Fourragères
15 Epinière à la Berbère
16 École de Botanique
17 Carré aux Roses
18 Vergers d'Hiver
19 Vergers d'Été
20 Vergers d'Automne
21 Vergers d'Été
22 Vergers de Printemps
23 Café Restaurant
24 Fosse aux Ours
25 Jardin de Rafraîchissement
26 Entrée du Soir
27 Entrée du Jardin principal
28 Nouveaux grands Serres
29 Ci devant Grande Serre
30 Cages de paon
31 Rotonde
32 Oiseaux Aquatiques
33 Lettres publiques
34 Col. Linéaires antiques

of a company, who were to keep it in repair for twenty years, and receive toll during that same time. In 1848, however, the bridge was thrown open, free to foot passengers. From this bridge, looking westward, a fine view of the back of Notre Dame, the Hôtel de Ville, the Pantheon, and different parts of the city may be obtained. Looking up the river, the eye follows it through Bercy, nearly to where the Seine joins the beautiful Marne. Opposite the Pont d'Austerlitz, is the principal entrance into the

Jardin des Plantes.—This botanical and horticultural garden was established by Louis XIII, in 1635, at the instigation of his physician, Guy de la Brosse, and contained then only seventy acres. Buffon, who was named superintendent of it in 1729, devoted himself to it, and enriched it by valuable additions. He collected here, from all parts, the most varied productions of nature, and established its museums, its galleries, and its hot-houses. All the dispositions of the gardens were his work. But, after him, the place languished until Bonaparte gave it a new impulse, and filled its flower-beds and museums with collections despotically brought from other countries. These were, however, restored in 1814, and the support of the gardens has been since provided for by an annual grant of the government. Here may be seen nearly every known kind of flower and shrub and tree, native or exotic, in existence, from the smallest bush, to the gigantic cedar of Lebanon, besides a variety of birds, beasts, and fishes, which represent the different species of the animal kingdom.

Besides these gardens and collection of living animals, there are also museums of geology, botany, comparative anatomy, and zoology; a fine scientific library, laboratories, and an amphitheatre, where lectures upon the different branches of natural history are delivered to the students of the university or others, whose business or inclination leads to pursue either of these studies. The buildings are complete for the development of that science, which Buffon and Cuvier so largely contributed to.

In the centre of the garden is a conical mound, on the summit of which is a pavilion, made of bronze, from which a fine view of this part of Paris, and the eastern environs may be had. All the prominent objects, that from the Arc de l'Etoile were indistinct, now become clearly visible; and the columns at the Barrière du Trône; the towers and wood of Vincennes; the heights of Belleville; and the landscape towards Sceaux and Fontenai-aux-Roses, may easily be distinguished. On one of the pillars of the pavilion is a sun-dial, above which is inscribed, the motto—*non numero nisi serenas*. Half-way up the ascent, is the fine cedar brought from Lebanon by an English physician, and planted where it now stands, in 1734. The gardens are open every day, from morning till sunset, but the animals can only be seen from eleven to three. The *Musée de l'Histoire Naturelle* is only to be seen on Tuesdays and Fridays by the public, but with a passport, admission is easy every day. The bureau for tickets is near the *Musée d'Anatomie Comparative*.

To the west of the Jardin des Plantes, is the *Halle-aux-Vins*, an extensive market for wines, covering an area of one hundred and thirty-four thousand square yards, and disposed to receive and store two hundred thousand pieces of wine. It was commenced by order of Napoleon, in 1803, on the site of the ancient abbey of St. Victor. The front facing the quay, from which it is separated by a very fine railing, measures eight hundred yards in length. Two pavilions, placed on either side of the façade, are occupied by the administration, and persons connected with the surveillance of the entrance and exit of wines. The interior is composed of five large masses of building, divided into streets, called after the names of different wines, as Rue de Languedoc, Rue de Bordeaux, Rue de Bourgogne, &c. These buildings serve for magazines, cellars, and halls. There are upwards of fifty magasins. Along the quay-side, are arranged, small offices, which form the counting-houses of the merchants. It is estimated that the Halle may contain four hundred and fifty-thousand casks, and sometimes as many as one thousand five hundred casks enter in one day. Behind is a warehouse for spirits. The public is admitted at all hours in the day.

One of the most interesting objects to be seen of its kind in Paris, and which we have left unavoidably to the last, is the

Manufacture des Tapisseries des Gobelins, No. 270, Rue Mouffetard, the reputation of which has long been universal. The best way to reach it from the gardens, is by taking the Rues Geoffry and Censier, the first of which runs at the back of the gardens. This manufactory was originated by John Gobelin, in 1450, who established here a celebrated dyeing factory. Afterwards, his successors brought from Flanders, the art of making tapestry—and in 1655, M. Gluck introduced the art of dyeing wool and cloths of a scarlet colour. Under Louis XIV. it received still greater development—the establishment became a *royal manufactory*, and the direction of it was given by the great Colbert to the celebrated painter Lebrun: from that time it has obtained a very high degree of perfection. Lately the *Savonnerie*, so renowned for the richness and variety of its products in carpets, and originally founded by Catherine de Medicis, has formed part of the establishment.

On entering, the visitor is introduced into rooms filled with specimens of tapestry, and then into the rooms, six in number, where the looms are fixed. There are altogether twenty-five looms. It is scarcely possible to conceive, how, by the simple process of weaving, the effects of painting, with all its purity and fineness of colouring, may be reproduced, with almost perfect exactness. The carpets take sometimes from five to ten years in making, and cost from one thousand four hundred, to six thousand pounds. The largest carpet ever made, measured one thousand three hundred feet, and consisted of sixty-two pieces. Not more than six hundred and twenty workmen are employed in this manufactory, who earn from sixty to one hundred pounds a year. When they are disabled by age or infirmities, they are allowed to retire on a pension of from twenty-four to forty pounds a year.

Visitors are admitted on Wednesdays and Saturdays, from two to six in summer, and from two to four in winter.

An omnibus will always be found outside the manufactory, which, by correspondence, will take the visitor to any part of Paris he may wish.

ENVIRONS OF PARIS.

To give a greater efficiency to this work, we subjoin a few of those spots in the neighbourhood of Paris, which, if the stranger have time, will amply repay a visit. To each will be given its peculiar feature of attraction.

Asniéres.—This place is situated on the left bank of the Seine, about five miles from Paris, and contains about 1200 inhabitants. It is noted for the beauty of its position, and the elegance of its houses, which become in summer the residences of wealthy Parisians. The park of Asniéres is celebrated for its gay amusements, fireworks, illuminations, concerts and balls, taking place there Sundays and fête-days. It is at Asniéres also that the boat-racing, a sport which is becoming much in vogue with the French people, takes place. It is reached by the Chemin-de-fer de St. Germain, Place du Havre.

Belleville.—This place, situated on the hills to the north-east of Paris, is much frequented on Sundays. From it may be obtained a fine view of the City. It contains about 24,925 inhabitants, and lies just outside the barrier-walls.

The omnibuses *Les Citadines* and *Les Excellentes* will take you there.

Bougival, pleasantly situated on a hill that rises above the Seine. It is one of the most romantic spots in the neighbourhood of Paris. The road leading from Bougival to Louvecienne is very picturesque, and on either side may be seen numerous country seats, amongst them the Chateau of Madame Dubarry, the Chateau of the Count Hocquart, and the Chateau de la Jonction. It is about 10 miles from Paris, and contains about 1,400 inhabitants. Route—Chemin-de-Fer de St. Germain.

Enghien.—About the same distance from Paris as Bougival, but on the great northern road. It is situated on the borders of a lake, whose mineral waters have long been celebrated. This lake is very beautiful, and surrounded with cottages romantically built. The afternoon of a fine day spent on its bosom, and in the bowers which are erected around it, will be found very agreeable. Route—Chemin-de-Fer du Nord.

St. Germain.—It would be a great omission on the part of any person who has the time, to fail in visiting this town, so celebrated as it is for its historical associations, and the beauty of the scenery of which it commands a view. Before the eleventh century there was no other habitation in the vast forest that covered this spot than a small chapel, dedicated to St. Germain. This was enlarged into a monastery, and in the 12th century, Louis Le Gros erected a chateau near it. This chateau was destroyed by the English, in 1346. It was rebuilt, but several times plundered by the English and Armagnacs, after which, it was left neglected until Francis 1st., taking a fancy to the spot, repaired the chateau and celebrated his marriage there. Henry II., however, laid the foundation of a new chateau, to which Charles IX. and his Court retired from the religious disturbances of the city. Henry IV. and Marie de Medicis took up their residences in the new building, whilst the old was repaired and fitted up, by the king's orders, for the beautiful Gabrielle d'Astrées. The magnificent Terrace, from whence an extensive prospect may be obtained, was laid out during this reign. Louis XIII. used St. Germain as his favourite residence, as did, likewise, Louis XIV., until the Chateau of Versailles was ready for his reception. After this, the Palace found an occupant in the dethroned King James II., to whom it was allotted by his generous friend. During the revolution of 1789 it was divided into the residences of private individuals, and during the empire became a cavalry barrack; after the restoration it was occupied by a company of the life-guards, but is now used as a military prison.

The terrace, which is everywhere celebrated for the magnificence of its view, is between two and three miles long, and looks down upon the winding Seine. Behind this commences the noble forest of St. Germain. The only remains of the Chateau Neuf, as it is called, is a tower in which Louis XIV. was born, now converted into a restaurant, under the name of the *Pavilion of Henry IV*. In the church on the *Place de Chateau*, is a monument erected by the late King George IV., to the memory of James II. It stands in a small chapel near the doorway, to the right on entering.

St. Germain is about 15 miles from Paris, with a population of about 13,000. A part of the railway from Pecq to St. Germain is on the atmospheric principle. Station, Place du Havre.

Joinville. Situated about six miles from Paris, and commanding a fine view of the Marne and the country beyond it. The road to it lies through Vincennes and the woods of Vincennes and Joinville. Omnibuses rom the Place de la Bastille may be found to take the visitor there.

Montmartre. Though lying outside the barrier-wall, Montmartre may almost be said to be a part of Paris. It derives its name of Montmartre, or Mons Martyrum, from the execution of St. Denis and his companions, which took place here. Its great height above the city makes it a favourable point from which to obtain a coup d'œil of the streets and public buildings of Paris. In a valley to the west of the hill is situated the cemetery of Montmartre, which may rival in the beauty of its position the cemetery of Père la Chaise. It contains, too, the remains of several celebrated personages.

Neuilly. About a mile and a half beyond the Barrière de l'Etoile stands the village of Neuilly, on the left bank of the Seine. It is elegantly built, and of rather modern date. From the bridge that here crosses the river, a fine view may be had of the islands with which it is sown, and the country seats that line its banks. The principal object, however, to be seen is the Chateau de Neuilly, situated in a beautiful park, the residence of the late royal family. The palace was built in the reign of Louis XV., when, and until the revolution, it belonged to private individuals. After that time it passed to M. Talleyrand; then to the Prince Murat and the Princess Borghese; and finally to Louis Philippe and his family. In February, 1848, this beautiful palace was nearly destroyed by a body of revolutionists, who left Paris, and breaking into it, gave themselves up to all kinds of scenes of destruction, riot, and drunkenness.

Half way between Neuilly and the Arc de l'Etoile, near the Porte Maillot, is the chapel erected by the late King of the French to the Duke of Orleans, on the spot where that unfortunate prince was accidentally killed. The interior is well worth examination. Amongst the group of statuary are two figures, beautifully executed, by Marie the lamented sister of the duke.

St. Ouen, situated 5½ miles from Paris on the right bank of the Seine. It was here that King Dagobert is supposed to have fixed his residence. In 1351 King John instituted in the palace the military and chivalrous order, afterwards so distinguished under the title of *Knights of Malta.* In 1482 Louis XI. annexed the royal property here to the Abbey of St. Denis, that its monks might pray for a prolongation of his life. It should be observed that the superstitious monarch died the next day. The chateau, from this time, passed through various hands, until it became the residence of Madame de Pompadour, who exhausted considerable sums in embellishing it. In 1814 Louis XVIII. sojourned here the evening before his entry into Paris, and signed the declaration called the Declaration of St. Ouen.

Close by is another chateau, formerly the property of M. Necker, where his daughter, afterwards the celebrated Madame de Stael, was born.

Rueil.—About 10 miles from Paris, with a population of 7,000. It is situated at the foot of a beautiful hill, covered with vines and fruit trees. It was here that Cardinal Richelieu had his residence during the stormiest period of his political career. Near to Rueil is the beautiful palace of Malmaison, so closely and dearly associated with the name of the beautiful Josephine. In the church of this village (where a beautiful monument is erected to her memory) the empress lies buried.

Sceaux.—The town of Sceaux now offers little of the attractions it did formerly. A chateau was built here by the celebrated Colbert, embellished with sculptures by Pujet and Girardon, and surrounded by a garden laid out by Lenôtre. This chateau was purchased in 1700 by the Duke du Maine, who enlarged and adorned it at an immense cost. As he and his son were men of enlightenment and taste, this chateau became the resort of the most distinguished literary men of the age, as well as of the most fashionable society of Paris. The revolution of 1798 put an end, however, to the splendour and magnificence of this establishment, the building was destroyed, and the grounds suffered to run to waste. Recently, however, the Maire of the place has purchased the park for the use of the inhabitants, and here several fêtes and festivals are held.

The railway from Paris to Sceaux is an experimental one. The object is to ascertain in how small a curve, and up how steep an ascent, a train may be conducted. The visitor will, therefore, be surprised to find himself winding up a steep hill, and turning very sharp angles, but he need be under no apprehension, as though the result has not been satisfactory for general purposes, the transit has been proved to be safe.

About a mile beyond Sceaux is a restaurant situated in a wood, called *Robinson.* To this place vast numbers of the Parisians flock. The principal attraction is a chesnut tree, sufficiently large to hold two pavilions, and upwards of 15 or 16 persons. From these pavilions, in which the visitor may dine, an extensive view of Paris and the intervening country may be had. Throughout the gardens numerous bowers and seats are distributed.

Route. Chemin-de-Fer de Sceaux. Barrière d'Enfer.

ADDRESSES OF EMBASSIES AND CONSULATES IN PARIS.

Embassies.

Austria, Rue de Grenelle St. Germain, 87.
Baden, Rue de la Ville-l'Evêque, 17.
Bavaria, Rue d'Aguesseau, 15.
Belgium, Rue de la Pépinière, 97.
Bolivia, Rue Laffitte, 31.
Brazil, Rue de la Pépinière, 106.
Central America or Guatemala, Rue de Provence, 21.
Chili, Rue de l'Université, 69.
Denmark, Rue de la Pépinière, 88.
England, Rue du Faubourg St. Honoré, 39.
Greece, Rue d'Anjou St. Honoré, 78.
Haïti, Chargé d'affaires, Place de la Madeleine
Hanover, Rue de la Ville-l'Evêque, 26.
Hanse Towns, Rue Trudon, 6.
Hesse-Darmstadt, Rue du Luxembourg, 25.
Hesse Electoral, Rue de Ménars, 4.
Mecklenburg-Schwerin, Rue du Faubourg St. Honoré, 35.
Mecklenburg-Strelitz and Saxe-Weimar, Rue Coumartin, 7.
Mexico, Rue de Tivoli, 10.
Naples, Rue du Faubourg St. Honoré, 47.
Nassau, Rue de la Ville-l'Evêque, 10.
Netherlands, Rue de Suresnes, 28.
Parma, Rue St. Dominique, 121.
Portugal, Rue de Lille, 77.
Prussia, Rue de Lille, 78.
Russia, Rue du Faubourg St. Honoré, 33.
Roman States, Nonciature, Rue de l'Université, 63.
Sardinia, Rue St. Dominique, 133.
Saxony, Rue du Faubourg St. Honoré, 179.
Sweden, Rue d'Anjou St. Honoré, 74.
Spain, Rue de la Chaussée d'Antin, 45.
Switzerland, Rue Chauchat, 9.
Tuscany, Rue Caumartin, 3.
Turkey, Rue des Champs-Elysées, 3.
United States, Rue de Matignon, 19.
Wurtemberg, Rue d'Aguesseau, 13.

Consulates.

Argentine Confederation, Rue St. Georges, 35.
Austria, Rue Laffitte, 19.
Brazil, Rue Castellane, 10.
Chili, Rue St. Lazare, 31.
Denmark, Rue de Trévise, 29.
England, Rue du Faubourg St. Honoré, 39.
Ecuador (Republic of), Rue du Sentier, 12.
Greece, Rue Basse-du-Rempart, 30.
Hanse Towns, Rue de Ménars, 4.
Holstein-Oldenburg, Rue St. Georges, 13.
Mexico, Rue Neuve St. Augustin, 50
Netherlands, Rue du Faubourg St. Honoré.
Peru, Rue St. Lazare, 31.
Persia, Rue St. Honoré, 371.
Portugal, Rue Louis-le Grand, 25.
Russia, Rue du Faubourg St. Honoré, 33.
Sweden and Norway, Rue Laffitte, 29.
Spain, Rue Miromesnil, 30.
Turkey, Rue de la Chaussée-d'Antin, 68.
United States, Boulevard des Italiens, 27.
Venezuela (Republic of), Rue du Faubourg-Poissonnière, 32.

FORTIFICATIONS.

Since the Revolution of 1789, the project of building fortifications round Paris, has been several times entertained. After the disasters of 1815, Napoleon expressed at St. Helena bitter regret at the Parisians having been forced to open their gates to the allied armies, for want of sufficient protection, and he repeated the regret in the *Mémorial de Sainte-Hélène*.

At length, after long parliamentary debates, the fortifications were voted in 1841. The building of them cost 140,000,000 fr. They form a gigantic undertaking.

They consist:

1. Of an *enceinte continue* of about 38 kilometres in length, which extends on the two banks of the Seine, surmounted with bastions, and terraces, and a wall 10 metres thick;

2. Of seventeen detached forts with several fosses. The whole is united by strategic roads.

The following is a list of the detached forts: Charenton, Nogent, Rosny, Noisy, Romainville, Aubervilliers, Est, Couronne du Nord, la Briche, Mont Valérien, Vanves, Issy, Montrouge, Bicêtre, Ivry, Stains, Rouvray.

The fort of Vincennes has also been strengthened.

GENERAL POST OFFICE.
RUE J. J. ROUSSEAU, 9.

In Paris there are seven deliveries of letters on week days and five on Sundays. There are two mails from England daily; letters by the earlier arrival (comprising London letters chiefly) before twelve.

As in England, the postage is paid by affixing stamps, which can be obtained at the post-offices, at tobacconists', and at most stationers' shops; the stamps are of the value of 5c., 10c., 20c., 40c., and 1fr. Those at 5c. are used for franking newspapers for England, France, or elsewhere. The postage of a single paid letter to England is 40c. (4d.), but if unpaid, the person receiving it will have to pay 8d. Letters may be posted for England to half-past 5 o'clock at the General Post-office, and till 5 at the Bourse, for the night's mail; at the receiving-houses till half past 3 only; at the district offices with their branches till 4 o'clock.

BUREAU A. Rue Saint-Honoré, 12.
BUREAU B. Boul'ev. Beaumarchais, 29.
— C. Rue du Grand-Chantier, 5.
— D. Rue de l'Echiquier, 26.
— E. Rue de Sèze, 24.
— F. Rue de Beaune, 8.
— G. Rue de Seine.
— H. Rue des Fossés-Saint-Victor, 35.
— J. Place de la Bourse.
— K. Rue de Rivoli, 10 bis.
— L. Au Luxembourg, Rue de Vaugirard, 19

Bureau du Corps législatif, Rue de Bourgogne.

ANNEXES, Rue Neuve-Bourg-l'Abbé, 1; Hôtel de Ville.
— Rue du Faubourg-Saint Antoine, 196.
— Rue Folie-Méricourt, 12.
— Faubourg-Saint-Martin, 162; Place Lafayette, 5.
— Faubourg Saint Honoré, 175; Rue de Londres 33.
— Petite Rue du Bac; Rue Saint-Dominique, 148.
— Rue de la Sainte-Chapelle, 15.
— Boulevard de l'Hôpital, 5; Rue Saint-Louis-en-l'Ile, 29.
— Rue Bourdaloue, 5.
— Rue de Chaillot, 6.

At the office, 22, Place Lafayette, letters for England, Belgium, etc., may be posted till 7 o'clock for the same night's mail.

The postage of letters in Paris is 10c. (1d.) prepaid, 15c. (1½d.) if unpaid. The uniform postage of pre-paid letters for all France is 20c. (2d.), unpaid one-half more.

LIST OF CUSTOMS DUTIES.

Payable in London, or at any Sea Port in the United Kingdom, on articles imported from the Continent, according to the last new Tariff.

THE FOLLOWING ARE ALL FREE OF DUTY:—

Bronze Works of Art.
Coins and Medals of all kinds.
Diamonds and other precious stones *not* set.
Flower Roots.
Furs and Skins.
Maps and Charts.
Mineral Water.
Pictures, Sketches, Drawings, or Sculpture, on a declaration by the Proprietor (being British Subject) that they are of his or her performance, and not intended for sale.
Vases, Ancient, not of stone or wood.

CUSTOMS DUTIES.

On the following the Duty is 10 per cent. *ad valorem*:—

Brass or Bronze Manufactures, not being Works of Art, such as Inkstands, Candelabra, and Articles of Furniture.
Cashmere Shawls, and other Articles and Manufactures of Goats' Wool.
China, or Porcelain Wares, painted or plain, gilt or ornamented, and Earthenware.
Clocks and Watches (must have the Maker's name, both on face, and on works.)
Frames for Pictures, &c.
Furniture.
Furs and Skins, all articles made up.
Jewellery.
Lace, viz.—Thread Lace, also Lace made by the hand, commonly called Cushion or Pillow Lace, whether of Linen, Cotton or Silken Thread.
Linen Articles, wholly or in part made up.
Musical Instruments.
Perfumery.

Plate of Gold or Silver, gilt or ungilt, in addition to 10 per cent., is liable to 1s. 6d. per oz. Stamp Duty.

LIST OF DUTIES CONTINUED.

	£	s.	d.
Books of Editions printed prior to 1801, the cwt.	1	0	0
In or since 1801, in foreign Living Languages, ditto	2	10	0
In the Dead Languages, or in the English Language, printed out of England in or since 1801, ditto	5	0	0
(N.B.—Pirated Editions of English works, of which the Copyright exists in England, totally prohibited since April, 1843)			
Boots, Ladies' untrimmed, the dozen pair	0	6	0
Boots, Men's ditto, ditto	0	14	0
Shoes, ditto ditto, ditto	0	7	0
„ Ladies' ditto, ditto	0	4	0
Cigars and Tobacco, manufactured (3lb. only allowed for passenger's baggage), the lb.	0	9	0
Tobacco, unmanufactured, ditto	0	3	0
(N.B.—Unmanufactured Tobacco cannot be imported in less quantity than 300 lb., or Cigars 100 lb. in a package; but small quantities are admitted for private use on declaration and payment of a fine of 1s. 6d. per lb. in addition to the duty.)			
Cordials and Liquors (for bottles, see Wine), the gallon	1	10	4
Eau de Cologne, in long flasks, the flask	0	1	0
(N.B.—If other than the ordinary long flask, 30s. 4d. per gallon and the Bottle Duty.)			
Embroidery and Needlework, for every £100 value	15	0	0
Flowers, Artificial, ditto	25	0	0
Glass—Wine Glasses, &c., the lb.	0	0	1
Gloves, Leather (not less than 100 doz. pairs can be imported in one package), the doz. pair	0	3	6
Marble, manufactured, the cwt.	0	3	0
Paper Hangings, the square yard	0	0	2
Pictures, each	0	1	0
And further, the square foot	0	1	0
Prints and Drawings, plain or coloured, single, each	0	0	1
Silk, Millinery, Turbans or Caps, each	0	3	6
„ Hats or Bonnets, ditto	0	7	0
„ Dresses, ditto	1	10	0
Hangings, and other Manufactures of Silk, for every £100 value	15	0	0
Velvet, plain or figured, the lb.	0	9	0
„ Articles thereof, ditto	0	10	0
Tea, the lb.	0	2	1
Wine in Casks, all except Cape wine, the gallon	0	5	6
Wine in Bottles, ditto	0	5	6
And further on the Bottles, the cwt.	0	0	9
Spirits in Casks (no Cask can be imported of less contents than twenty gallons), the gallon	0	15	0
Spirits in Bottles (the additional Duty on the Bottles, as on Wine Bottles).			

ADVERTISEMENTS.

H. P. TRUEFITT'S

THE TOILET CLUB

HAIR CUTTING SALOON,

20 & 21, BURLINGTON ARCADE.

The magnificent Saloon, for which this Establishment has always been famous, has just been re-decorated, and fitted with every requirement and comfort, in a style unequalled for business purposes. An Annual Subscription of **10s. 6d.**, or **1s.** for a Single Attendance, includes Hair Cutting, Use of Papers, Periodicals, &c. Private Rooms if preferred.

TO WIG WEARERS.

H. P. TRUEFITT can offer advantages not attainable in any other Establishment, and would particularly notice several recent improvements.

CERTAINTY IN DYEING THE HAIR

Is at last thoroughly effected by the "TINCTURA," a fragrant extract, by which any shade of Brown or Black is produced instantly and permanently. Those who have been deceived by any of the Dyes in use at present will appreciate the value of this happy discovery.

PRIVATE ROOMS, replete with every convenience, are reserved for its application.

N.B.—The Nos. are 20 & 21 only.

MOUSTACHES.

THE SARDINIAN POMADE,

The same as used by the KING OF SARDINIA, is the only article which, by fixing the Moustache or Whisker, gradually trains the growth in the desired form. In stopper'd bottles 2s. each. Colour: White, Brown and Black.

Sold Wholesale and Retail only by H. P. TRUEFITT, 20 and 21, Burlington Arcade. [2-Lo

ANTWERP.

HOTEL ST. ANTOINE, PLACE VERTE; MR. SCHMIDT SPAENHOEVEN, Proprietor. English Travellers will find this Establishment deserving their patronage, and equal to the best of English Hotels, combining comfort with superior accommodation, but at Continental prices. [M.

BRUSSELS.

THE GRAND HOTEL DE SAXE, RUE NEUVE, 79, is admirably situated, near the Boulevards, Theatres, and Railway Stations, and offers to Families and Single Travellers spacious, comfortable and airy apartments, newly furnished and decorated. There is also a garden for the use of visitors.
FIXED PRICES.—Breakfast, 1 franc. Table d'Hôte at half past four o'clock, 3 francs. Sitting Rooms, 3 to 5 francs. Bed-rooms, 1½ to 2½ francs. Excellent Wines, and good attendance. [M.

PARIS.

GRAND HOTEL DE FRANCE and D'ANGLETERRE.—IMPORTANT NOTICE TO TRAVELLERS VISITING PARIS.
EXTRACT FROM THE "*Independance Belge.*"
"To Travellers visiting Paris we can particularly recommend the Grand Hotel de France and d'Angleterre, 72, Rue Richelieu, and Rue des Filles St. Thomas, situated on the side of the Bourse, the Palais Royal, the Boulevards, and the Theatres."
Irrespective of its admirable situation, Travellers will find at this splendid Hotel one of the best Table d'Hôtes in Paris, at 4 francs, including a bottle of Bordeaux. Excellent private Dinners at all hours, from 3 to 4 and 5 francs. Comfortable Bed-rooms at 2, 3, 4, or 5 francs, and upwards. [M.

HOTEL DES ETRANGERS, 3, RUE VIVIENNE, M. GIRARD, PROPRIETOR, near the Palais Royal, the Bourse, the Boulevards, and the Theatres. Restaurant—Table d'Hôte, 4 francs. Large and small well-furnished apartments. Bed-rooms at 2, 3, or 4 francs. French, English, and German newspapers. M. GIRARD requests Gentlemen and Families who are recommended to this Hotel not to allow themselves to be misled by touters or other interested persons, who frequently deceive passengers by conducting them to other establishments of the same name as the above respectable Hotel. [M.

HOTEL DE NORMANDIE, 240, RUE ST. HONORE.—The above Hotel possesses advantages for Travellers rarely to be met with. It is in the vicinity of the principal Public Establishments, in the most favourable situation for pleasure as well as business, and it is the constant aim of the Proprietor to merit patronage by affording every comfort at the most moderate charges. N.B.—English spoken by the landlord and servants. [M.

CUVILLIER, 16, RUE DE LA PAIX.
GENERAL PROVISION WAREHOUSE,
Agents to MESSRS. DOMECQ, of Xeres de la Frontera.

Wines, Guiness' Stout, Ales, Teas, Groceries, Pickles, Sauces, and Sundries from all parts of the World. Orders taken in Town. Exportation. [M.

MADAME CLEMENCON,

STAYMAKER to several Courts. It is to this house that we owe the invention of the "*Corps Pompadour,*" so necessary to stout persons; and the "*demi corps chatelaine,*" which gives so much grace, elegance, and dignity. MADAME CLEMENCON, as mistress of her profession, is capable of affording additional grace to every form, and of combining all the freedom required for the promotion of health. [M.

PARIS—Continued.

BRITISH ACADEMY.

LEMONIER, ARTISTS, DESIGNERS, AND JEWELLERS IN HAIR.

Prize Medal at the London Exhibition, and Gold Medal at the Paris Exhibition.

New models for bracelets, brooches, rings, watch-guards, necklaces, bouquets, and cyphers. 10, Boulevards des Italiens, corner of the Passage de l'Opera, formerly Rue du Coq, St. Honoré. [M.

ARTIFICIAL FLOWERS.—TILMAN, 104, RUE RICHELIEU.—Purveyor, by letters patent, to Her Imperial Majesty, the Empress. Manufactory and Warehouse for flowers, hair dresses, and trimmings for dresses, Ladies' ball and wedding head-dresses, court ornaments.

The *Page-Agrafas*, or patent hook, for holding up Ladies' dresses in bad weather, can be had at this establishment. [M.

STRASBOURG.

GRAND HOTEL DE LA FLEUR.—W. A. DOERR, Proprietor. In a centrical situation, near the Cathedral. Table d'Hote at One and Five o'Clock. Travellers will find the accommodation combines elegance with comfort and prompt attendance. Excellent cuisine and good apartments. This Hotel is celebrated as having been inhabited by the principal persons connected with the project of Prince Napoleon in 1836. The apartments are still shewn which those personages occupied at that period. English spoken. [M.

COMFORT TO THE FEET

THE LEATHER CLOTH or PANNUSCORIUM BOOTS and SHOES are the easiest and most comfortable ever invented for tender feet; a valuable relief for Corns, Bunions, Gout, Chilblains, &c., having no drawing or painful effect on the wearer. A Boot or Shoe sent for the size will ensure a fit. The material sold by the yard in any quantity.

HALL & CO, Patentees, Wellington Street, Strand. London, leading to Waterloo Bridge. [12.Lo

W. F. ROE (late Freeman Roe),

HYDRAULIC & GAS ENGINEER AND FOUNTAIN MAKER,

70, STRAND, LONDON.

THE HYDRAULIC RAM, For raising Water without manual labour, where a small fall can be obtained. Estimates given upon receipt of the following particulars:—the fall in feet—the horizontal distance—the perpendicular height, and the quantity of water, in gallons, flowing per minute.

FIRE ENGINES & PUMPS, Pumps for deep & other Wells, &c. Gas Fittings, Glass Chandeliers. Mansions fitted up with Gas. Gas and Water Works erected.

FOUNTAINS OF EVERY DESCRIPTION, For Lawns, Conservatories, or Drawing Rooms. ROCKS AND GROTTOES. Every ORNAMENTAL DESIGN of Jets d'Eau. [8.Lo

ADVERTISEMENTS.

FLAVEL'S PRIZE KITCHENER.

The only Kitchen Range which obtained a Prize Medal and Special Approbation at the Great Exhibition, 1851.

These Ranges are strongly recommended for their simplicity of construction and their economy and cleanliness in use.

It is made from 3 feet to 18 feet in width, suitable for large or small establishments, and may be arranged to supply a Bath, Steam Kettles, Steam Closet, &c.

It is an effectual cure for Smoky Chimneys.

BENHAM and SONS,
19, WIGMORE STREET,
CAVENDISH SQUARE,
LONDON;

Also in the Hardware Court of the Paris Exhibition, and the Crystal Palace, Sydenham.

WALTERS' RAILWAY CONVENIENCE.

THESE most useful Instruments have now stood the test of experience. Their inventor, F. WALTERS, can therefore recommend them confidently to Railway Travellers and Invalids, as the more they have become known to the public the greater has been the demand. They are made entirely of India Rubber, with a patent valve to prevent the escape of the fluid. They may be worn by ladies, gentlemen, and children, both while travelling and in bed, and are perfectly comfortable and imperceptible. Price 15s., 17s. 6d., & 20s.; Postage, 1s. 6d.

PATENT JACQUARD ELASTIC STOCKINGS.

F. WALTERS begs to invite all those who suffer from weak legs or varicose veins to come and examine those bandages, when he will be happy to explain the great advantages which they possess over all other descriptions hitherto invented. The peculiarity of this patent is, that the full elasticity of the vulcanized India Rubber is not in the slightest degree restrained by the non-elasticity of the silk which is woven with it. They are woven without seam, so that the pressure is perfectly equable over the whole of the surface. They are much thinner than any ever yet made, and therefore do not obstruct the action of the skin. Manufacturers of Walters' Hydrostatic Truss &c.

FREDERICK WALTERS, 16, Moorgate Street, City.

N.B.—*Entrance for Ladies, Private Door.—A Female Attendant for Ladies.*

NOTICE.

FOUNTAINS, FIGURES, VASES, BALUSTRADING, AND TRACERY,
All sizes, manufactured in Imperishable Stone, warranted to stand all weathers.

Architects and Builders supplied with any quantity of Soffits, Bed Mouldings, Centre Flower Patress; Corinthian and Ionic Pilaster Capitals, Trusses, Scrolls, and every description of Architectural Ornaments, at

TWENTY PER CENT. CHEAPER THAN ANY HOUSE in LONDON,

At 74, BOROUGH ROAD, SOUTHWARK.

N.B.—An illustrated Pattern Book, with List of Prices and Sizes of each article, sent Free by Post, on receipt of thirteen postage stamps.

JOHN SMITH, Proprietor.

Bradshaw's Guides, British and Continental.

BRADSHAW'S ENGLISH & FOREIGN HANDBOOKS
ARE TO BE HAD AT EVERY
RAILWAY STATION, BOOKING OFFICE, AND BOOKSELLERS
THROUGHOUT THE UNITED KINGDOM,
AND THE PRINCIPAL CITIES OF THE
CONTINENTS OF EUROPE AND AMERICA, INDIA AND AUSTRALIA.

ON THE FIRST OF EVERY MONTH:

BRADSHAW'S RAILWAY AND STEAM NAVIGATION GUIDE OF GREAT BRITAIN AND IRELAND, with splendid Map of Great Britain, with all the Railways and Lines of Navigation. 6d.

BRADSHAW'S THREEPENNY GUIDE for all the Railways, with Map.

BRADSHAW'S CONTINENTAL RAILWAY, STEAM NAVIGATION, AND GENERAL CONVEYANCE GUIDE OF EUROPE, including every useful and practical information for Visitors to all parts of the Continent, with splendid Map of Northern and Central Europe. 1s. 6d.

BRADSHAW'S CONTINENTAL RAILWAY GUIDE AND GENERAL HAND-BOOK, giving, in addition to the Railway and Steam Information, a Descriptive Guide to the most frequented parts of the Continent, including the Overland Route to India; Guides to Turkey, Algeria, &c. Illustrated with clear Travelling Maps of EUROPE; also Maps of France, Belgium, Switzerland, Panoramic Map of the Rhine, and Plans of Paris, Lyons, Marseilles, Brussels, Antwerp, Ghent, Mayence, The Hague, Ostend, Cologne, Frankfort-on-the-Maine, Berlin, Hamburgh, Munich, and Dresden. 3s. 6d., bound in cloth, with pockets, &c.

ANNUALS.

BRADSHAW'S ILLUSTRATED HAND-BOOK OF FRANCE, with Maps, Town Plans, and Illustrations. 5s.

BRADSHAW'S ILLUSTRATED HAND-BOOK TO BELGIUM AND THE RHINE, and through Rhenish-Prussia, with Splendid Maps and Illustrations. 5s.

BRADSHAW'S GUIDE THROUGH PARIS AND ITS ENVIRONS, with a new and beautiful Steel-Engraved Plan of the French Metropolis and Environs, exhibiting, in a novel and comprehensive form, all that can be seen, and how to see it, with the least fatigue, time, and expense, forming a complete and indispensable Companion to the Visitor to Paris. 2s. 6d., cloth.

BRADSHAW'S COMPANION TO THE CONTINENT. By EDWIN LEE, Esq. A Descriptive Handbook to the Chief Places of Resort, their Characteristic Features, Climates, Scenery, and Remedial Resources: with Observations on the Influence of Climate and Travelling. Cloth, 7s. 6d.

BRADSHAW'S HAND-BOOK TO THE MANUFACTURING DISTRICTS OF GREAT BRITAIN. Furnishing a very instructive detail of the various Branches of Trade of Lancashire, Cheshire, Staffordshire, and Warwickshire; with well-executed Maps and Engravings. 3s. 6d., cloth.

BRADSHAW'S (ILLUSTRATED) GUIDE THROUGH LONDON AND ITS ENVIRONS, giving in a new and comprehensive form, all that can be seen in the British Metropolis and its vicinity for thirty miles round. Illustrated with Oil-Coloured Prints, Wood and Steel Engravings, and beautiful full Maps of London and its Environs for thirty miles round. 3s. 6d., cloth.

BRADSHAW'S GUIDE THROUGH EDINBURGH, with Illustrations. 1s.

BRADSHAW'S (6d.) GUIDE TO THE NEW CRYSTAL PALACE AT SYDENHAM, with Map and Exterior view of the Palace and Grounds, Park, &c.

BRADSHAW'S NEW LARGE SPLENDID RAILWAY MAP OF GREAT BRITAIN (size 6 feet 2 inches by 5 feet 1 inch), exhibiting at one view, all the Railways, Railway Junctions, Railway Stations, Tunnels, the Lines of the Electric Telegraph, the Canals, Navigable Rivers, and the Mineral Districts, with their Geological distinctions clearly and accurately defined, from the latest and most approved authorities, reduced from the Ordnance Survey. Mahogany Rollers, Varnished, £4 4s.; Library Case, £4 4s.; Sheets, Coloured, £1 15s.

BRADSHAW'S NEW RAILWAY MAP OF GREAT BRITAIN AND IRELAND, showing the Stations, Distances, &c., &c., with Plans of the Principal Towns. 2s. 6d., Case.

BRADSHAW and BLACKLOCK'S Copy Slips, Atlasses, Maps, and the Shilling Volumes of their POCKET LIBRARY, their improved and beautiful selection of Oil-Coloured Prints (Baxter's Process), always on sale at BRADSHAW'S RAILWAY GUIDE OFFICE (W. J. ADAMS), 59, Fleet Street, London; and at their Establishment, 47, Brown Street, Manchester.

JUST PUBLISHED, Price 7s.; Post Free, 7s. 6d.,

BRADSHAW'S RAILWAY MANUAL,
SHAREHOLDERS' GUIDE,
AND GENERAL RAILWAY DIRECTORY FOR 1856;

BOUND IN CLOTH, WITH SPLENDID ENGRAVED

MAPS OF THE RAILWAYS OF GREAT BRITAIN, IRELAND, AND THE CONTINENT OF EUROPE

THE PRINCIPAL FEATURES OF BRADSHAW'S MANUAL ARE—

A CONCISE HISTORY OF ALL EXISTING RAILWAYS—THEIR PROGRESS DURING THE PAST YEAR—THEIR CONDITION AND INCREASE OF TRAFFIC—THEIR INCOME OF EACH HALF-YEAR AS CONTRASTED WITH THE WORKING EXPENSES—THE AVAILABLE BALANCES, BOTH BEFORE AND AFTER THE PAYMENT OF DIVIDENDS—THE INCOME AND EXPENDITURE OF THE LARGE COMPANIES (EVEN TO PARTICULARS OF ITEMS)—THE RELATIONS IN WHICH COMPANIES STAND TOWARD EACH OTHER AT THE PRESENT TIME—A CAREFUL DIGEST OF THE PARLIAMENTARY CONTESTS OF THE PAST YEAR—A CLEAR AND STATISTICAL ACCOUNT AND DESCRIPTION OF THE

FOREIGN AND COLONIAL RAILWAYS,

AND ALSO OF THE RAILWAYS OF THE UNITED STATES UP TO THE LATEST MOMENT

A COMPLETE RAILWAY DIRECTORY,

Giving the Names and Addresses of the Directors and Principal Officials of every Existing Railway, including a Unique Alphabetical Arrangement of the same.

LONDON:—W. J. ADAMS, 59, FLEET STREET; MANCHESTER:—BRADSHAW & BLACKLOCK, 47, BROWN STREET, AND ALL BOOKSELLERS.

JUST PUBLISHED, Price 2s. 6d.; Cloth, 4s.; Post Free, 2s. 8d. and 4s. 2d.,

BRADSHAW'S RAILWAY ITINERARY
AND
GENERAL CONVEYANCE GUIDE
TO EVERY TOWN, VILLAGE, AND PARISH IN GREAT BRITAIN, FOR 1856;

GIVING THE MODE OF ACCESS, MILEAGE, &c. FROM THE METROPOLIS; THE NEAREST RAILWAY STATION AND DISTANCE THEREFROM TO THE ADJACENT TOWNS, VILLAGES, PARISHES, &c.; THE SITUATIONS, COUNTIES, AND POPULATION FROM THE LAST CENSUS;

TO WHICH IS ADDED

A GENERAL RAILWAY STATION LIST:

Where Situated, the Route thereto, and the various Companies' Lines by which to travel; also a complete

ELECTRIC TELEGRAPH DIRECTORY,

Shewing the nearest Telegraphic Stations to the places of destination, with the mode of transit of Messages, and other valuable information, illustrated with a beautiful Steel-Engraved and complete

MAP OF GREAT BRITAIN, WITH PART OF IRELAND,

Shewing every Line of Railway; the Lines of Navigation from every Port in the Island; the Lines of the Electric Telegraph; and, in order to enable the stranger to find, on inspection, the situation of any Town, &c., this Map divided into Squares by means of Vertical and Horizontal Lines.

LONDON:—W. J. ADAMS, 59, FLEET STREET; MANCHESTER:—BRADSHAW & BLACKLOCK, 47, BROWN STREET, AND ALL BOOKSELLERS.

RIMMEL'S TOILET VINEGAR

(As exhibited in the Fountains at the Crystal Palace),

IS far superior to Eau de Cologne, as a Tonic and refreshing Lotion, for the Toilet or Bath, a reviving perfume, a pleasant Dentifrice, and a powerful disinfectant for Apartments or Sick Rooms. Its numerous useful and sanitary properties render it an indispensable requisite to all Travellers. Price 1s., 2s. 6d., and 5s.

Rimmel's Toilet Vinegar, Hair Dye, Toilet Soaps, and other Perfumery, may be obtained genuine on the Continent from the following Agents:—
Amsterdam, Etienne. Laurent; *Bâle*, Burckhardt; *Berlin*, Ludwig, Henry; *Boulogne*, Brydaine; *Brussels*, Lelorrain, Woolbert; *Dresden*, Kressner and Voldih; *Frankfort*, Breul; *Geneva*, Pfister; *Havre*, Smith; *Lahaye*, Mulders; *Liege*, Thomas; *Moscow*, Darzens; *Munich*, Breul; *Paris*, Caumont, Clery; *Petersburg*, Duchon; *Posen*, Desfossé; *Rotterdam*, Klinger; *Stettin*, Müller; *Stockholm*, Bégat; *Turin*, Ancarani; *Utrecht*, Brandon; *Vienna*, Weisse; *Warsaw*, Schlenker.

EUGENE RIMMEL, PERFUMER, 39, GERRARD STREET, SOHO, LONDON.

WALTERS' HYDROSTATIC TRUSS.

F. WALTERS begs to call the attention of those suffering from Ruptures to his newly-invented HYDROSTATIC TRUSS. By means of a pad filled with water, the pressure in this truss is rendered uniform under every and any movement to which the body may be subjected. The truss has met with the strongest recommendation from Mr. Gay and other surgeons whose attention has been specially directed to the subject of hernia.

Manufacturer of Walters' Celebrated Railway Convenience.

N.B.—Ladies' entrance at the private door, where a female attends.

TO BE OBTAINED ONLY OF

F. WALTERS, 16, Moorgate Street, City.

IMPROVED RADIATING STOVE GRATES.

THESE Grates have met with universal approbation, being simple, effective, and economical.

They are particularly adapted for *very cold rooms*, and for *Smoky Chimneys*.

BENHAM & SONS

Invite attention to their SHOW ROOMS, where may be seen the largest and best selection of Stove-Grates, Fenders, and Fire Irons, for Drawing Rooms, Dining Rooms, Bed Rooms, &c. Also Kitchen Ranges of the most approved construction.

BENHAM & SONS,
WIGMORE-ST., CAVENDISH SQUARE,
LONDON;

Also in the Hardware Court of the Crystal Palace, Sydenham.

BRADSHAW'S

OIL-COLOURED PRINTS

(BY BAXTER'S PATENT PROCESS).

Messrs. BRADSHAW AND BLACKLOCK beg to call attention to the following

SUBLIME CARTOONS OF RAFFAELLE

(Engraved from the original pictures at Hampton Court Palace),

Beautifully executed, both in respect to the correctness of the Colours and elaborateness of the Engravings. Price TWO SHILLINGS each, or FOURTEEN SHILLINGS the set.

No. 1. THE DEATH OF ANANIAS.
" 2. ELYMUS THE SORCERER STRUCK BLIND BY ST. PAUL.
" 3. THE BEAUTIFUL GATE OF THE TEMPLE (The Lame Restored by St. Peter and St. John).
" 4. THE MIRACULOUS DRAUGHT OF FISHES.
" 5. ST. PAUL AND ST. BARNABAS AT LYSTRA.
" 6. ST. PAUL PREACHING AT ATHENS.
" 7. THE LAST CHARGE TO PETER.

"The Peculiar genius of *Raffaelle* is evidenced in these Miracles of Art, in various respects, in the most extraordinary degree. His power of invention appears in the most brilliant light, and nowhere do we feel so correctly how deeply *Raffaelle* has penetrated into the pure spirit of the Bible, as in these designs, in which the few and simple words of Scripture have been developed in his creature fancy into the richest pictures, but which correspond in all their parts with the sense of their words."

Also,

HER MAJESTY and PRINCE ALBERT—The PRINCE OF WALES and PRINCESS ROYAL—The late DUKE OF WELLINGTON—and

NUMEROUS BEAUTIFUL AND INTERESTING SUBJECTS.

LONDON:
W. J. ADAMS, 59, FLEET STREET;
ACKERMANN AND CO., STRAND AND REGENT STREET;
AND ALL PRINTSELLERS IN TOWN AND COUNTRY.

ADVERTISEMENTS.

TOURISTS, TRAVELLERS,

And others exposed to the scorching rays of the Sun and heated particles of Dust, will find

ROWLANDS' KALYDOR

A most refreshing preparation for the complexion, dispelling the cloud of languor and relaxation, allaying all heat and irritability, and immediately affording the pleasing sensation attending restored elasticity and healthful state of the skin. Composed of choice exotics of balsamic nature, and free from all mineral admixture, ROWLANDS' KALYDOR tends to neutralise the action of the atmosphere upon the skin, and to promote that healthy action of the minute secretory vessels, by which its general well-being and the beauty of its appearance are so essentially promoted. Freckles, Tans, Spots, Pimples, Flushes, and Discolorations, fly before its application, and give place to delicate smoothness, and the glow of beauty and of gloom. In cases of Sunburn, or Stings of Insects, its virtues have long been acknowledged. Price 4s. 6d. and 8s. 6d. per bottle.

The heat of summer frequently communicates a dryness to the hair, and a tendency to fall off, which may be completely obviated by the use of

ROWLANDS' MACASSAR OIL,

A delightfully fragrant and transparent preparation, and, as an invigorator and purifier, beyond all precedent. Price 3s. 6d. and 7s. Family bottles (equal to 4 small), 10s. 6d., and double that size, 21s. per bottle.

Nor at this season can we be too careful to preserve the Teeth from the deleterious effects of vegetable acids (the immediate cause of tooth-ache), by a systematic employment, night and morning, of

ROWLANDS' ODONTO,

OR PEARL DENTIFRICE,

A White Powder, compounded of the rarest and most fragrant exotics. It bestows on the teeth a Pearl-like Whiteness, frees them from Tartar, and imparts to the gums a healthy firmness, and to the Breath a grateful sweetness and purity.—Price 2s. 9d. per box.

BEWARE OF SPURIOUS IMITATIONS!!! The only GENUINE of each bears the name of "**Rowlands**" preceding that of the Article on the Wrapper or Label.

Sold by A. ROWLAND and SONS, 20, Hatton Garden, London, and by Chemists and Perfumers.

BRADSHAW'S CONTINENTAL HAND-BOOKS for 1856.

BRADSHAW'S (ILLUSTRATED)

HAND-BOOK OF FRANCE,

Elegantly Bound in Turkey Red, Price 5s.; Illustrated with a

SPLENDID TRAVELLING MAP OF FRANCE;

PLANS OF THE PRINCIPAL CITIES,

And numerous well-executed Steel Engravings of the

CHIEF PLACES OF RESORT IN FRANCE.

"The most convenient comprehensive Travellers' Hand-Book for France hitherto published:—Vide PUBLIC PRESS

BRADSHAW'S (ILLUSTRATED) HAND-BOOK FOR

BELGIUM AND THE RHINE,

AND THROUGH

RHENISH PRUSSIA,

With numerous Engravings, illustrative of the Scenery and Architectural Beauties of

BELGIUM AND THE RHINE,

With Splendid Steel-Engraved Travelling Maps and Town Plans of the various Cities, &c., elegantly and conveniently bound in Turkey Red.

Price 5s.

LONDON:—W. J. ADAMS (Bradshaw's British and Continental Guide Office), 59, Fleet Street.
MANCHESTER:—BRADSHAW and BLACKLOCK, 47, Brown-street; and all Booksellers.

ADVERTISEMENTS.

THE GORGET SHIRT 6 FOR 42 SHILLINGS

Sample Shirt forwarded upon receipt of a Post Office Order for 8s. 6d.

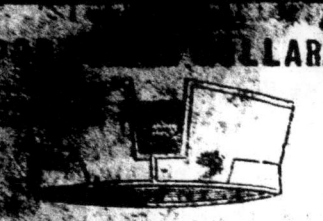

THE GORGET combines novelty with perfection of Fit, is acknowledged by all to be the easiest fitting Shirt yet made, and, by a simple invention of the Patentees, adjusts itself to all movements of the body, either, walking, sitting, or riding.— Price, including the REGISTERED ELLIPTIC WRISTBAND, 42s. the half dozen.

The ELLIPTIC three-fold COLLAR, quite unique, in all shapes, with PATENT ELASTIC FASTENING, 12s. the doz. The PATENT ELASTIC COLLAR FASTENING can be attached to any Collar.

THE ELLIPTIC COLLAR, TO FASTEN IN FRONT, With Patent Elastic Fastening.

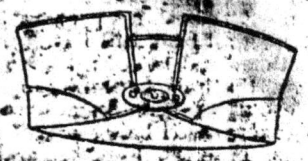

Opening back or front. Sent by Post on receipt of 13 Postage Stamps.

Directions for Measurement.—
1. Round the Chest, tight over the Shirt.
2. Round the Waist, tight over the Shirt.
3. Round the Neck, middle of Throat, tight.
4. Round the Wrist, tight.
5. Length of Coat Sleeve, from centre of Back, down seem of Sleeve to bottom of Cuff.
6. Length of Shirt at back.

To insure a Fit, the above measure should be taken without any allowance being made for shrinking, &c.

Say if the Shirts are to open back or front. If with Collars attached (3s. the half-dozen extra). If Buttons or Studs in Front. If Buttons or Studs at Wrist.

Patentees, **COOPER** and **FRYER**, next door to the
HAYMARKET THEATRE, LONDON,
AND AT SOUTH WEST GALLERY, CRYSTAL PALACE, SYDENHAM.
MANUFACTORY, 18, SUTHERLAND SQUARE, WALWORTH ROAD.

AGENTS.

Aylesbury, Connor.—Bath, W. Tuck, 15, Milsom St.—Birmingham, J. Hollingsworth, 63, New Street.—Boston, Lincolnshire, J. H. Small, junr., Market Place.—Bradford, Yorkshire, Smith & Son, Tailors, of Leeds.—Brighton, —Bristol, —Cambridge, —Canterbury, W. Claris & Son.—Cardiff, —Carlisle, —Cheltenham, C. Brimal, 2, Promenade Villas.—Chester, —Colchester, —Coventry, Thomas Morris, Hertford Street.—Derby, C. Gamble, Sadler Gate.—Devizes, Chas Roach, Brittox.—Exeter, —Gloucester, N. G. & C. Washbourne, Westgate Street.—Helston, Cornwall, Curry & Son.—Hereford, —Horncastle, Lincoln, J. Parish.—Hull —Ipswich, —Kendal, Westmoreland, J. Younghusband.—Leamington, W. H. Haynes, Tailor, &c., 3, Victoria Parade.—Leeds, Smith & Son, Tailors, Bond Street, and at Bradford.—Leicester, Joseph Carryer, Market Place.—Lincoln, G. R. Trafford, 2, Exchequer Gate.—Liverpool, Jackson Brothers, 46, Castle Street.—Manchester, H. R. Freeborn, Royal Exchange Arcade.—Nottingham, M. Vowles, Long Row.—Norwich, —Newcastle, —Newport, Monmouth, B. Evans.—Newbury, —Oxford, —Poole, Richard Fryer.—Peterborough, James Aitken, Bridge Street.—Plymouth, —Portsmouth, —Reading, —Salisbury, —Scarborough, —Sheffield, —Shrewsbury, Thomas Hall, Market Square.—Southampton, —Stamford, R. Bromhead.—Sunderland, —Swansea, —Ulverstone, Lancashire, Town & Fell.—Weymouth, —Wolverhampton, T. L. Shaw, 20, Dudley St.—Worcester, Bennett & Son, opposite Town Hall.—York, G. Bland, County Mantle Rooms.

Agents will shortly be appointed for the Towns not filled up.

By Her Majesty's Royal Letters Patent (Cooper's Patent).
THE PATENT PORT-HOLE COLLAR
IS NOW READY FOR DELIVERY, WHOLESALE, BY
WELSH, MARGETSON and COMPANY, LONDON.
RETAIL, BY ALL HOSIERS, &c., IN THE UNITED KINGDOM.

ADVERTISEMENTS.

CITY SOAP WORKS, LONDON, ESTABLISHED 1712.

NAPLES TRAVELLING TABLET.

THE refined habits of English Travellers as yet but imperfectly understood or provided for, particularly by Continental Hotel-keepers, render a COMPLETE TOILET EQUIPMENT one of the first essentials of the Tourist; and amongst those equipments, nothing holds so important a place, as regards both the health and comfort of the voyager, as a thoroughly good SOAP, in a compact and portable form. The objection to carrying Soap on a JOURNEY, has hitherto been the difficulty of putting it up whilst wet from use (as must frequently be done in hasty travel), without danger of spoiling whatever it comes in contact with. Messrs. GIBBS believe they have entirely obviated this difficulty, by the adoption of an ELASTIC CASE (similar in construction to that invented by them for their SHAVING TABLETS) to contain a Tablet of their well-known NAPLES SOAP—a Soap compounded with the greatest care, and of the choicest materials, and which, having been now for many years before the Public has never in a single instance failed to give entire satisfaction.

Each Tablet and Case is Stamped "**CITY SOAP WORKS**," LONDON.

Each Wrapper bears the Signature of the Inventors and Sole Manufacturers,

Manufactured and Sold Wholesale only by D. & W. GIBBS, and Retail by CHEMISTS and DRUGGISTS and the usual Vendors of Toilet Soaps.

Passport Agency Office, London, 59, Fleet Street.

Parties residing in any part of the United Kingdom or London, who desire to avoid delay or trouble, can have their Passports obtained and duly vised, with the utmost expedition and despatch, upon application by Letter, or otherwise, to Mr W. J. Adams (Bradshaw's British and Continental Guide Office), 59, Fleet Street, as above.

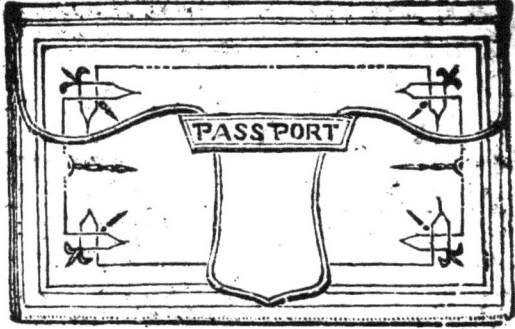

Ladies and Gentlemen resident in the Country, by this arrangement are saved the trouble of coming to London about their Passport, as it can be forwarded to them by Post (*En Regle*).

For Full Particulars respecting Passports, see Bradshaw's Continental Guide, p. 18, 19, 20, 21, and 22.

Passports carefully mounted, and Names Lettered thereon in Gold.

Passport Cases from 1s. 6d. to 6s. each.	Cash Belts
Travelling Desks.	Cash Bags and Purses.
Travelling Bags. (Leather.)	Students' and Portable Travelling Cases.
Travelling and Pocket Inkstands.	Pocket and Memorandum Books.
Travelling Soap. (Gibbs'.)	Polyglot Washing Books for Ladies or Gentlemen—English and French—English & Italian—English and German—English and Spanish—English and Portuguese, at 1s. each.
Travelling Roll-up Writing Cases.	
Travelling Pocket Memorandum & Writing Cases	
Travelling Luggage Labels, adhesive.	
Do. do. do. Parchment.	Foreign Post and Note Paper.
Courier Bags.	Envelopes, &c., &c.

And every Description of Stationery, British and Foreign.

The Latest Editions of *Bradshaw's Handbooks to France, Belgium, and the Rhine; Paris, Switzerland, &c.* French and German Dictionaries, Phrase-Books, and every description of English and Foreign Guide Books, &c.

W. J. ADAMS (Bradshaw's British and Continental Guide Office), LONDON: 59, Fleet Street.

Milton Keynes UK
Ingram Content Group UK Ltd.
UKHW052101310524
443378UK00008B/519